THE SELFIE VOTE

KRISTEN SOLTIS ANDERSON

THE

SELFIE

VOTE

Where Millennials Are Leading America

(And How Republicans Can Keep Up)

BROADSIDE BOOKS

An Imprint of HarperCollins*Publishers*

HarperCollins books may be purchased for educational, business, or sales promotional use. For information, please e-mail the Special Markets Department at SPsales@harpercollins.com.

Broadside Books™ and the Broadside logo are trademarks of HarperCollins Publishers.

FIRST EDITION

Designed by Jessica Shatan Heslin

Library of Congress Cataloging-in-Publication Data has been applied for.

ISBN: 978-0-06-234310-9

15 16 17 18 19 OV/RRD 10 9 8 7 6 5 4 3 2 1

CONTENTS

THE SELFIE VOTE

A Front-Facing Picture of a Generation: How Millennials Show Us Where We're All Going

"MOM. STOP."

We're about sixty seconds away from being instructed to turn our personal electronic devices into airplane mode, and the passenger at the other end of my row has pulled out her phone to take a picture. I'm surrounded by teenage cheerleaders and their chaperones heading from Washington to Los Angeles, and the mother-daughter pair next to me is engaged in a technology lesson.

"I want to take a selfie before we take off!"

"Ugh, you're holding it wrong."

The daughter grabs the phone, pokes the screen, and hands it back.

"You have to turn the camera around," she points out, obviously frustrated that her mom has pulled her away from the game she was just playing on her own iPhone.

The mom takes the picture but then decides that she doesn't like the way her own smile looks. "Let's take it again." The daughter resists. "MOOOOOOOM. It's fiiiiiine."

I say nothing, poking around on my own phone, trying to eke out my final moments of Twitter access before losing contact with the world for the duration of the flight. But I can't help being incredibly amused. To see that the selfie has finally made the leap from "supposedly annoying thing kids do" to "embarrassing thing parents ask their kids how to do" feels too perfect.

For those eager to dismiss millennials—those born in the 1980s and 1990s—the selfie is the ultimate symbol of an "It's all about me" younger generation that cares primarily about documenting and broadcasting its own greatness. After years and years of researching my generation, the millennial generation, I can't even count the number of times I've heard of selfies referenced to demean and diminish the value of young people and their opinions. *Those kids and their selfies. Ugh. Who cares what they think? They only care about themselves and their phones.*

Like the older folks of yesteryear complaining about how the young were on the road to hell because of their love for rock and roll, one can hear echoes of generational condescension throughout the cultural debate over the selfie. There have been plenty who see the rise of the selfie as a surefire sign that the apocalypse is nigh.

"Some social scientists lump the selfie trend—which is most popular among younger social media users—into the larger narcissism that they say is more prevalent among today's preteens and adolescents, arguing that the self-portraits are an extension of their self-absorption," wrote Alexandra Sifferlin at *Time*.[1] Leave it to the British *Daily Mail*— never a publication known for understatement—who declared in a headline: "Take a Lot of Selfies? Then You May Be MENTALLY ILL."[2] Even academic researchers have studied the psychology of selfies, ominously noting that young men who post selfies are more likely to exhibit psychopathic behavior. (Thankfully, they are apparently not more likely to exhibit Machiavellian tendencies. Whew.)[3]

In 2013, "selfie" was added to the Oxford Dictionaries and was named word of the year. Selfies were mainstream. Older generations had started to take cues from their kids and grandkids. Millennials were leading the way.

And it didn't take long for the selfie to go presidential.

In December 2013 an extraordinary cast of leaders and icons came to South Africa to mourn and honor Nelson Mandela, South Africa's first black president. Musicians like Bono, actresses like Charlize Theron, and former and current world leaders like George W. Bush and President Obama came to celebrate Mandela in a memorial service attended by thousands.

And it was here that the firestorm erupted. The image was soon splashed on news sites and newspapers worldwide: Danish prime minister Helle Thorning-Schmidt, flanked by British Prime Minister David Cameron and President Obama, leaning in to take a photo using the front-facing camera on Thorning-Schmidt's phone, wide smiles on their faces as they sat in the stands during the Mandela funeral program. Before long, the president taking a picture of himself at a funeral with other major leaders had become the subject of everything from amusement to outrage around the world. Countless op-eds were written attacking and defending the leaders for the gesture, and both Cameron and Thorning-Schmidt were pressed to answer questions back home about their involvement.

Roberto Schmidt, the Agence France-Presse photographer who captured the moment from a distance, took to the news service's blog to defend Obama, Cameron, and Thorning-Schmidt. "At the time, I thought the world leaders were simply acting like human beings, like me and you. I doubt anyone could have remained totally stony faced for the duration of the ceremony, while tens of thousands of people were celebrating in the stadium. For me, the behaviour of these leaders in snapping a selfie seems perfectly natural. I see nothing to complain about, and probably would have done the same in their place," he wrote shortly after the controversy emerged.[4]

Shortly thereafter, even more selfies made the news. At the Academy Awards in early 2014, host Ellen DeGeneres stood in the theater aisle and snapped a photo with a collection of Hollywood stars. DeGeneres posted the photo on Twitter, where it rapidly became the most shared post ever on the site.

In the 2014 midterm elections, one of the best campaign ads I saw was the final television spot by Republican Charlie Baker, running for governor of Massachusetts, featuring clip after clip of the candidate posing for selfies with voters across the state. "My iPhone's filled with the new friends I've met," he said in the ad.[5] Baker would go on to win despite being a Republican in a deeply liberal state.

Political selfies aren't exclusively an American phenomenon, either. During the March 2015 elections in Israel, *Tablet* writer Yair Rosenberg reported that "some Israeli voters attribute long lines & wait times to the fact that so many people are taking selfies of themselves voting."[6]

Of course, there's also a debate about what "selfie culture" means for the future of our nation's politics.

"Only pot, selfies and Facebook will abide," wrote *New York Times* columnist Ross Douthat in a column entitled "The Age of Individualism," which examined the political implications of rising individualism as the creed of the younger generation.[7] Another *Times* columnist, Charles Blow, concluded a piece about the politics of young Americans with the line "This is not only the generation of the self; it's the generation of the selfie."[8] In response to both columns, Nick Gillespie, editor in chief of Reason.com (the online version of the libertarian *Reason* magazine), wrote a column in the *Daily Beast* entitled "There's Nothing Wrong with Being Your Best Selfie," an ode to the supposed embrace of libertarian, limited-government, individualistic values prevalent among the young.[9]

Somehow, the humble, silly selfie was no longer just a convenient way to take a picture. It had become a symbol for our nation's young voters' deeply held values and, therefore, the country's political future.

☆

Like taking a selfie, eating a spicy tuna roll hardly seems like a profound act of political expression. Since the 1960s, when the Japanese cuisine hopped the Pacific and began to permeate American restaurants and grocery stores, the sushi industry in the U.S. has grown enormously. In 2001, when the new SuperTarget opened near my childhood home in Orlando with its own sushi counter, it seemed extraordinary if not bizarre that we'd be able to pick up salmon *nigiri* at the same time we were picking up paper towels or batteries. Yet, a decade and a half later, I can walk into just about any suburban grocery store and find a California roll as easily as I can find milk or eggs.

I *love* sushi. The concept of raw fish does not bother me in the least. The same cannot be said of my parents. Mom is fine with California rolls, but those don't actually involve raw fish. Dad was amused when the cafeteria at his workplace began bringing in a sushi chef on Mondays about a year ago, but he and his engineer friends do not partake. (Asked directly, he told me "I have yet to see any sushi at my old geezer table in the cafeteria." His characterization, not mine.)

It turns out that I am not particularly alone as a younger sushi lover, nor are my parents so unusual for their age in their apprehensive approach to the cuisine. Younger people are much more likely to say they are fine with trying sushi than are those from older generations. There's a reason why Google, on a quest to recruit and retain the best and the brightest young workers, has offered employees fresh sushi and an incredible multitude of culinary options in their cafeterias: young people tend to have adventurous palates and an appetite for new experiences.[10] While nearly six out of ten adults under age 30 say they'd be open to trying sushi, only four out of ten from their parents' generation—those aged 46 to 65—said the same. Seniors are even less excited about giving sushi a whirl: fewer than three out of ten senior citizens say they'd be willing to give sushi a try.[11]

Age, it turns out, is not the only characteristic that is in some way correlated with openness to sushi. The researchers behind the survey also sliced their data on comfort with sushi by how their participants identified politically. Sure enough, while a majority of Democrats said they'd eat sushi, 64 percent of Republicans said they would not.

So it comes as no surprise then that when Dave Gilson, an editor at *Mother Jones* magazine, lined up the data on attitudes about sushi with data from the Pew Research Center on attitudes about same-sex marriage, he found that "age-based unwillingness to put delicious uncooked fish in your mouth correlates nearly perfectly with existing data about who disapproves of marriage equality."[12]

Correlation is not causation. Whether one does or doesn't like spicy tuna is not necessarily a cause (or effect) of one's attitude toward politics or same-sex marriage. Similarly, it's unlikely that a single voter has walked into a voting booth in America and selected a candidate based on their preference for (or aversion to) a particular food.

But our political attitudes are rooted somewhere, and often the same things that drive our politics drive our attitudes in other areas of our lives. Our consumer and lifestyle choices may seem at first blush to have nothing to do with our politics. Whether we eat sushi or take selfies seems totally separate from how we vote. Yet all three of those elements—our shopping, our lifestyles, and our political views—influence, and are influenced by, how we see the world.

For instance, research has found a relationship between political conservatism and feelings of "contamination disgust"—being repulsed by having contact with the toilet seat in a public restroom or drinking a soda someone else has already started drinking. Conservatives, it is said, place greater value on things like purity and tradition than their liberal counterparts, and this doesn't just show up at the voting booth.[13] It shows up in how you feel about watching someone double-dip a chip.

Our political choices do not exist in a vacuum. Google brought in sushi to adapt to the preferences of the younger generation, which was clamoring for something different and expected lots of choice. We also expect change and choice from our political leadership. The line between the consumer and the voter is increasingly blurred, and the same values that lead to us making certain consumer or lifestyle choices are not so different from those values that drive our political views as well.

Like the selfie, sushi did not begin as mainstream in America. And, like the selfie, the rise of sushi in America does not necessarily have one big lesson to teach us about our politics. More selfies may mean we as a nation are becoming more individualistic. More sushi may mean we are more open to trying new things. Watching the trends that start off more popular with the new generation and ultimately spread upward and outward can give us small clues about where our country is headed.

But for each of these relatively minor lifestyle or consumer choices people make, there are even bigger ones at hand—the decision to own a home, to go to church, to buy a car, to join a union, to invest in stocks, to get married—that speak volumes about who we are and what we stand for. Following all of these trends, from the silly to the serious, can actually tell us a lot about where our nation's politics are truly heading.

☆

"It's been long enough; I think the statute of limitations on this one is up. I can tell you this story now," says Alex Lundry, the chief data officer of the Romney 2012 campaign and cofounder of Deep Root Analytics.[14]

"In 2008, we were building microtargeting models for Romney in one of the primary states, and, depending on the model you're building, sometimes you have more control over what goes in and what doesn't, and in this particular instance one variable kept coming up and coming up and coming up. It was a variable I would normally never use in the modeling—I'd just disregard it, assume the model is overfitting—but it came up so frequently and in so many instances. What was it about this one variable?"

Lundry, a veteran of Republican microtargeting efforts going back nearly a decade, has seen a lot of data in his day. He did not set out initially to become a Republican data pro, but while in graduate school at Georgetown "I discovered there was this great job called 'the pollster' in the political realm," he says. After a year or so working for Frank Luntz, the infamous GOP überpollster, Lundry joined a firm called TargetPoint, where he became one of the party's primary analytics gurus.

Analytics and modeling, a now-booming field in the marketing and political world, very simply is a way for a company or campaign to use an enormous amount of data about an individual to make an educated guess about how that person will behave. Researchers can survey thousands and thousands of people and then use the results of how people responded in that survey to make informed guesses about how other voters who have similar characteristics will behave too. They see what factors, for example, make someone more likely to support a particular candidate or issue position. Campaigns then build statistical models that try to predict how each individual voter will behave.

Think of a model like a recipe: a bunch of different ingredients are all included in different amounts to create something useful at the end. What are the ingredients that, if you mix them together, mean someone will probably be a Republican?

Each person is defined by a large number of ingredients, or "variables," characteristics about their demographic or consumer profile. Usually variables like age, gender, voting history, and party registration are obvious indicators of whether you will turn out to vote or whether you'll choose a particular candidate. Whether you're married, have a high income, or live in a certain neighborhood might all give an analytics expert like Lundry additional clues about your potential behavior. Nowadays, thousands upon thousands of variables might be at a campaign's disposal, ranging from the type of car you drive to the hobbies you have.

When it came to Mitt Romney, in this particular recipe in 2008, one weird ingredient—an unusual variable—stood out.

"It turned out that dog owners were breaking consistently against Romney," Lundry observes. "I made the connection in my mind between that and the negative press around Seamus. And so 'dog owner' went into the model."

Ah, the Seamus story. In 2007, in a profile piece on the Romney family in the *Boston Globe*, the world first learned the story of Seamus, the Romney's family dog during the 1980s.[15] The Romneys brought Seamus on the road with them for the daylong journey in a carrier strapped to the roof of the car. The profile noted that Mitt Romney had attempted to put a windshield on the crate so that Seamus wouldn't be blasted by the rushing air during the drive, but during the trip, poor Seamus became ill and relieved himself in the crate. The tale of the dog on the car roof followed Romney through both of his presidential campaigns.

All right, this explains why some dog owners might be slightly less enthused about voting for Mitt Romney. But how did the Romney campaign know that people were dog owners in the first place? People today may have some awareness that nearly every transaction they make is logged somewhere, that every mouse click or card swipe is probably feeding information to someone. They may know that the data goes to their credit card companies and maybe to the stores where they shopped.

Fewer people are aware of how that data is used. When your grocery store has you sign up for that discount card, you're exchanging data about your shopping habits for a few bucks off your grocery receipt. When you sign up for the mailing list of your favorite clothing store, information about your purchases gets linked up with the name and phone number you put down, and that data is used to make guesses about how rich you are and what your fashion sensibilities are. Suddenly you start getting coupons in the mail from your grocery store that just happen to be tailored to the sorts of things you buy, or other clothing retailers similar to the one you shop at start sending you catalogs in the mail. Did you sign up for a loyalty card at your pet supply store and then buy a new collar for your puppy? Buy dog food at the grocery store? Order some doggie treats online? That may be enough to get you flagged as a dog owner, and you may start to see more ads about pet-related products.

All in all, that's not so surprising. But what very few people realize is that the same consumer data that is purchased by corporations to try to get you to buy soda or cashmere sweaters is also purchased by political groups, and it is used to make assumptions about if and how you will vote.

That piece of campaign mail that came in last week, talking about how a particular candidate *slashed* education funding? Those nice kids who came to your door the other day to talk to you about how Candidate So-and-so is an experienced small businesswoman who wants to bring jobs to the area? Your next-door neighbors probably didn't get the same brochure in the mail. Those nice kids probably didn't stop by the house next door—or if they did, they might have had a slightly different sales pitch to deliver.

None of that happens by accident, and the science behind it tells us a lot about where the future of politics is heading.

Margaret Scammell, a lecturer at the London School of Economics, published a paper titled "Political Brands and Consumer Citizens: The Rebranding of Tony Blair" in 2007 that dove into the emerging concept of "political branding" as the modern approach to how our leaders would win votes. Scammell studied the way that Tony Blair had campaigned for office and noted that as politics shifted "from a mass media model to a consumer model of political communication," branding would become an even more important element of political campaigning.

What does it mean to move from a "mass media" model to a consumer model? Essentially, Scammell said that the campaigns of the 1980s and 1990s were characterized by the rise of spin and media manipulation by broad-based advertising campaigns. Today that model "is in decline." This seems to make perfect sense given how trust in mass media in general has plummeted. For instance, trust in television news media is at record lows, with only 18 percent of Americans saying they have a great deal of confidence in it, down from 36 percent in the mid-nineties.[16] Newspapers barely fare better. Instead, Scammell notes, it is more advantageous for campaigns to focus on pitching directly to voters (their "consumers"), which requires targeting and more refined approaches to understanding an individual's attitudes.

"There is a perfect circle in the brand approach: campaigners research citizens as though they were consumers, and their research tells them that citizens' attitudes toward politics are profoundly shaped by their experience as consumers," wrote Scammell.[17]

As someone coming from the political opinion research realm, I can attest to the way that political polling these days closely parallels corporate brand research. For instance, a question favored by some pollsters in focus group settings involves asking participants what automobile model or brand a particular candidate is most like; in 2012, voters told the Republican polling organization Resurgent Republic that President Obama was like a Jeep, a Chevy Volt, and a Yugo, each of those associations linking the characteristics of a corporate brand (ability to navigate rough terrain, innovative but untested, faulty) with the brand of a candidate.[18]

But there's also the other aspect of the "voter as consumer" approach, and that's understanding how the same values and preferences lead to individuals' choices about both politicians and purchases. And just as data analytics have reshaped the consumer landscape, they have also made it possible for political campaigns to know about you *as a consumer*. Not just that you are a Democrat, or that you live on Spruce Street, or that you voted in the last presidential election. They can know if you like technology. They can know if you have high-end culinary tastes. They can know if you have a gun. They can know if you like to knit. And, as a result, they can make very, very good educated guesses about if and how you'll vote before you even do it.

Our political choices are driven by our emotions and our values. Voters are consumers and essentially wear both of those hats at the same time. What we buy, who we know, where and how we live our lives, are all reflections of the values that shape our shopping habits as well as our partisanship. Whether we're taking a selfie or ordering sushi or donating to charity or buying cat food, we are giving off signals about our values, big and small. By studying lifestyle habits and the changing lifestyle habits of the next generation, we can begin to learn more about what they expect out of their leaders and what ideas might have the most positive impact on their lives.

Often the trends that shape our society start out as among young adults. That generation is a leading indicator of where things are heading. And better understanding the lives and choices of young Americans is absolutely essential to any political party that wants to thrive in the future.

Especially the Republican Party.

☆

It's no secret that the GOP has had a hard time winning over the millennial generation—the newest voters in the electorate—and that this has made it increasingly hard for Republicans to win elections.

I am young and I am a Republican. I don't view these things as in any way contradictory or unusual. During November of 2002, when I was 18 years old, I walked down to the Reitz Union on the campus of the University of Florida to cast my very first ballot, voting for Governor Jeb Bush to return for a second term as governor of my state. I had old friends from my high school debate days who, as Democrats, would engage me in good-natured political arguments, but I never felt that being conservative marked me as bizarre in any way. Sure, it was a little bit weird to be a young person deeply interested in *politics*, but it wasn't necessarily weird to be a young person who was *Republican*.

At 20 years old, I loaded up my personal belongings into my beloved Ford Mustang and drove up I-95 to begin an adventure in Republican politics in Washington. When I came to work in Washington as a young pollster and public opinion researcher in early 2005, there was a palpable sense that Republicans were invincible. Shortly after the reelection of President Bush in 2004, Republicans were dominant and jubilant. They'd just secured the White House for four more years. They'd picked up a handful of seats in the U.S. Senate (while losing just one, a previously Republican-held seat in Illinois, to none other than a newcomer named Barack Obama) and they'd taken out then Senate minority leader Tom Daschle in the process. In the U.S. House of Representatives, the Republican majority grew by a few seats.

That feeling of invincibility did not last long. Over the next few years Americans soured on the Republican Party, and by the time the 2008 election rolled around, the GOP was ushered out of the White House with resounding force. In the run-up to the 2008 election, anecdotally, I started to feel a shift in how my friends *outside* of politics were looking in at the parties. I started getting asked different versions of the question: *How can you be Republican? You seem nice and normal!* Friends who had previously thought I was an oddball for being so interested in politics *now* thought I was odd for being *Republican*. They were tuned in, fired up, and ready to go for Barack Obama, and couldn't fathom why someone would choose to associate with the GOP.

I've spent the last six years trying to crack the code on young voters. I've pored over countless public opinion surveys, conducted focus groups all over the country, and taken a deep dive into all of the data about where my generation stands and what we believe.

What I have found should terrify Republicans.

Not all of my fellow partisans share my fears. I can't tell you the number of times in the last few years I've been told that the GOP doesn't need to worry about all these young people voting for Democrats. After all, they say, people become more conservative as they get older, throwing around a version of the line "If you're young and conservative, you have no heart, and if you're old and liberal, you have no brain," usually falsely attributed to Winston Churchill. They're eager to make the case that all is well. Surely, these crazy kids with their sushi and their startups and their selfies will one day grow up, move out of Mom and Dad's basement, get married, get a *real* job, start paying taxes, and, *voilà*, they'll become Republicans!

Not quite.

Republicans shouldn't hold their breath waiting for my generation to grow up and age into conservatism on their own.

There are three reasons why Republicans need to get past the idea that losing millennial voters is no big deal.

The first is that this moment is not normal. In the past, while Democrats have often done *very slightly* better with young voters, we have not seen the sort of enormous, sustained generational political divide that we are seeing today. Even as recently as fifteen years ago, young voters behaved generally like their grandparents at the polls. Today that is unfathomable.

The second reason why Republicans need to pay attention to winning young voters today is that we can't count on them naturally becoming Republican tomorrow. Across a whole host of cultural factors, today we are seeing a decline in the sorts of behaviors that might have lent Republicans a more natural advantage with millennials as they age.

When I conduct a survey of voters, I often ask a series of demographic questions in order to segment and analyze the results. The most common demographic items that pollsters like me look for include age, race, marital status, religion, income, education level, and type of location where one lives. These factors alone can tell you a lot about how someone might vote. Republicans, for instance, do well among married voters; Democrats do well among voters who aren't married. Republicans do well among voters who go to church every week, but lose voters who go to church less often. Republicans do well with voters who live in more spread-out or rural areas, while Democrats do well in denser areas and city centers.

So what trends are we seeing among millennials? They're flocking to denser areas, they're less likely to go to church regularly, and they're less likely to get married, just to name a few. Republicans are potentially on the losing side of a whole host of social trends, and need to be certain they can reach voters who don't have the normal "Republican" cultural and demographic indicators. Many of these voters are millennials.

But the final reason why Republicans need to actively seek to understand young people and to work hard for their support is because many Republicans fundamentally misunderstand millennial values and where the opportunities—and challenges—exist. They often take too simplistic a view of what young people want.

Young Americans are more diverse and complicated than most—including and especially the Republican Party—give them credit for. When I hear Republicans talk about winning over young voters—which, sadly isn't often—it often focuses on a need to be more present in social media, to evolve on "social issues" like same-sex marriage, and to emphasize individual liberty and fiscal conservatism. Fine, but this idea is too narrow, too simple, and far too incomplete.

Republicans haven't always been the party of the old or the party of the past. There hasn't always been a stark divide between young voters and their grandparents. And the cultural and technological trends that make up millennial life in America today suggest that if Republicans don't gain an understanding of what values are driving this generation, they are at serious risk of being left behind.

The case I will lay out in this book is not just one about winning votes and elections, however; it is about governing well. It's about understanding how younger Americans are driving cultural, technological, and lifestyle changes that will affect politics *and* policy. It's about understanding the emerging, exciting tools that policy makers have at their fingertips to better learn about and engage with those whom they represent, particularly the young Americans who are most highly connected and tech savvy. To get to that understanding, we'll explore many of the most basic demographic factors that analysts use to make predictions about how voters will behave: race, family structure, workplace and income, education, religion, and neighborhood. We'll learn how trends in these areas are remaking our politics and what marketers, campaigners, and leaders ought to do about it.

We live in an era when political movements and leaders have an unprecedented ability to learn about their voters and to reach out to them in a personal way. We live in an era when cultural norms about religion and virtue are changing, yet loving one's neighbor remains the core of a generation's moral code. We live in an era where the public sector increasingly represents an old way of thinking and problem solving, and when changes in people's lifestyles show the need for reforms in outdated systems. We live in an era ripe for disrupting old ways of doing things, whether they're being protected by unions or regulations or simply inertia.

The opportunities embedded in this landscape for Republicans are incredible, and I hope to shine a light on the ways that Republicans should not fear change; they should embrace it.

I don't just want to figure out how someone or some party can win more votes. I want to explore what the next generation of voters expects—and what the next generation of thinkers is doing to bring about that change. And I want to understand what people need to know in order to understand and connect with my generation.

The world is changing.

Don't you want to see where we're headed?

ONE

The Election of 2076:
Why Republicans Should Think
More Like McDonald's

In 2003 the *New York Times Magazine* covered an emerging phenomenon of rightward-leaning youngsters in a piece by John Colapinto entitled "The Young Hipublicans."

The piece outlined the growth in organizations like the College Republican National Committee during the early 2000s. "Today's surge reflects a renewed shift pronouncedly to the right on many defining issues, after several years during the Clinton presidency when students gravitated toward more liberal political labels," wrote Colapinto.[1]

Today it is almost comical to consider such a sentence. The "Young Hipublicans" didn't last long. Even in 2003 the seeds of a potential liberal resurgence down the road were possible to see. "Like the rest of their generation, [the young conservatives have] been trained, from preschool onward, in the tenets of cooperation, politeness and racial and gender sensitivity. As much as they would hate to admit it—as hard as they try to fight it—these quintessential values have suffused their consciousness and tempered their messages," noted Colapinto.

The "Young Hipublicans" were on the leading edge of the millennial generation, and a decade later those seeds of liberal values had fully bloomed. The 2008 and 2012 elections highlighted a generational political divide never before seen in modern American political history. Republicans lost young people by historic margins. The "Hipublican" story was now happening in reverse, and the millennial exodus from the GOP was in full force.

No longer were there intrepid reporters exploring what was pulling young people rightward. Instead, a *New York Times Magazine* headline in 2013 asked:

"Can the Republicans Be Saved from Obsolescence?"[2]

In early 2013, I flew from Washington to Columbus, Ohio, with journalist Robert Draper, who would be writing the aforementioned *New York Times Magazine* piece on what was driving young people away from the GOP. We were on our way to a focus group facility in the suburbs where that night I would moderate two focus groups of voters under the age of 30, asking them about their views on politics, policy, and media. Draper was coming along to sit behind the one-way mirror and observe firsthand what I had been seeing in the data and to see if there was any way that young people could be pulled back to the Republican Party. What we discovered on that trip, and what I observed in the rest of my research on young voters, was striking.

The young voters I spoke to that night in Columbus viewed the Republican Party as old-fashioned, out of touch, from a different era. While not necessarily enamored of the Democratic Party, the consensus was that Republicans represented an old-school approach to life that didn't mesh with the more diverse, tech-savvy, open-minded millennial generation. They couldn't connect with a party they felt was disconnected from and disinterested in their generation.

When Draper's article was published, the artwork accompanying the story focused in on the notion of the Republican Party as outdated. It featured an antiquated typewriter with the caption "G.O.P. Laptop" and a filing cabinet labeled "G.O.P. Hard Drive." The Republicans' problem wasn't about a single issue, a single piece of technology or single candidate. The problem with the Grand Old Party was right in the name. It was *old*.

Draper chronicled my thoughts from that night in his story:

" 'There is a brand,' the 28-year-old pollster concluded of her party with clinical finality. 'And it's that we're not in the 21st century.' "[3]

The title of Draper's piece posed an interesting question: *Can* the Republicans be saved?

If the young Republican moment of the early 2000s failed to stick, will the Democratic moment of the late 2000s and early 2010s simply fade too?

Or is something more powerful happening here that spells trouble down the road for Republicans over the long term?

☆

It wasn't always this way. In the 2004 election, for instance, Republicans were widely touted as being the more tech-savvy team, having pioneered practices of microtargeting and online organizing. George W. Bush lost young voters to John Kerry, yes, but by a margin that was minuscule compared with the Obama wave to come.

Even before 2004, Republicans typically fared well with young people even if they didn't win them outright. Grandparents and their grandchildren were not polarized against one another. Put simply, from 1980 through 2000, whether you were young or old had little bearing on your vote. Plenty of young people voted Republican, old people voted Democratic, and there was very little "age gap" in any major presidential election.

In 1980, Jimmy Carter and Ronald Reagan ran neck and neck among young people.[4] By 1984, Reagan was winning voters under age 30 by enormous margins, and the "age gap" between the oldest and youngest voters was minimal.[5] Young people were more likely to vote for George H. W. Bush in 1988 than were senior citizens.[6] Bill Clinton won the votes of more young people than did his opponents, but he won all age groups, not just the young.[7] Even George W. Bush in 2000 ran about the same among young people as he did among senior citizens.

In short: the idea that young people are always solidly Democratic and that old people are always solidly Republican is nonsense.

What happened in 2008, the year that young voters played a monumental role in the fate of our nation and elected Barack Obama to the presidency—the year that young voters broke for the Democratic candidate by over a 30-point margin—was way, way, way, outside the norm.

Despite the fact that Barack Obama was in his forties when he was elected, some called him "the first Millennial president."[8] He was young, and he ran on the promise of a more optimistic brand of politics. He ran on hope and change. He ran a tech-savvy operation that understood how to use social media to organize support. He spoke directly to disaffected young people. Running a campaign explicitly aimed at energizing groups of voters who had tuned out or felt cut off from politics, Obama turned the tide on youth participation in politics.

First, he got them to the polls.

In the presidential elections of the late 1970s through most of the 1980s, according to the national exit polls, voters under the age of 30 made up approximately 23 percent of all voters. Through the 1990s and early 2000s, youth participation fell and young people constituted only around 17 percent of the vote.

In the 2008 election, young voters bounced back. Big-time. They accounted for roughly 23 million of the votes cast, about 18 percent of voters.[9] It wasn't just a onetime surge, either; despite a rough economy, along with disappointment with and sagging enthusiasm for President Obama, young voters continued to be an important force in the 2012 election, with exit polls estimating that those under age 30 cast 19 percent of all votes.

But the notable trend in the youth vote in the last two presidential elections wasn't just about a supposed uptick in participation. It wasn't just that Obama got young people out to vote.

It was the extent to which they turned out to vote *for him*.

In the presidential election of 2008, according to the National Election Pool exit polls, Barack Obama defeated John McCain among young voters by a nearly two-to-one margin, an historic feat and one that was key to Obama's victory. In 2012, President Obama continued to win significantly among young voters. Poll after poll showed the millennial generation breaking with the GOP.

But something had happened even before the rise of Barack Obama, before hope and change. Obama rode the wave, but he did not start it. It's true that the 2008 election is the one that is most associated with the big "breakup" between the Republican Party and the millennial generation, and it was the Obama campaign that did activate young voters to turn out in an historic way. But one needs to go back even further to see what set the scene for the split between Republicans and young people.

We need to go back to that moment when the Republican confidence was at its peak. We need to go back to 2005.

Starting with the Bush administration's unsuccessful attempt to reform Social Security, exacerbated by the deteriorating situation in Iraq and capped by the response to the devastation of Hurricane Katrina, 2005 and 2006 were disastrous years for the GOP. Favorability toward Republicans across all age groups fell off a cliff. Republicans started 2005 being viewed favorably by 56 percent of Americans and ended 2006 being viewed favorably by only 35 percent.[10]

In the 2006 elections that followed, Republicans lost their House majority and lost voters nationwide by an 8-point margin. But something peculiar emerged when the exit poll results were broken out by age. Of course, Republicans lost young voters in that election, just as they lost all age groups. But the size of the deficit with the young was striking. Republicans won only 39 percent of the votes of those under age 30—the worst result for *either* party among *any* age group going back over two decades.[11] Even in previous huge-wave elections, there had never been a generational break quite like this.

Barack Obama wasn't a major national figure yet. Young voters weren't caught up in Obamamania. Obama's name wouldn't even be *tested* in a major presidential election poll until 2007.

This was not about Obama.

Yet here, in 2006, young voters spoke loud and clear: they had simply rejected the Republican Party.

That's what should make the results of the last two presidential elections so alarming to Republicans.

This is *not* the norm. And it is *not* just about Obama.

Of course, Republican dominance in the 2014 midterm elections has temporarily alleviated the concerns about the party's future. Far exceeding the expectations of most pundits and prognosticators, Republicans retained and gained a number of governors' offices across the country while also gaining control of the U.S. Senate. Republicans had a great election night and were justifiably jubilant. The discussion of two years earlier, about how Republicans were in trouble and destined to go the way of the dinosaurs, almost felt silly. Extinction? Hardly. They were back at the top of the food chain.

Politics can feel quite cyclical. One party is in power while the other fades, only to see the tables turned a few years later. In 1969, Nixon strategist Kevin P. Phillips wrote *The Emerging Republican Majority*, laying out the story of how Republicans would supposedly control the next few decades of politics. In the early 2000s, we had Karl Rove's goal of a "durable Republican majority," and Republicans found success in three successive election years.[12] (Perhaps ironically, during the *Meet the Press* appearance where Rove spoke of that durable majority, then senator-elect Barack Obama joined him as a round-table guest on the program.)

In 2006 and 2008 the narrative of Republican dominance was turned on its head, and suddenly we were talking about "the emerging Democratic majority," as it was first dubbed by researchers John B. Judis and Ruy Teixeira in 2002. It seemed that demographic and cultural shifts meant a Democratic victory was destiny.[13] In *40 More Years: How the Democrats Will Rule the Next Generation*, famed Democratic operative and pundit James Carville in 2009 wrote about how Democrats were poised to be victorious in American politics for the foreseeable future.[14] Then came the 2010 elections and the significant Republican wave of that year, in which Republicans won a multitude of races across the country. Suddenly it seemed that not all hope was lost for the GOP. The pendulum quickly swung back, of course, and by the 2012 election the Republican "brand image" was worse than ever, with Democrats retaining the White House. Come 2014, we were right back to Republican euphoria, with election victories that lent credence to the theory that it is *Democrats* who are doomed in the long run because of their declining appeal with a large swath of white working-class voters.

On and on, round and round we go.

But while the notion that politics is cyclical may offer comfort when you're out of power, it can also lend the impression that you need only wait around long enough and surely your party will be back in fashion. Wait long enough, and people will tire of the people running the show and will give you another shot.

This is how I hear many people think about the politics of the young in America. Sure, Reagan won over a generation, but then a decade later Bill Clinton pulled young adults leftward. Behold the early George W. Bush era, with those "Hipublicans" and their growing campus conservatism! But give it a few more years, and suddenly you have the Obama generation putting up "CHANGE" posters in their dorm windows.

Why bother trying to win young voters if they're going to ultimately come around to your side anyhow? Inevitably, we will return to favor, right? Won't the pendulum come back around?

This attitude is dangerous. It is particularly dangerous for today's Republicans in large part because it's hard to see how the "brand damage" being done today might lead to negative consequences later on. It's the sunburn that you think is gone when it stops hurting and being pink, forgetting that you've still done lasting and irreversible damage to yourself. Assuming that young people will naturally come back to the right one day ignores the risk of the real, lasting electoral impact of badly losing a generation in the first place.

Political views are sticky. Gallup has tracked political partisanship and ideology for decades. Its data tell an interesting story about how we hang on to the political attitudes we form when we're young. During the summer of 2014, they released a chart showing political partisanship broken down by age in America today. As you'd expect, today's young voters are much more Democratic than Republican. However, the party gap comes to a close when looking at voters in their mid-forties. But for voters in their mid-fifties and early sixties, the baby boomer generation? *Democrats* pull back slightly into the lead. It isn't until we get to those in their late sixties that Republicans gain the edge again.[15]

So what's going on here? Why is it that a voter who is in his or her late forties today—who would have first earned the right to vote during Reagan's presidency—is still more likely today to be Republican than voters who are ten or twenty years *older*? Why is it that a voter in his or her early sixties today, who would have first earned the right to vote around the Watergate era, is so much *less* likely to be a Republican than the Gen Xers? Do political attitudes and preferences take shape when you're young and stick with you as you age? Are we *really* seeing Reagan and Watergate continuing to ripple through people's party affiliations decades later?

For decades, political scientists have studied how political attitudes are formed, how they persist, and what causes them to change. In 1987, academics Keith R. Billingsley and Clyde Tucker wrote in the journal *Political Behavior*: "We believe that the early adult years are the most important ones for 'shaping' an individual's political behavior." They go on to note that "the historical events which take place during early adulthood go a long way toward determining the political experiences of the young adult. When the character of these events is such that the political behavior of young voters is different from that of their predecessors, a new political generation is born."[16]

Nearly thirty years later, it turns out that early adulthood is still a hugely influential period for someone's lifetime political views. The *New York Times* blog "The Upshot" illustrated this phenomenon elegantly in 2014 with an interactive chart developed by academics Andrew Gelman of Columbia University and Yair Ghitza of data firm Catalist, relying on Gallup data as well as other proprietary survey work.[17] They built a model that looked at hundreds of thousands of pieces of data about political partisanship and age, and plotted out the expected lifetime pattern of political partisanship of those born in each individual birth year from 1937 to 1994. Each year, or "cohort," is looked at individually. While the baby boomer generation certainly undergoes a partisan transformation as they near retirement, for the most part the research does not show a consistent trend of voters getting more Republican as they get older. Instead, there's wide variation in the very early years, with each cohort eventually making up its mind and stabilizing in later years. Like cement that starts out being malleable but ultimately hardens, young people may bounce around in their views at first but pretty quickly pick a side and tend to stick there.

"Events at age 18 are about three times as powerful as those at age 40, according to the model," say Ghitza and Gelman.

It turns out first impressions mean a lot.

☆

Buried somewhere in the back of the closet in my old bedroom in my childhood home in Florida, likely wedged beneath an old Mall Madness board game or a bin of Nintendo games and "treasure troll" dolls, are an awful lot of old Happy Meal toys. Most prominently, of course, are the "Teenie Beanies" (miniature Beanie Babies collectable plush toys) of the late 1990s, a craze that gripped children and grown adults alike (even causing altercations between adults on the hunt for the toys, either for profit, for their kids, or for their own collections).[18] My childhood in the 1980s and 1990s involved a fair share of tiny Happy Meal Barbies and plastic McNugget characters and tiny versions of McDonald's food favorites called Changeables that could transform from burgers and french fries into robot figurines. McDonald's wasn't a constant staple in my home growing up, but it was a nice treat every so often, and pursuit of those Happy Meal toys certainly accounted for some of the begging and pleading for a trip to the Golden Arches that I did as a child.

The McDonald's Happy Meal first debuted in 1979, and the company's appeal to the very young consumer has not stopped since, although it has run into criticism along the way.[19] In fact, McDonald's has been sued on the relatively ridiculous grounds that it ought not to market its products so successfully to kids.[20] San Francisco tried and failed to stop the sale of Happy Meals by prohibiting free toy giveaways.[21] McDonald's is, of course, not the only food purveyor to aim for kids, but it was among the most prominent early adopters of the strategy of marketing to children not just to win them as kid customers today but to hang on to them for a lifetime, winning brand loyalty that will stick with a child as he or she matures and becomes an adult consumer.[22]

It's not hard to see how this might seem sinister. But it undoubtedly works. To this day, I prefer Pepsi over Coca-Cola, in large part because it was the soda in my household as a kid. I grew up going to Publix supermarkets and would do just about anything to get the company to open a store in the mid-Atlantic states. And though I don't eat them regularly, I still have a strong affinity for those McDonald's cheeseburgers. The habits, preferences, and behaviors that shaped me when I was young continue to have an impact on my choices decades after my first Happy Meal toy.

The formative years in our lives, when we first start to remember the foods we will love for our lifetimes or the laundry detergent we'll prefer using into adulthood because it smells like home, are called formative for a reason: they do much to form the people we will be throughout our lives. We aren't frozen in time, of course, and our tastes and preferences and values can change, but loyalties and habits are hard to break.

Of course, when it comes to politics, one would hope that a voter is putting more thought into his or her choice of political party than into his or her choice of soda or fast-food joint. But the same sorts of forces that will, for better or worse, forever link McDonald's with happiness in my mind are not so terribly different from the forces that make me think of Republicans as being strong or responsible, or that might make someone else think of Democrats as being caring and tolerant. Once a brand is associated with certain attributes in our minds, it is tough to break that first impression, to change those initial loyalties.

Corporations and consumer brands get that the formative years are among the most critical. And it is precisely the formative years where voters are being most neglected by political leaders.

In my research in 2013 for the College Republican National Committee, the research trip that took me to Columbus and a handful of other cities, I was on a quest to find out what the Republican and Democratic "brands" were in the minds of young people who were just beginning to form their impressions and establish their loyalties. I set out to speak with young voters who had cast ballots for President Obama but who were not liberal Democrats, and conducted a series of focus groups across the nation. One of the most important exercises in each group was to ask the handful of respondents in my sessions to free-associate, shouting out the first words that came to their minds when I named each political party.

For Democrats, the answers were a mix of positive and negative characteristics. Some said that Democrats were soft or that they were weak. Others noted that Democrats liked to spend tax dollars. Still others said they viewed Democrats as tolerant, open-minded, and diverse.

For the Republican Party, the mix of words was not nearly so positive. As I wrote in the 2013 "Grand Old Party for a Brand New Generation" report for the CRNC, "The responses were brutal: closed-minded, racist, rigid, old-fashioned."[23]

Republican hand-wringing over the party "brand" isn't particularly new. In 2008, former congressman Tom Davis (R-VA) compared the GOP's brand to dog food, saying that "the Republican brand is in the trash can . . . [I]f we were dog food, they would take us off the shelf."[24] Four years later, the notion that the Republican brand was *still* in bad-dog-food territory was often discussed.[25] After the electoral defeat in 2012, the RNC compiled and released the "Growth and Opportunity Report," which references rebuilding the party "brand" numerous times.[26] And despite good news in the 2014 elections, the Republican "brand" is still viewed quite poorly. On the eve of the huge Republican victories in the 2014 midterm elections, Senator Rand Paul (R-KY) was still adamant: "The Republican Party brand sucks and so people don't want to be a Republican."[27] And despite the big wins Republicans saw in that election, Senator Paul was right: the exit polls showed that the voters who turned out in the midterm elections nationwide and mostly cast their ballots for Republicans still held little love for the Republican Party.

For those young voters who are first awakening to politics, who are first coming of voting age, and who will be participating in our nation's politics for decades to come, the way they view the GOP today will create impressions and loyalties that are increasingly hard to shake.

Being the party of yesterday is hardly the way to win the elections of tomorrow.

Republicans in the U.S. aren't the only ones who are facing a challenge with young voters. Conservatism around the globe is facing a challenge in reaching out to the young, particularly as the global economic crisis has caused many—particularly in Europe—to look askance at the virtues of capitalism and the free market.

In early 2013 the International Democrat Union (IDU) Young Leaders Forum was hosted in London, bringing together representatives of center-right political parties from around the world. The IDU, founded by Prime Minister Margaret Thatcher, then vice president George H. W. Bush, and other world leaders in 1983, is a global coalition that includes Germany's Christian Democratic Union, Sweden's Moderate Party, Australia's Liberal Party, and many others. Attending the summit over the course of four days, I was fortunate enough to meet rising stars from conservative parties around the world. I was both comforted and alarmed to hear that they were encountering similar challenges to those I was observing back in the United States: conservatives were viewed as culturally disconnected from young people and representing the past rather than the future. All were eager to help connect their parties with their generation.

Michelle Rempel, an energetic and sharp member of the Canadian Parliament, is at the forefront of the charge in her own country. Despite being the youngest of the Conservative MPs, Rempel was appointed minister of state by Prime Minister Stephen Harper and is unquestionably a rising star in Canadian politics. Upon meeting her, you immediately recognize Michelle as wonderfully different, a breath of fresh air, hyperintelligent and laser focused on bringing about change.

Michelle and I met and bonded at the London IDU event, swapping tales of what it is like to be a young female conservative in a party or industry where we are thought of as a rarity.

Michelle's insights on what conservatives need to do to reach young people are certainly applicable in the U.S. and beyond. "Part is having the awareness that you need young people *in* office. Part is policy that is cognizant of what matters to that cohort, and then making sure that cohort knows why that policy matters." She notes that her campaigns have been particularly data-driven and have made the effort to really understand how things like news consumption have changed dramatically. "How do you get someone to pay attention? There's no silver bullet. Being blunt and direct, and using creative means to do so," she suggested.

The good news for Republicans is that nowadays we have an opportunity to deploy just the kind of strategy Rempel proposes. I often find that discussion about winning back young voters goes to two unhelpful extremes: either the conversation gravitates toward the totally vacuous—for example, how having pop stars send out a campaign endorsement is the key to winning over the kids these days—or it becomes entirely wonkish, focused on appealing to young voters as strictly rational beings who waltz into the voting booth with a list of pros and cons about tax cuts and entitlement reform and Obamacare premiums. Neither of these approaches hits the mark.

Voting is an emotional act as much as a rational act. Voters are not as dumb as political consultants think they are, and they are not as rational as think tank scholars hope they are. Young voters, in particular, are still figuring out which party and candidate works for them, who represents their values and preferences. And what I have heard, through years and years of studying young voters of all stripes, from all walks of life, from all across the country, is simple:

"I wish someone actually understood my life and what I'm going through."

And thus, here lies the disconnect, the root of so much of the frustration and disappointment and now detachment from politics today. Even well-intentioned politicians and candidates with their hearts in the right place—people who truly do care about the next generation— are often confused or unaware of the significant way that the world has changed since they were young adults.

The way today's 18-year-olds will grow up and establish their lives is quite different from the way that their parents and grandparents did. They don't remember the Cold War and barely remember September 11. They know they won't get a pension, they'd rather live where they can walk to the grocery store, they might not bother getting cable TV. They probably won't get married as early, and they might not wait until they're married to have kids. They're probably not going to go to church every Sunday. They might postpone buying a house.

These changes aren't just superficial. This isn't about bell-bottoms versus skinny jeans. When your best friend comes out to you as gay, that has a fundamental impact on how you think about family values. When you can't get a job after graduation and decide to freelance to pay down your student loan debt, you think differently about how the economy works. When you see the street on which you grew up dotted with foreclosure sign after foreclosure sign, it profoundly affects how you view homeownership and the American Dream.

So when political leaders go on TV and talk about family values, or the economy, or the American Dream, those leaders oftentimes have no idea why what they are saying doesn't resonate. They're perplexed that their talk about "big government" hasn't rallied the young masses. They wonder why their plan to cut corporate taxes hasn't earned them widespread adoration. *Maybe if we just post it on Twitter, then the kids will love it.*

This isn't a uniquely Republican problem by any means, but as of late it is Republicans who appear less and less attuned to these generational shifts, and it is Republicans who are paying the price at the ballot box when young people show up to vote. While many of these losses are being offset by Republican gains among older voters today, that will not always be the case, particularly as millennial voters constitute a greater and greater share of the nation's voters.

For Democrats, these millennial voters are the backbone of their coalition, a necessary piece of their long-term electoral strategy. For Republicans, these millennial voters are the future—a way out of the wilderness.

Someone who turns 18 on the eve of the 2016 presidential election will, based on average life expectancy, continue to vote until the presidential election of 2076.

That's a lot of votes.

TWO

Snapchats from Hillary:
How Video Games and Cat Videos
Are Changing Campaigns

"I'm watching the debate at my condo, recording it on my VCR so that I could upload a RealAudio file of the thing afterwards, because who the fuck has video back then, right? And all of a sudden, he says it. We didn't know he was going to do it. It wasn't planned. And so the cup I'd been holding in my hand crashed to the floor and I'm, like, 'What the fuck just happened?'"

As architect of the Bob Dole 1996 presidential campaign website, Rob Kubasko was there at the beginning, the dawn of the campaign website age. He's seen how much things have changed. He's also seen what hasn't.

"We had this beat-up Sun SPARC workstation, and we set it up in my business partner's parents' basement," says Kubasko, recounting the way the Dole '96 website was hosted. "They had to use a backhoe to put in a T1 line and to get power to it. The Internet service was awful and was supposed to cost over a thousand dollars a month. They had to put a transformer on the back of the house to handle the extra power. And then, every day, the campaign would *fax me a printout of every page of the website*, with handwritten edits on the pages.

"So Dole is up there on the debate stage, and as he's finishing up he tells the viewers to go to his website, and says the URL. Of course, the site immediately crashed, because, like, five thousand visitors was enough to crash a website in 1996."

When one tries to think of a time where Republicans have been the more groundbreaking, innovative, youthful team, perhaps Bob Dole's presidential bid does not come to mind. Nonetheless, during a presidential debate in October 1996, it was Dole who made campaign tech history by being the first man to ever note the address of his campaign website in his debate remarks.

"This is important business—this election is important," Dole said, wrapping up his closing statement at the October 6, 1996, presidential debate in Hartford, Connecticut. "I ask for your support, I ask for your help. And if you really want to get involved, just tap into my home page at w-w-w-dot-dolekemp96-oh-ar-gee. Thank you and God bless America."

As a Dole spokeswoman put it after the fact, "Sen. Dole's mention of the address during the debate was arguably the single biggest advertisement for a Web site in history."[1]

Yes . . . or, alternatively, this was the moment that Kubasko dropped his drink and let the expletives fly.

You can still visit dolekemp96.org today. When you do, you first arrive at a landing page saying that the site is preserved for educational purposes by an entity called "4President.org." Clicking through, you are transported back in time. There are old-school animated GIFs, "Today's Headlines" from November 1996, and transcripts of remarks from Dole's debates and appearances, including, of course, that October 6 debate in Hartford—with one minor, barely noticeable edit.

In his statement at the end of the debate, Dole accidentally neglected to say the final "dot" before "org," sending many viewers to an error message. Kubasko tried to fix Dole's error the day it happened. "I took the audio file I had created from the videotape and edited it so it was correct—basically adding in the extra dot and smoothing it out—[then] I went ahead and posted it to the splash page and the campaign *flipped their shit* at me," he said. "I made the case that it would be unusable . . . it wasn't accurate and as a result we NEVER used it or referenced that he did it again on the site."

The lede of the *Chicago Tribune*'s story about Dole's website name-drop is amusing in hindsight, of course. "Bob Dole's attempt during Sunday's presidential debate to connect with the Internet generation by mentioning his home page got nothing but an error message."

That one of the earliest Republican advances in technology ran into hiccups at the hands of an old-fashioned candidate who likely didn't understand the first bit about technology is almost poetic.

It was certainly prophetic.

☆

In 1996, when Bob Dole was trying to "connect with the Internet generation," nobody who we today think of as a millennial was eligible to vote yet. Some hadn't even been *born*. I was in the Hunter's Creek Middle School computer club that year, wearing out a *Command & Conquer* game demo CD-ROM and making silly BASIC programs out of my *Teen* magazine quizzes. I'm fairly certain I was not Bob Dole's target audience. In fact, it is astonishing to think that less than twenty years ago not many people at *all* were able to access the exciting and mysterious "World Wide Web." The U.S. Census Bureau estimated that, in 1997, less than 37 percent of households had a computer, period.[2] Only 18 percent of households had Internet access.

By the year 2000, that number had effectively exploded, with over 41 percent of households having Internet access and over half having a computer.[3] By 2012, three out of four homes had the Internet and nearly 80 percent had a computer.[4] (That's a higher proportion, by the way, than households who had landline phones.)[5] When you take a step back to really consider how rapidly this radical change has taken place, it is breathtaking.

This extraordinary transformation happened so quickly and so recently that few young adults today really remember a world without the Internet. They've been dubbed "digital natives," because, unlike their parents, they didn't have to *adapt* to today's technology; it's just the reality they've always known. (Consider a 2011 YouTube video that went viral, featuring a toddler who is utterly confused about how to handle a print magazine. The child repeatedly tries to "swipe" the physical pages and treats the magazine like it has a touch screen. Hard copies of books are a mystery; a tablet like the iPad is the norm. Welcome to the future.)[6]

In nearly every focus group I have done of young people, whenever I've asked what they think makes their generation special, they inevitably bring up their own comfort with technology. Every major corporate or PR firm research study on young adults that I have ever been a part of or have had a chance to review names connectedness and technological aptitude as a core defining attribute of this generation. Being a connected, technologically savvy candidate is a necessary though not sufficient condition these days for being acceptable to young voters.

Political figures have long looked to the latest innovations in communication technology to reach voters. The fact that many homes had electricity and radios in the 1930s made it logical for FDR to hold his "fireside chats" over the airwaves, and the fact that most people had computers and an Internet connection at home by the mid-2000s made it sensible for Hillary Clinton to announce her 2007 bid for president by posting "I'm In" online.[7]

Yet widespread changes like the adoption of the radio or the television unfolded over decades. Today, how we connect with each other seems to change significantly in the blink of an eye. Take the rise of the iPhone and Android: in early 2006, of the subset of Americans who had cell phones, only 14 percent used their devices to browse the Internet.[8] By 2013, 56 percent of *all American adults* had a smartphone of some kind, including eight out of ten of those aged 18 to 34.[9]

Every election, there's a new advance in technology that is credited with having given one side an advantage over the other. In 2006, George Allen, a U.S. senator from Virginia (and, at the time, possible 2008 Republican presidential contender), was campaigning for reelection, when he was caught on camera bizarrely insulting a student; the clip's circulation on YouTube doomed Allen to defeat, leading the election to be dubbed "the YouTube Election."[10] By 2008 we had "the Facebook Election," where President Obama's victory was credited in part to the campaign's savvy at leveraging social networking tools to build support.[11] In 2010 the big story was the Tea Party but also Twitter, which academics at the University of Michigan found conservative and Tea Party candidates were particularly adept at using and doing so prolifically.[12] The 2012 election was the "big data" election, for which both on- and off-line data about individual voters was used to build a more effective and efficient campaign.[13]

Every year, it seems there's something.

So what's next?

In 2013 the *Economist* wrote that, "rather as electrification changed everything by allowing energy to be used far from where it was generated, computing and communications technologies transform lives and businesses by allowing people to make calculations and connections far beyond their unaided capacity." Electricity is omnipresent in our lives and facilitates almost everything we do today, and we don't even really notice. It is invisible and it does everything.

The ability to be constantly connected to the rest of the world digitally is gaining that same status. Experts expect that, in the next few years, most things in our lives—from our home appliances to our own bodies—will be seamlessly connected to the Internet, sharing data and interacting, without us really noticing.[14] Ever heard of "the Internet of things," a term used nowadays to describe the increasing digital connectedness of traditionally "off-line" things like our daily exercise routines or home thermostats? Very soon, digital life won't just be about looking at a screen, checking your e-mail, grabbing a quick stock quote, browsing Facebook. It will be integrated, almost invisibly, into everything you do.

This doesn't actually make it more important than ever that a campaign have a large digital department.

It means very soon it will be completely ridiculous that a campaign would have a stand-alone digital department at all.

Today, nearly *everything* is digital.

☆

Inside every campaign lives a turf war.

It may be civil and polite. It may be unspoken. It may be loud and destructive. It may spill out into the pages of *POLITICO* or it may happen behind closed doors, but make no mistake: there is always a turf war afoot.

Think about all of the consultants involved in a campaign who play a role in the process of reaching and persuading a voter: there's the direct mail consultant, whose job it is to send brochures and mailers to voters' houses. Then, there's a different consultant, the media consultant, whose job it is to put together TV and radio advertisements. There's a pollster who does the surveys and focus groups to figure out what the message ought to look like and how best to portray the candidate. These days, there ought to be a data or targeting firm that builds and enhances the campaign's list of voters that they want to reach. Then there's the digital consulting firm that usually does the website, the Facebook page, the YouTube advertising, the banner ads . . .

Each of these things costs money. And despite rising levels of spending on elections, campaigns do not in fact have unlimited money.

If you think about the way incentives work, each of those consultants—the media person, the direct mail person, the digital person—is pretty likely to tell you that *their* piece of the equation is the most important or deserves a bigger slice of the campaign's budget. Someone who works in the world of campaign direct mail will tell you the campaign should spend more there because you're guaranteed to reach exactly the voters you want with a perfect level of efficiency, something neither the TV folks nor the digital team can promise. The media consultant will say the media team should have the vast majority of the budget because TV is the medium that truly "moves numbers"—meaning that if you put enough money into television advertising, you'll always see the polls shift your way shortly thereafter. And then, the digital team will argue that mail gets thrown away and TV ads get skipped on the DVR or are shown to tons of people who are tuned in but aren't target voters. The digital folks point out that—with people spending increasing amounts of time online and with massive improvements in how we can follow and target voters online with our message—the digital piece of the campaign deserves more investment.

This is not necessarily nefarious; it's likely that each of the consultants genuinely believes the work his or her team does is critical. But it does mean that, in a campaign with finite resources, there are winners and losers. And particularly on the Republican side, too often, the digital folks wind up the losers.

For a long time, when "digital campaigning" was new in the world, the "digital department" struggled to find a proper "home" in the organizational chart of many campaigns, because it doesn't neatly fit into the usual buckets that a campaign has carved out. Take fundraising: campaigns will have a "finance team" whose job is to raise as much money as possible. Particularly since 2007 and the birth of the "money bomb"—an intensive online fund-raising push over a brief period of time—campaigns have turned online to raise huge volumes of cash, usually in the form of many, many small donations.[15] There's an obvious digital component of fund-raising. But fund-raising isn't the only thing that can be done online: there's advertising to voters, there's organizing of voters, there's communicating with the media. Digital fits everywhere, so the solution in the past has been to make "digital" its own department, often stuffed into the communications team as a subsidiary. This can mean the digital team is walled off or treated as a second-tier entity.

Of course, having a stand-alone digital team works out just fine if the campaign has made a commitment to prioritizing what the digital and technology team is doing in all areas of the campaign. My current partner at Echelon Insights, Patrick Ruffini, released a report titled "Inside the Cave," a detailed analysis of how the Obama campaign had structured their digital, data, and analytics efforts. He noted that "most campaigns talk about giving the Internet a seat at the senior staff table. Obama for America had two."[16] Both the digital team, handling all of the ways that a campaign interfaces with voters, and the technology team, the group tasked with making the campaign run at maximum efficiency, had a voice at the highest levels of the campaign. "Inside the Cave" estimated that the digital team had two hundred staff members, while technology and analytics had another hundred, and that in total these staffers made up 30 to 40 percent of the people working out of the Obama campaign's Chicago headquarters.

Sure, it's OK to have a "digital department" when what you're essentially talking about is *four out of ten of the people working in your building.*

This has not been the norm on the Republican side. Ruffini's analysis suggested that the Romney team had far, far fewer staff in these areas. In an interview with *POLITICO* in 2014 about the Republican Party's "tech deficit," one unnamed Republican digital strategist noted: "I'd say there's only 10 people [on the Republican side] who are capable of overseeing a team and fighting with all the other departments for budget." The story noted: "One Republican digital operative working on the 2014 midterms said he'd work for a White House contender in 2016 only if he was assured a seat at the table for key tech decisions with the candidate, campaign manager and top general consultant."[17]

They're absolutely right. That's an important step. But building a huge digital team and having a seat at the decision-making table would just be catching up to what Democrats already did in 2012. The future is having every single piece of a campaign fully integrated with what a "digital team" would do. It's not about having one digital team person with a seat at the senior staff table. It's about having *everyone* at the senior staff table with an understanding and appreciation for what digital can do, with digital embedded in every single function of the campaign.

At its core, "digital campaigning" is about looking at all of the ways that the Internet and new technology enhance how we can identify, persuade, and activate people. At every level of a campaign, from campaign manager to intern, and in every department of a campaign, from fund-raising to field organizing, staff and consultants need a clear understanding of how new technology enables a campaign to achieve its goals.

The campaigns that will win the youngest generation today and win the elections of the future won't view digital as a sideshow; they'll see it as part of the campaign's DNA.

☆

I am no longer Kristen Soltis Anderson, normal human being.

I am Emmastone, a redheaded fire mage, fighting proudly for the Alliance against the Horde across the plains of the lost world of Pandaria.

Intending to embark on casual research mission into the world of "massively multiplayer online role-playing games" (MMPORGs), I subscribed to Blizzard Entertainment's popular *World of Warcraft*, or *WoW*. Video games today are a way that many people stay connected with each other, and I thought I'd explore whether or not there was any way a smart campaign could tap into these digital networks.

I soon came to discover that signing up for *WoW* was akin to saying, *I think I will try hard, addictive drugs . . . just once . . . for research.*

Launched in 2004 and a decade later boasting millions of subscribers, *WoW* involves creating a character and entering the online world of Azeroth alongside everyone who is playing around the world at that moment. You explore the world, meet others, go on quests, battle enemies, develop trade skills, try to collect interesting loot.

Like real life, but with more orcs.

While your average American probably thinks *WoW* is a weird online enclave of freaks and geeks, Blizzard Entertainment has evolved the game to keep up with changing computing capabilities and to broaden its base of users. *WoW* subscribers now range from hard-core gamer kids to adults who occasionally pop in to participate in a "raid," an organized effort of anywhere from ten to twenty-five players all trying to progress through a level to defeat a particular enemy "boss" in a battle at the end. Far from the traditional stereotype of gamers as loners and debunking the notion that video games make people more isolated, the game requires and encourages people to interact with one another. Sometimes those interactions aren't confined to the screen: "You see spouses who met playing the game and are now married," lead game designer Ion Hazzikostas told CNET.[18]

Ostensibly, my goal in registering for *WoW* was to figure out if there was anything campaigns can or should be doing through these games to engage with voters. After all, the NSA had thought it a worthwhile place to go hunting for good intel, though of a very different sort: in 2013, documents leaked by Edward Snowden revealed that intelligence agencies created characters in MMPORGs including *WoW* with the intent of gathering information and identifying informants.[19]

Maybe I'd discover political discussions happening in the game's chat channels. After all, during the 2012 election, researchers had used surveys on the Xbox console to study public opinion about the upcoming presidential election.[20] Maybe there were ads or references to politics woven in to the game's landscape. Maybe I'd stumble across a secret Democratic effort to recruit voters through the game's "guilds," communities where members work together to gather resources or defeat enemies.

Instead, I wound up running a relatively serious jewelcrafting empire out of the auction house at Stormwind City and day trading ghost iron ore. (Even in a video game, I gravitate toward the charms of the free market.) I'd sell my wares to other players who could embed the jewels into their pieces of armor to improve their character's "stats," or their chances of winning in battle. I started up a farm in the virtual town of Halfhill where I grew pumpkins and carrots. I burned an incredible number of hours I'll never get back on the game's appropriately named Timeless Isle, trying to obtain an electrified rideable dragon. I'd gone way off course in my mission, with no politics to be found.

"*WoW* provides respite from the incessant advertising which is the backdrop of so much contemporary activity. Most of the Internet can no longer be experienced without a barrage of ads; *WoW* has none. It is restful, even old-fashioned," writes anthropologist Bonnie Nardi, recounting her own research mission into the game.[21]

Clearly, American political campaigns have not arrived in Azeroth. (Yet.)

Plenty of video games are certainly *political*. We talk a lot about the political messages embedded in our movies, TV shows, and music, but there's just as much of that going on in the stories of our video games. *BioShock*, released in 2007, explores the libertarian philosophy of Ayn Rand and "aggressive Darwinian capitalism" as your character navigates a radically experimental underwater city that has been taken over by drug-addled zombie inhabitants.[22] Driving around in *Grand Theft Auto V*'s vast virtual world of Los Santos, a near copy of Los Angeles, one can listen to "Weasel News," a thinly veiled parody of modern cable news and talk radio, complete with plenty of material lampooning both parties.[23]

But that's not the only way video games are political. Today, even the stadium ads in *Madden NFL* aren't safe from the reach of politics. In 2008, the Obama campaign made history by purchasing in-game advertising spots through video game company Electronic Arts in over a dozen different games.[24] Because of the relative ease of geographical targeting, the Obama team was able to focus their video game ads on voters in battleground states.[25] Players from states like Ohio and Colorado logging on to a game like *Need for Speed: Carbon* may have found themselves racing down the highway, only to pass a billboard advertising "voteforchange.com" with Obama's face on it.[26]

Not all video game campaign activity has been particularly successful. Perhaps the funniest example comes courtesy of failed Democratic presidential candidate John Edwards, whose campaign established an office in the weird online world of Second Life in 2007. It was mostly notable because it wound up being vandalized by pranksters in-game.[27] Virginia senator Mark Warner appeared in Second Life for an awkward in-game campaign rally. None of these efforts were particularly successful, to say the least, and some platforms or hot gaming trends can fizzle quickly. Furthermore, making politics work in the world of video games requires more thoughtfulness than the aforementioned examples.

For video game advertising or engagement, context matters. Researchers in 2005 studied how gamers reacted to and recalled advertisements embedded in different types of video games, and discovered that ads could be effective only if they made sense in the world of the game. "Just as a McDonald's logo has no place in *World of Warcraft*, certain products should not be advertised where they do not normally belong," the researchers noted.[28] Yet they also noted that playing video games is a deeply immersive experience and the games offer advertisers a real opportunity to reach consumers—or, perhaps, voters—if the ads are crafted to work with the world in which they'll be displayed. Consumer brands have responded to the new advertising opportunity, with huge conglomerates like Unilever inking deals to have their products integrated into games like the popular *Sims* franchise.[29]

There's more to video games, though, than just fighting space aliens or going on quests through magical forests. Sometimes you just want to play a quick game of Scrabble on your phone. There, too, the Obama team in 2012 had purchased ad space, inserting their advertising into people's matches.[30] And it's these more casual gaming worlds, in things like online board games and word puzzles you can solve with friends, where most video game playing occurs these days. For instance, half a billion people had downloaded 2012's popular *Candy Crush Saga* game for their mobile devices, according to paperwork filed by the game's parent company, King, in early 2014 ahead of that company's IPO; at the time, they estimated 125 *million* people played the game *every single day*.[31] While there may not be tons of grandmothers playing *Gears of War*, the explosion of casual and social gaming has helped dramatically change the population of game players, making it a ripe arena for reaching target voters. "Women age 18 or older represent a significantly greater portion of the game-playing population (36%) than boys age 18 or younger (17%)," according to a report by the Entertainment Software Association in 2014, noting that in just one year, between 2012 and 2013, the number of female gamers *over age 50* increased by a third.[32]

There's likely to be a new *Candy Crush* or *Angry Birds* "freemium" game out there every few months to absorb our attention and monopolize our time. (Both *Angry Birds* and *Candy Crush* got a spin-off, and supermodels like Kate Upton can now be found starring in ads for addictive phone-based games.) Yet, even as individual games come and go in popularity, the platforms on which people play them—mobile devices, personal computers, and gaming consoles—aren't going anywhere.

Half of American households have some kind of video game console like an Xbox or PlayStation. Even if it isn't being used to play *Halo* or *Call of Duty*, these gaming consoles have a multitude of other uses, like letting people watch streaming video on their TVs. Sony announced that they want to give the PlayStation its own channel, creating original content in the same way that Netflix has made its own shows, like *Orange Is the New Black* and *House of Cards*.[33] In 2014 Microsoft tried to encourage campaigns to deploy ads on the Xbox dashboard, touting the diversity of the console's users and the ability of campaigns to match up target voter lists with the Xbox Live subscriber base.[34] Campaigns today have TV advertising strategies built around getting the message out over a medium that people turn to for entertainment; smart campaigns should start thinking about how to deploy ads that work in everything from mindless "freemium" iPhone games to blockbuster console video game releases.

It's hard to imagine a day when political candidates and leaders throw on a headset and log in to the world of Azeroth to go on quests to fight demons alongside targeted swing voters. (I admit, however, that I'd find it highly amusing if nothing else. If you'd ever like to do a raid, Joe Biden, *I'm in*.) But as we live more and more of our lives online, and as our social interactions increasingly involve communicating, connecting, and competing through games from Scrabble to immersive fantasy world MMPORGs, political leaders should seriously consider ways to engage with voters across these platforms.

The goal of campaign advertising has always been to get a message in front of voters where they're paying attention. Walk into most American homes and there will be some kind of gaming console. Walk into any room of young adults today—or, frankly, adults of *all* ages—and the odds are decent that at least half of them will be staring at their phones. We're surrounded by screens, and, for better or worse, that means campaigns and marketers have an enormous number of new ways to get their ads in front of consumers and voters. But if all we are doing in digital advertising is replicating off-line advertising— radio-style ads on online streaming radio services like Pandora, TV-style ads during streaming video on services like Hulu—we're missing the full potential of how we can reach people. Whether it's thought-ful, context-appropriate in-game advertising using console and mobile game advertising platforms, or organizing communities who are al-ready connected via games, campaigns who want to reach voters where they are need to be creative and open to diving into the worlds of gaming and online entertainment. Wherever people are fighting aliens or crushing candies, if there's a way for a company or brand to adver-tise and win over consumers, campaigns should take a good, hard look at how they can be there too.

☆

"I am Tim Berners-Lee. I invented the WWW 25 years ago and I am concerned and excited about its future. AMA."

On March 12, 2014, the father of the Internet took to Reddit, the self-proclaimed "front page of the Internet," to take questions from anyone, about anything. Reddit is a site that allows users to post what-ever they find interesting—photos, links, etc.—in hopes of sharing it with the interested Reddit public. On Reddit, posts and comments made by users are voted up or down, giving anyone the opportunity to participate but ensuring the cream of the comments rises to the top. Within Reddit there are also "subreddits," pages where users can post more topic-specific items, such as /r/space for space-related links and photos, or /r/LifeProTips for things like tips on how to keep celery crisp in the fridge or how to break free from duct-tape-bound captiv-ity. The "Ask Me Anything" subreddit, or "AMA," is where Reddit's millions of users from around the world can do just that: pose questions to whoever has volunteered.

Think it sounds silly? Not exactly. Barack Obama and Bill Nye are among those who have popped on over to Reddit and made the offer: Ask Me Anything.[35] The Reddit AMA may one day become a rite of passage for major national candidates, but not every political figure who has tried an AMA thus far has thrived in the format; just ask the former governor of Maryland. "Martin O'Malley did a Reddit AMA. It didn't go very well," wrote Abby Phillip of the *Washington Post*, noting that the format is one where authenticity and honest answers are expected and where O'Malley's talking points and formality fell utterly flat.[36]

During the Tim Berners-Lee Reddit AMA, Berners-Lee was asked by a Reddit user: "What was one of the things you never thought the Internet would be used for, but has actually become one of the main reasons people use the Internet?"

Berners-Lee replied: "Kittens."

Indeed, kittens do seem to run the Internet. Popular websites like BuzzFeed essentially print money by posting articles that are, quite literally, just a series of pictures of cats with captions. ("21 Cats Who Are Totally Empowered by Their Halloween Costumes" is an honest-to-goodness real thing that has appeared on the site.)[37] YouTube is full of cat videos. "Grumpy Cat," a cat famous for looking perpetually unhappy, became an icon and was featured in McDonald's advertising. Blogs are full of animated images of cats doing funny things. Entire major Internet humor websites have been built around cat-related jokes. Reddit itself is a major hub of cat-related Web content where the /r/cats "subreddit" hosts photos people upload of their cats and elevates those with the most votes to the top of the page. "Cats" not specific enough for you? There's a subreddit called StartledCats where tens of thousands of people have subscribed to see pictures of, yes, *startled* cats. Even politics is not immune from the weird feline domination of the digital arena: Democrats have sent out fund-raising e-mails including kitten photos in their appeals for donations, and Republicans have made a BuzzFeed copy-cat site with headlines like "13 Animals That Are Really Bummed on ObamaCare's Third Birthday"—including cats, of course.[38]

Given that cats are really, perhaps disturbingly, behind most of what seems to happen in the digital world these days, it should be unsurprising that it was a cat that led me to finally break down and join in on another digital trend: Snapchat.

Let me explain.

Snapchat, launched in late 2011, is an app that lets you send picture messages to your friends. The catch? The photos vanish a few seconds after being viewed. Being slightly older than the target market for Snapchat at the time, everything I knew about Snapchat I heard from the news, which essentially portrayed Snapchat as a way for college-age kids to send one another provocative photos.[39] After all, why else would you want to use a service that specifically erases your photos shortly after you send them? This did not really sound like my particular area of interest.

And then my sister got a cat.

I first got acquainted with Mimi, my sister Jen's new kitten, in the summer of 2013, during the festivities leading up to my sister's wedding in our hometown. Mimi and I did not particularly get along. Then, on Jen's big day, as we all had lunch and did our makeup in preparation for the wedding, Mimi and I had an altercation over who had rights to my turkey sandwich. Over the holidays, we arrived at a sort of détente, but Mimi's insistence on unexpectedly leaping at my face as I sat on the couch watching football really ruined the chances that we'd ever be close companions.

But Jen loves Mimi, and loves taking pictures or short videos of Mimi doing amusing things. And she loves sending them off to friends via Snapchat. Mimi chasing a string. Mimi jumping for the doorknob.

Mimi meowing. And then I discovered my other sister, Heather, was in on the game. Heather would take photos of, say, whatever she was eating and, *poof*, off they'd go into the ether, presumably to whichever friend would be interested in knowing what Heather had eaten for lunch.

These were not profound statements or heartfelt conversations. It was pictures of cats and pictures of food. And it was *weightless*. It was stupid. But it was a way I could keep in touch with my sisters. Frankly, it looked fun. I joined.

Once I had the app, I discovered that every morning I'd be the lucky recipient of a Snapchat from Jen featuring none other than her beloved Mimi. Mimi watching something on TV. Mimi making a weird noise. On my birthday, I got a Snapchat from Jen featuring Mimi in a drawn-on birthday hat, using the app's built-in photo editing and captioning functionality.

When you post a photo on Facebook, chances are you put at least a little thought into how you'll present it. Maybe not a lot, but at least a little. You want to make the caption just right. You hope your friends will "like" it. Is it a good picture? Should I tag people in it? Or take Twitter, where posts have limited text, but where posting typically means blasting your item out to the world, and where even deleted tweets can live forever. I may not really care to share with the entire world that I just ate French toast *and it was awesome*. If I feel strongly that I need to share with someone, I could e-mail it, but that's a hassle. I could send it as a regular text, but that feels . . . permanent. The photo sticks around. Not that there's anything incriminating about me and my French toast, but . . . is it really that big a deal?

Thus, the appeal of Snapchat. You fire and forget. A Snapchat is fleeting and therefore perfectly acceptable for total frivolity. It is ephemeral (even if it technically isn't necessarily as ephemeral as users are led to believe). And laugh all you want about how dumb it is that people these days are using the incredible, revolutionary technology at their fingertips to swap cat pictures and brunch photos, but this is what we as a society are doing to connect with each other, for better or worse.

Around the same time that I was finally jumping on the Snapchat bandwagon and getting my daily dose of Mimi, the app was blowing up into something much bigger than a small digital fad; it was home to about half of all photos being uploaded every day, period. More photos were being uploaded to Snapchat than were being uploaded to Facebook, more than were going to Instagram, more than were being sent to photo-sharing sites like Flickr. The founders of Snapchat were offered $3 billion *cash* by Facebook to sell the company, *and the Snapchat guys said no*, viewing the company as having even greater growth potential.[40] At least for the moment, they appear to have made the right call: less than a year later, the *Wall Street Journal* reported that the company's latest round of funding had garnered them a valuation of $10 billion.[41]

Once it became clear that Snapchat wasn't just a way to transmit naked pictures, the big brands started to show up.

Taco Bell was the first major national brand to get into the Snapchat game, urging people to "friend" them on Snapchat and then sending those new friends a simple image of a Beefy Crunch Burrito with a hand-drawn "Hi Friend" scrawled across the photo.[42] In February of 2014, *Advertising Age* reported that McDonald's would launch a promotion over Snapchat featuring LeBron James, using the app's "Stories" feature to broadcast brief, evaporating clips of the basketball superstar with the chain's latest bacon cheeseburger.[43] A few months later, *Variety* reported that Marriott was getting into the Snapchat business, launching its own "in-house branded entertainment division" that would work on projects like a series of Snapchat stories showcasing just how cool it is to travel to Marriott hotel destinations.[44]

There are a handful of politicians and political groups on the service, but—like political groups and video game advertising—engagement is not yet widespread. Generation Opportunity, a conservative group focused on persuading young Americans to support limited government, hopped onto Snapchat via the character of "Creepy Uncle Sam," a fairly unsettling version of the patriotic icon whose mission was to persuade young people to "opt out" of the Affordable Care Act's health insurance exchanges.[45] Senator Rand Paul soon followed, joining Snapchat in early 2014 ostensibly to connect with younger voters and to make a point about privacy and surveillance.[46]

Why would a politician bother with something like Snapchat? Peter Hamby of CNN, in his coverage of Senator Paul's Snapchat debut, put it thusly: "Politicians—at least the smart ones—aren't just flocking to new platforms because they're trying to be hip, though that's certainly part of the calculation. They're joining them because that's increasingly where the voters are." At least, it's where *young* voters are—for now. Harvard's Institute of Politics' fall 2014 survey asked respondents if they had accounts across a variety of platforms, and 37 percent of those aged 18 to 24 and 28 percent of all of those under age 30 said they were on Snapchat.[47] Researchers at CivicScience who studied even younger respondents found that 57 percent of those aged 13 to 18 either use or plan to start using Snapchat soon.[48] Anecdotally, during my brief stint at the Institute of Politics at Harvard University, I saw firsthand the ubiquity of Snapchat: when ESPN's College GameDay came to campus for the Harvard-Yale football game, students I spoke to were particularly hopeful that they'd be the chosen "Our Story" event on Snapchat that day, meaning users could upload their photos and short videos from the game and be featured on the phones of Snapchat users everywhere. Snapchat began as a private messaging medium and appears likely to expand as a way for people, brands, and possibly candidates, to share *their* stories to millions.

It's always risky to declare a particular app or service the next big thing, because the pace of change is so rapid and new services can fall out of favor quickly. For instance, a few years ago, the mobile check-in app Foursquare, which let users "check in" at locations and notify their friends, was the hot new company; Facebook even launched their own competitor with Facebook Places. Today, the social "check-in" trend has faded and Foursquare has refashioned itself into a service that helps people find dining and entertainment destinations that will meet users' tastes. The point isn't necessarily that Snapchat itself is *the* future of political communication. The point is that nowadays people are eager to weightlessly, casually share their lives, feelings, and opinions with the world. Young Americans in particular are living their lives on their phones. They don't need things to be formal and highly produced and retouched. (Exhibit A: selfies.) They just want things to be personal and available. Campaigns should be sure to meet them there.

The way campaigns are used to communicating involves spending the vast majority of campaign dollars on television ads. Typically, around four out of five dollars a campaign spends wind up going to TV ads, while online communication accounts for about one out of ten. Sure, some politicians and campaigns have gotten savvy about using services like Facebook and Twitter, or about how they communicate via e-mail or Web ads. But, frankly, those platforms should be a given. And just having your campaign doing things in the digital space doesn't mean you're doing them right. During the 2012 election, for instance, the Facebook page for Mitt Romney primarily featured posts about campaign messages and fund-raising, but after the election ended, it changed tone by posting photos of Governor Romney on vacation with his grandkids, showcasing the "softer side" of Mitt. Given that this is how *most* people use Facebook, doesn't it make sense to have the message match the medium, to sprinkle in the personal with the political on these platforms?

You don't get a gold star for having ads on YouTube and a well-managed Facebook page. Running ads on Pandora and Hulu isn't an advance in campaigning; it is an expectation. If you want to reach the *next* generation of voters, those steps are just the start. For instance, among voters under age 30, nearly four out of ten say they are on Twitter, but the same number say they use Instagram, the Facebook-owned photo-sharing site that lets people easily upload artsy photos on which their friends can comment. Nearly every politician and campaign has a Twitter account these days, but precious few use Instagram to share the more personal side of a candidate or to offer followers a firsthand look at the campaign in action. A notable exception was Elise Stefanik, elected in 2014 from upstate New York as the youngest woman ever in Congress; she often Instagrammed photos from rallies, visits to local small businesses, and meetings with voters. Any campaign looking for a good model of how to use Instagram for more than cats and brunch photos should start with her example of how to do things right.

This isn't a call for campaigns to slash their TV budgets and pour their efforts into Snapchat or Xbox ads. But why do campaigns buy TV ads? They do it because they want to reach voter eyeballs. They want to catch people where they're paying attention and get a message to them. Entertainment and social communication platforms, which today may seem like they are primarily useful for swapping pictures of parties and food and pets or for playing word games and fighting aliens, are where an awful lot of voters' eyeballs and attention are these days. The campaign "turf wars" over which communication medium is best—TV, radio, mail, digital—are too often about who gets what dollars and not about the best, most cost-effective way to reach the right eyeballs, the right voters. Decisions about how to reach voters should be driven by data and should be open to creative use of new channels and technology. And "digital" shouldn't just be viewed as a one-way street where campaigns can send *out* a message, like TV or mail. Digital is a two-way street where voters can talk back, pledge their support, share a message, or contribute. Digital today may only be a small sliver of a campaign's budget or a small department within a broader campaign effort; smart campaigns will make digital a part of every single thing they do.

☆

Rob Kubasko kept working in politics after the Dole '96 campaign, all the way through the ill-fated McCain campaign against Barack Obama in 2008. I met Rob in July of 2009 at a PechaKucha event for young Republican strategist types hosted by some mutual friends in Alexandria, Virginia. PechaKucha (from the Japanese term meaning chitchat) is a highly structured, fast-paced presentation style that was developed in the early 2000s and has become popular in tech circles around the world. At these events, everybody gives a brief slide presentation that is twenty slides long and where each slide automatically advances after twenty seconds. The point of the event where I met Rob was to get the young Republican digital nerd crowd to gather around a bucket of beer, a laptop, and a projector screen to talk about where the GOP ought to go after defeat in 2008.

It was a fun evening, though I admit I forget almost everyone's presentation. But I remember Rob's. It was gorgeous in its design, compelling in flow, and it was one of the first things I'd seen that actually got to the heart of the problem facing Republicans. Our problem wasn't just about websites or about Facebook, Rob said. Those were excuses. In his opinion, the problem was that we as a party didn't have compelling content or ideas to sell to voters, and so of course our brand would be terrible. It is a view Rob continues to hold.

"Apple has taken twenty years to remake their brand by building kick-ass products that work. Not by *saying* they build kick-ass products that work, but by actually *building* kick-ass products that work."

Kubasko, today, does not think Republicans have kick-ass products that work.

Rob has worked in the world of campaign digital strategy essentially ever since there was such a thing as campaign digital strategy. He's seen it all. He's designed it all. And, sadly, he's decided he's had enough. He decided he was done with it all when he was asked by a campaign policy staffer to put together the design for a policy paper the campaign was going to release. "The guy tells me he doesn't care what it looks like, he just wants it to be triple-spaced so it looks bigger. He grabs a phone book that was sitting around the office, and holds it up, and says he wants it to look like this. It didn't matter what was in it—just the optics. It was like, 'Ah, this is a campaign about nothing.' That was it for me."

You won't find a bigger advocate for the importance of digital campaigning, of meeting voters where they are, than Rob Kubasko. But he is adamant—and absolutely right—that the medium is just part of the story. Getting on Snapchat or putting up ads on the Xbox means you're using new channels—which is great, but an old message on a new channel is a wasted opportunity. The tools campaigns have at their disposal are evolving constantly, and the ways that technology can enhance how campaigns communicate with their audiences are countless and expanding. Certainly, the medium *is* the message: candidates who run truly modern digital campaigns and reach voters in new ways can much more credibly say that they understand how America is changing and that they are looking to the future. And especially for Republicans, who are so often viewed as old-fashioned, trying to break that stereotype by being effective at using new digital tools to reach young voters is key. But what we *say* with those tools is even more important.

Thus far, we've seen why it is so important for political leaders to focus on the next generation, on the cultural and demographic trends that are reshaping the political landscape. We've seen how technology and data are giving campaigns deeper insights into how voters think and behave, and how these new tools can give a candidate the ability to get their message out in more efficient, more effective ways. We've touched on how things like consumer preferences reflect characteristics and values that connect to political behavior. And finally, we've taken a peek at just a few of the new ways that campaigns can respond to the changing communications landscape out there by following voters onto new digital platforms.

But understanding how *information* travels today is just the beginning. We can be smarter than ever about *who* we want to reach and *how* we want to reach them. But *what we say* and *what we plan to do* is the most crucial piece of the puzzle. In order to best understand what the next generation of voters is hungry to hear, we have to start at a much more basic place: we have to understand where their lives are headed.

And we have to prove we have ideas that can enable them to lead fulfilled, healthy, happy lives.

THREE

Saying No to the Dress
(but Yes to the Diapers):
The New Shape of the American Family

"It's a gift that we can all appreciate—and goes a lot further than a gravy bowl," declared the Obama campaign's website in June 2012, announcing the launch of its newest fund-raising initiative: a wedding registry. "It's a great way to support the President on your big day." Happy soon-to-be-wed couples could forgo pots and pans and napkin rings and instead direct friends and loved ones to BarackObama.com to make a contribution in honor of their pending nuptials. By mid-July, the *New York Post* reported that the "bizarre marriage-theme fund-raising scheme . . . has been a total flop."[1]

The evolution of the wedding registry in the United States over the last century provides a glimpse at how the institution of marriage itself has changed through the decades. In 2011 the *Wall Street Journal* reported that as the average age when someone first gets married has increased, cohabitation has become the norm, and as men have become more involved in domestic household chores, what couples register for has adapted as well.[2] No longer is the wedding registry the place where most new couples make requests to help launch their joint household. Nowadays some couples set up registries to "upgrade" to nicer household items or to fund Jet Ski rides and massages through sites like Honeyfund. High-profile weddings of 2011 showcased the extremes of unique approaches to the wedding registry concept, ranging from the over-the-top wish list of Kim Kardashian and NBA player Kris Humphries (where thousands of dollars' worth of vases were requested to celebrate a marriage that would last only seventy-two days) to the Royal Wedding Charitable Gift Fund, where over £1 million was raised for charitable causes from well-wishers in honor of the marriage of Prince William to Kate Middleton.

Whether viewed as a desperate fund-raising ploy or an interesting use of a shifting societal norm, the Obama campaign wedding registry reflected, in some small way, the campaign's assumption that the soon-to-be-wed might value Change over cutlery as a way to celebrate their special day. Even if the tactic wound up lampooned as an embarrassing late-night talk show punch line more than anything else, the changing shape of marriage in American society, along with trends in division of household labor, workforce participation, and childbearing, are having a dramatic impact on the way American voters think about the concept of "family values."

Three months before my own wedding, and five months before the Obama wedding registry would launch, I tweeted at a friend of mine, Alex Lundry, who would go on to become the chief data scientist for the Romney 2012 campaign. "Thought: Can @alexlundry predict my vote based on the contents of my wedding registry? What does my china pattern say about my politics?" His response: "You've already given me 3 great data points! 1) you're getting married, 2) you have a registry, 3) you've put china on it."

While it is unlikely that the color of my dishes really has any meaningful relationship to my political leanings, Alex's point was a crucial one. Campaign microtargeting rose to prominence in the 2000s, touting the ways in which lifestyle and purchasing habits can identify which voters might be likely supporters of your candidate. If I had to guess, I'd say registering for china is a signal that I'm ripe for a Republican campaign appeal. (After all, Mitt Romney's campaign once pinpointed supporters in Iowa by mining data about who was shopping at Williams-Sonoma.)[3]

But what does the simple fact that someone is getting married mean to a political campaign? In general, those who are married and those who are not married vote differently. Just as political coverage sometimes talks about a "gender gap" in politics, there's a marriage gap—and it is growing. In 2012, 60 percent of the American voters told network exit pollsters that they were married, and these married voters broke for Mitt Romney by a 14-point margin. Yet, among the four out of ten voters who were not married, Romney only garnered 35 percent of the vote, including only 31 percent of unmarried women. Married people were much more likely to vote for Mitt Romney. In 2008, the "married gap" was still present, though slightly less pronounced: John McCain enjoyed only a 5-point advantage over Barack Obama among married voters while losing unmarried voters by a two-to-one margin.

Trends in who is (and who isn't) heading to the altar have something to do with this widening gap. Race, income, religion, and education level are but a few of the factors that influence how likely you are to marry. Take differences based on race: in the 2008 election, 70 percent of white voters were married, a slight increase from the 68 percent of white voters who said they were married in 2000. Yet the proportion of Hispanic voters saying they were currently married ticked down very slightly, from 60 percent in 2000 to 59 percent in 2008. Among black voters, the proportion saying they were married went from 50 to 46 percent. White voters are more likely to be married, nonwhite voters less so. If the voting behavior gap between white and nonwhite voters has grown, one would expect the gap to grow between married and unmarried voters. Yet, even when you take race out of the equation, the marriage gap still persists. Take just white voters, for instance. In 2008, there was a 31-point difference between John McCain's advantage among married white voters and his loss among unmarried white voters.

If marriage is associated with voting Republican, and the gap between married and unmarried voters has grown, trends in participation in the institution of marriage in the U.S. could paint a difficult picture for the GOP down the road. Data point after data point suggests a decline is coming for the married share of the electorate. For instance, the median age at the beginning of a first marriage for women has risen as much in the last twenty years as it did over the previous hundred. According to the U.S. Census Bureau, in 1900 the median first-time bride was 21.9 years old. In 1990, she was 23.9 years old. Fast-forward to 2010, and the median first marriage came after her twenty-sixth birthday. Men, too, have been tying the knot later and later, from a median age of 25.9 in 1900, up only very slightly to 26.1 in 1990, then rising to 28.2 by 2010.

Not only is the median age of marriage increasing, but fewer Americans are married at all. The General Social Survey, a major ongoing decades-long study conducted by the National Opinion Research Center at the University of Chicago, indicates that since 1972 there has been a dramatic drop in the percentage of people who are married, with a significant uptick in divorced and never-married people over the last few decades. This is not just a trend among the very young. While there have been dramatic drops in the percentage of those under age 35 who report being married, that persists into the late thirties and early forties. Pew Research Center analysis of U.S. Census Bureau data estimates that while 86 percent of those aged 35 to 44 were married in 1960, that number had fallen to 62 percent by 2010.[4]

Given that societal trends in marriage have been so dramatic, with such huge shifts even in just the last decade, it is perhaps remarkable that the portion of the electorate that reports being married has stayed as stable as it has, and one can expect that future elections will involve many more voters who have not tied the knot—not to mention the fact that shifts in who marries and when are just the beginning when it comes to describing the new face of the American family. As one of the young women I spoke with during a January 2013 focus group in Columbus, Ohio, put it:

"It used to be everybody had 2.5 kids and a dog and a white picket fence and that was what everybody worked towards. But now I think what family is isn't necessarily classified as that. You can have a family and have your boyfriend and live with him and have a kid and that can be considered family, whereas in the older generations you had to be married, you had to have two kids and you had to have all these different things."

☆

In September 2009, ABC launched *Modern Family*, a now Emmy-winning sitcom about the "modern" American family. Chronicling the lives of three related families, the show covers the challenges and joys of holding a family together in the era of smartphones and "Spanglish." The show's portrayal of Cameron Tucker and Mitchell Pritchett, a same-sex couple raising an adopted daughter, won great praise and has been credited with contributing to rapidly changing public opinion on the same-sex marriage debate. (In the show's fifth-season premiere, coming on the heels of a summer of landmark court rulings expanding same-sex couples' rights, Cameron and Mitchell took the plunge and proposed to each other.)

Another of the families on the show, Jay Pritchett and his second wife, Gloria, together are presented raising Gloria's wise-beyond-his-years young son Manny Delgado, a nod to the increasing cultural diversity within American families and communities and the warm, close-knit bonds that can form between stepparents and stepchildren.

Yet despite billing itself as "modern," many of the show's family units are surprisingly traditional: the adult women are stay-at-home moms and each family has a primary breadwinner. Nowhere to be found are single parents or two-income households. Over a decade after the historic coming-out episode of *Ellen*, nearly two decades after Murphy Brown decided to become a single mom, and almost forty years to the day after two families were stitched together in *The Brady Bunch*, does *Modern Family* really break new ground in its effort to showcase the changing face of the American family?

The way in which Americans structure their families influences not just culture but politics. Political leaders are keen on talking about promoting "family values" and saying they are looking out for "hard-working American families," but what that word—"family"—means to a 65-year-old white male running for political office in Kentucky may be a world away from what "family" means to a young Hispanic mom raising two sons in San Antonio with the help of their *abuela*. In a focus group of young Hispanic voters in Orlando, Florida, that I conducted in January 2013, one of the participants put it succinctly: "There is no definition of family." Trends in who is getting married and when, who is having kids and how many, and how families are sticking together and coming apart all have an impact on how Americans have political conversations.

Perhaps the most high-profile political expression of shifting cultural norms around how to define families is the debate over gay marriage. On June 26, 2013, the Supreme Court handed down two landmark decisions on the subject of gay marriage and gay rights, overturning the Defense of Marriage Act and effectively affirming a lower court's decision that California's Proposition 8 should be struck down. The decisions in both *Hollingsworth v. Perry* and *United States v. Windsor* opened the door for same-sex marriages to resume in California, and also removed the federal government's definition of "marriage" as between one man and one woman.

The decisions came just over a year after President Obama made headlines by reversing his position on the issue. Perhaps prompted by Vice President Joe Biden's earlier declaration that he was "absolutely comfortable" with same-sex marriage, President Obama's views evolved. In an interview with ABC News, President Obama noted, "Some of this is also generational . . . [Y]ou know, when I go to college campuses, sometimes I talk to college Republicans who think that I have terrible policies on the economy, on foreign policy, but they are very clear that when it comes to same-sex equality or, you know, sexual orientation, they believe in equality. They are much more comfortable with it."[5]

Perhaps no issue has a stronger generational relationship than gay marriage. Three months before the Supreme Court issued its rulings, the court heard oral arguments on the cases. The Human Rights Campaign, a pro–gay rights group, launched an effort to get supporters to change their Facebook profile photo to a red and pink version of HRC's equal-sign logo as a public display of solidarity with the cause. Facebook's data science team released data on the profile update activity that occurred on Tuesday, March 26, and noted that—compared with the prior Tuesday—2.7 million more Facebook users updated their profile pictures that day, with this activity particularly occurring on profiles of those near age 30 and in counties with college towns.[6]

In 2013, Pew Research Center found that 66 percent of "millennials" favored same-sex marriage, while only 35 percent of the "silent generation" (those born between 1928 and 1945) and 41 percent of baby boomers (those born between 1946 and 1964) concurred. Harvard's Institute of Politics' spring 2013 survey of young Americans found that only 27 percent viewed homosexual relationships as morally wrong.[7] Even among young Republican voters, in a survey I conducted for the College Republican National Committee, some 46 percent said they thought that same-sex marriage should either be legal across the country or that states should be able to decide to recognize same-sex marriages if they want to. Looking beyond just voters, Pew found that 54 percent of those under age 30 who are Republicans or who lean toward the Republican Party "favor allowing gays and lesbians to marry legally."[8] While young Republicans are certainly more inclined to view homosexuality as immoral or to want to define marriage as only the relationship between a man and a woman, it is far from the uniform view of young people who identify themselves as Republicans.

The shift in public opinion on this issue has happened rapidly. Josh Barro, a writer for *Business Insider* whom I admire greatly, tweeted from the October 2013 Human Rights Campaign gala: "If you told someone in 1990 a gay rights org would have a mile-long list of corp sponsors for a fundraising gala, you'd have been laughed at," following it up with a photo of the sign thanking the many National Corporate Partners of HRC, including American Airlines, Chevron, Nike, and IBM. As recently as 2001, 57 percent of Americans said that they opposed legal same-sex marriage, with only 35 percent favoring it. Twelve years later, half of all Americans favored same sex marriage, with 43 percent opposing. Even among those who oppose it, 59 percent say that legal gay marriage is "inevitable."[9]

These shifts are not just occurring because millennials have entered the electorate; even senior citizens are growing more and more favorable. Recall that 35 percent of the "silent generation" today supports same-sex marriage; that is a significant increase from the 21 percent who said they supported same-sex marriage in 2001. Rising support for marriage equality has been paired with more and more people saying that they know someone who is gay. In 1993, four years before *Ellen's* on-air coming out, about 61 percent of Americans said they personally knew someone who is gay or lesbian. By 2013 that number had risen to 87 percent. In Pew's research, of those who report that they have changed their mind on the issue of gay marriage, the most commonly cited reason is that they have a friend, family member, or acquaintance who is gay or lesbian. Even as the courts have worked to resolve the legal definition of marriage, the issue has been largely decided in the court of public opinion—resolved in support of same-sex marriage.

☆

One of the primary arguments voiced by conservatives opposing same-sex marriage was concern about the separation between marriage and children. Unfortunately for those conservatives, that trend was already well under way before the Supreme Court overturned the Defense of Marriage Act and California's Proposition 8. Even in 1988, the General Social Survey showed that only 12.1 percent of Americans agreed that the "main purpose of marriage is kids." That same year, the General Social Survey showed 73 percent of respondents saying that "those wanting kids should get married," a proportion that had fallen to 62 percent by 2012. And even as marriage rates have declined, having children still remains a major aspiration of many: in 1988, 87 percent of Americans said that they agreed with the statement "Kids are life's greatest joy," a sentiment that was echoed by 87 percent of respondents again in 2012.

Exit polls show that this trend is also reflected in who is voting. During that 1992 election, only 5 percent of voters said they were single parents, while 36 percent said they had a child at home under the age of 18. While in the 2008 election some 36 percent of voters had children under 18 at home—the same as in 1992—the proportion of *unmarried* parents in the electorate had nearly doubled. Your average voter is just as likely to be a mom or dad as in years past, but whether or not that mom or dad is married has changed. In fact, Pew Research Center analysis of U.S. Census Bureau data shows that in 2008 fewer than two out of three children in America were being raised in a home with two married parents and that a quarter were being raised by a single parent.

In March 2013, the National Marriage Project at the University of Virginia, the National Campaign to Prevent Teen and Unplanned Pregnancy, and the Relate Institute released *Knot Yet: The Benefits and Costs of Delayed Marriage in America*, an examination of trends in marriage and childbearing in the United States.[10] The thirty-nine-page report highlights what the authors call "The Great Crossover," referring to charts plotting out the median age of a woman's first marriage and the average age at which she has her first child. Since at least the 1970s, the report says, women without a high school education have on average had their first child earlier in life than their first marriage. For women without a high school diploma, in 2010, some 83 percent having their first child were unmarried. And for college graduates the "First comes love, then comes marriage, then comes the baby in the baby carriage" sequence overall still holds true, with only 12 percent of first births by unwed mothers.

The "Great Crossover," the authors note, is being driven primarily by what they call "Middle American" women, defined as "moderately educated women with a high-school degree and perhaps a year or two of college." Among these women, the median age of first marriage "crossed over" the age of first birth around the year 2000, and now a solid majority (58 percent) of first-time mothers with a high school diploma or some college are unmarried when their first child is born. "How did twenty-somethings become the new teen moms?" asks W. Bradford Wilcox, one of the primary authors of *Knot Yet* in an article for *Slate*. A blend of economic pressure and a culture that views marriage as something you do *after* you've "made it" have driven these trends, and while many young Americans do want to marry one day, the reasons not to marry often prevent them from making the commitment.[11] The new "modern family" isn't necessarily Murphy Brown, nor is it *Teen Mom*; it's much more likely to be a woman in her twenties raising a child with her boyfriend, balancing late-night baby feedings with a shift at a part-time job.

Survey research points out a few reasons why childbearing and marriage are becoming decoupled for this generation. In 2010, some 39 percent of Americans told the Pew Research Center that marriage is becoming obsolete, including 44 percent of those aged 18 to 29. These under-thirty-somethings were also the most likely to say that "children don't need a mother and father to grow up happily."[12] Yet, beyond even the cultural factors that make marriage seem less relevant to many young Americans, the economy is also driving young people away from making the commitment to marry. Just for starters, the average cost of a wedding in 2012 was $28,427.[13] But even beyond the wedding day itself, there is an understanding that marriage is a financial commitment, hence its status as a "capstone" achievement according to *Knot Yet*. During a focus group in Orlando, Florida, I sat down with a group of young aspiring entrepreneurs and asked what they thought were the biggest challenges for our generation. One of our respondents, a young man who had recently changed his party registration from Republican to Independent (and had voted for Obama in the 2012 election), explained the dilemma clearly:

> The state of the economy is turning us into the slow and steady generation. We're having to wait a lot longer to make the big commitments: buy a car, buy a house, get married, because we don't have the money, and it's not coming in. At least for most of us that have graduated from college, we have student loan debt. I'm planning on going to law school. That'll be another $100,000 at least. I've been dating my girlfriend for almost five years now, and we're still not even really thinking about getting married because we don't have the money for it. We live together and everything, but I think that financially we're in a bad spot, as a whole generation.

Later in that focus group, another participant chimed in that the economy was generating greater financial pressure and had led to a conversation with his girlfriend about whether they would move in together. "It's like everything is leaning more toward the money aspect and not really the relationship of it," he said.

The millennial generation has come to find that nothing kills romance quite like stagnant economic growth.

☆

In the spring of 2012, the tension over the way Americans structure their families was front and center in the campaign for president of the United States. In a CNN discussion about the economic woes facing American women, Democratic strategist Hilary Rosen declared that Republican presidential candidate Mitt Romney's wife, Ann, "has never actually worked a day in her life," igniting a firestorm of criticism. Swiftly, Ann Romney tweeted her response: "I made a choice to stay home and raise five boys. Believe me, it was hard work." Within days, Ann Romney was speaking to the National Rifle Association conference, declaring, "All moms are working moms." The Romney campaign began selling "Moms Drive the Economy" bumper stickers. The Obama campaign knew that engaging in a battle over the importance of stay-at-home moms was a surefire loser, and top campaign officials immediately disavowed Rosen's comments.

In most elections, certain voter groups are seen as a great prize to be won, and the "mom vote" is a highly sought-after bloc. Many note that the 2004 election hinged in large part on what strategists called "security moms," a term coined by Republican strategist David Winston to describe women who could recall the fear they felt picking up their children from school on September 11 and who never wanted to feel that sense of terror again.

So what may come as a surprise is that whether or not a woman has children under age eighteen in her home, in the aggregate, has had shockingly little relationship to how she voted in the last two elections. In the 2008 election, Barack Obama won 57 percent of women with children, and won 56 percent of women without children. This phenomenon persisted into 2012, with Obama winning 56 percent of women with children and 54 percent of women without children. This didn't just apply to moms but dads too. Looking at both genders together, Mitt Romney won 47 percent of those with kids and 47 percent of those without kids.[14]

So why do campaigns focus on "moms" if women with children don't vote very differently from their counterparts without kids in the home? The answer has a lot less to do with the kids that they have and a lot more to do with whether or not they've walked down the aisle. Having kids exacerbates the voting marriage gap. For instance, unmarried moms broke for Obama 74–25 in 2008, and unmarried dads broke for Obama 68–26. In both cases, single parents were *more supportive* of Obama than were unmarried people without kids at home. On the other hand, married men became slightly more pro-McCain if they had kids at home.

If single moms are such a strong Democratic constituency, why the focus on moms as a swing group at all? First, because *married* moms are a serious swing group, making up about 15 percent of the electorate. And they always seem to pick the winner. In the 2008 election, married women with children broke for President Obama by 4 points. In the 2004 election, married women with children broke for Bush by a 14-point margin. In the 2000 election, married women with children broke for Bush by a 6-point margin. In 1996 they broke for Clinton by 6 points. While married dads always break for the Republican, and while single moms and dads always break heavily for the Democrat, it is these married moms who tend to pick presidents.

The second factor is that the emerging group of "Middle American" single moms identified by the *Knot Yet* report may prove a constituency that, in the longer term, could go either way. *National Journal*'s Ronald Brownstein has noted that "non-college white women, the so-called waitress moms, have also leaned Republican, but they have been much more volatile . . . [T]hese women are typically economically strained, and although they are often more culturally conservative than their white-collar counterparts, they are less likely to vote based on social issues because they face so many pocketbook concerns."[15] For these moms, issues like child care are much more front and center than monetary policy, and with good reason.

The *Palm Beach Post* in December 1980 ran a story entitled "Some Employers Helping Couples with Day Care." "Business is slowly waking up—and responding—to the reality that the two-income family is here to stay," the article declared. "Joan Lunden, a high-draw attraction on 'Good Morning America,' persuaded ABC to set up two nurseries in her office and at the studio, for her infant daughter Jamie. No nurseries, said Mrs. Lunden's lawyers, no Joan Lunden. ABC chose to keep its star."[16] I recalled Joan Lunden when, some thirty-three years after it was written, I ran across a story about Megyn Kelly's new prime-time show launching on Fox News, moving her from the afternoon to the coveted 9:00 p.m. time slot. "[Ms. Kelly] hopes the new schedule will be more family friendly . . . On her second day back at work last week, she brought baby Thatcher (and a baby sitter) in with her."[17] This story came on the heels of a *Vogue* cover story about Yahoo CEO Marissa Mayer, who also has "a private nursery in her office."[18] With the spring 2013 release of the book *Lean In: Women, Work, and the Will to Lead*, written by Facebook COO Sheryl Sandberg, the nation entered into that major conversation about how women can (or can't) "have it all" when pursuing family and career. And though three decades may have passed, the challenges of childrearing and great professional success seem to have changed little at all.

Much of the criticism of the *Lean In* phenomenon was its focus on high-achieving, top-of-their-game professional women and their challenges, rather than on the struggles of the average working mom. Not every woman is Joan Lunden or Megyn Kelly; not all women want to be Sheryl Sandberg or Marissa Mayer. Nonetheless, the number of moms who are playing an active—if not leading—role in providing for their families is on the rise. In 1980, business may have been slowly waking up to the reality of the two-income family, but "family" still largely meant a couple—a man and his wife—trying to care for their children. Today, how "family" is defined is quite different, and with that have come shifts in who is handling the bulk of the breadwinning and the domestic work for a particular household.

In 2013 the Pew Research Center made headlines by releasing a report entitled "Breadwinner Moms" showing that four out of ten mothers are the sole or primary provider in their households.[19] While the majority of these "breadwinner moms" are single moms who may not have another solid option for providing for their families, some 15 percent of moms are both married and are their families' primary providers. The median personal income of married mothers who outearn their husbands was $50,000, over twice the median income for their single-mom breadwinner counterparts. Pew also points out that, while most two-parent families today have a mother and father with a similar education level, there are actually more families where Mom has more education than Dad (23 percent) than the inverse (16 percent). In general, this trend toward married moms "bringing home the bacon" is looked upon favorably; in fact, in 2011, some 62 percent of people said that the best kind of marriage is one in which both parents work and both take care of the household—up big from 48 percent in 1977. Some 63 percent disagreed that it is better for a marriage if a husband earns more than his wife. Though the General Social Survey has actually shown an increase in the proportion of Americans saying that "being a housewife is as fulfilling as paid work," up from 53 percent in 1988 to 58 percent in 2012, working moms seem to be interested in taking on an even greater share of the paid work burden, with 37 percent of working mothers in 2013 saying they want to be working full-time, compared with only 21 percent just a few years earlier in 2007.[20]

Take women and the workplace as a starting point: in the 1992 national election exit poll, 8 percent of voters were identified as "home-makers" and 29 percent of voters were identified as "working women." By the time of the 2008 election, "homemaker" had been eliminated entirely as a breakout group from the exit polls, and less than 6 percent of women voting in that election were married with children and not working full-time for pay. Meanwhile, three out of ten voters were working women.

The flip side of the situation is the increase in the role men are playing in child care. In 1965, fathers on average spent less than three hours a week on child care and only four hours on housework; by 2011 they were spending seven hours on child care and ten on housework.[21] Some 46 percent of fathers told the Pew Research Center that they feel like they spend too little time with their children, and 50 percent say that they feel that juggling work and family life is difficult for them. In recent years some companies, like Yahoo and Bank of America, have announced or expanded "paternity leave" policies, offering new dads paid time to stay at home with their children.[22] Additionally, both 60 percent of fathers and 63 percent of mothers report that they find child care "very meaningful," while only a third of fathers say that "paid work" is very meaningful—a smaller percentage than the 36 percent of moms who feel the same about paid work. In the hit television show *Breaking Bad*, the main character, Walter White, is persuaded to continue cooking crystal meth by local kingpin Gus Fring with a simple argument: "A man provides." It may have kept Walter White churning out pounds of his signature blue methamphetamine, but, increasingly, "A man provides" is less and less the core of what it means to be a father in America.

In 1996, Maureen Dowd wrote in the *New York Times*, "Historically, the Republicans have always been the Daddy party . . . and the Democrats have been the Mommy party . . ." before asserting that the parties in that election were upending the norms, with Republicans putting on a nurturing face while Democrats took a tougher approach on issues.[23] Today, it's the role of what it even means to be "Mommy" and "Daddy" that look quite different.

☆

Barack Obama's campaign in 2008 was wrapped up in a single word: "Change." Acceptance of or resistance to change is in some ways an inherent component of the right-left divide in politics. Ever since Edmund Burke voiced his concerns about the pace and nature of change taking place in revolutionary France in the eighteenth century, conservative philosophy has been linked with the preservation of tradition. Ideological conservatism and the conservative temperament are not necessarily linked these days, but it is somewhat understandable for a conservative political party to look askance at societal change, asking, *Are we sure this is a good idea?* And indeed the research shows that not all Americans are enthusiastic about the major ways in which the structure of the American family is changing.

In 2011 the Pew Research Center conducted a study on how Americans felt about some of the changes happening to the structure of the family. They asked a variety of questions about certain changes: whether they were good or bad or if they made no difference; trends included mothers of young children working outside the home, people of different races marrying each other, and gay and lesbian couples raising children. Pew then used cluster analysis to break respondents into three groups: "accepters," "skeptics," and "rejecters." On the whole, some 31 percent of respondents were "accepters," meaning they generally viewed changes such as unmarried couples having children or mothers working outside of the home as a neutral thing or more positive than negative. Another 32 percent were "rejecters," believing that most changes to the American family structure are bad things. Finally, the largest group, the "skeptics," made up 37 percent of respondents, tend to "share most of the tolerant views of the Accepters," yet "they also express concern about the impact of these trends on society."[24]

What is interesting is that, even among the "accepters," overwhelmingly the responses to many of the changes were that they would make no difference, rather than embracing them as good things. Only 15 percent of the accepters thought that unmarried couples raising children was good for society, and the same number thought that more people living together without getting married was a positive. Only 22 percent of these "accepters" think society would be better off with more gay couples raising children.

Where is society heading, then? Should we expect the number of "accepters" to increase with time? Perhaps. Pew asked their questions about family structure in early 2007 and in late 2010, and in just that relatively short span the proportion of people saying that unmarried *couples* raising kids was a bad thing for society fell from 59 to 43 percent.[25] Similarly, the percentage of respondents saying that more gay and lesbian couples raising children was a bad thing fell from 50 to 43 percent.

On the other hand, even more people said that single women having children without a male partner to help them was a bad thing, trending up from 66 percent in 2007 to 69 percent in 2010. Even as society becomes more accepting of unmarried or same-sex couples raising children, the preference is still for a *couple*—however comprised—rather than an individual, to handle the task of childrearing.

Given the data showing the significant changes in marriage rates among younger Americans, one might expect that those under age 30 would be mostly "accepters," warmly embracing change just as they embody it. However, Pew's cluster analysis actually places a plurality of 18- to 29-year-olds—46 percent of them—in the "skeptics" category. That even young people were more likely to fall into the "skeptic" category than the "accepter" indicates that even as young adults in society move to structure their families in new ways, their *attitudes* toward those changes may remain uncertain. Young people are taking a "Wait and see" approach, and while they may be taking a different path themselves, they are still unsure how these large-scale trends will impact society as a whole.

☆

"They came across this past time with making every woman feel like they were going to make them be a housewife again and you're not going to have a job and all this stuff and we're going to take your equality away," said one of the young women in the postelection focus group of swing voters I was moderating in Columbus, Ohio. The "they" in question was the Republican Party. And these women were not thrilled with the GOP.

For the political party most closely associated with cultural conservatism, is there any way forward in the conversation around the role of the family that doesn't hearken back to a 1950s view of America? After all, it isn't as though Americans have given up on "family values" or that they are warmly embracing all forms of change in how people structure their families. As another young woman in my Columbus focus group put it: "I think that strong families and communities are the core of our society, but I think that's more an 'us' issue, not a 'government' issue, on why those things are not there . . . I don't think that's the government's job."

Therein lies the dilemma for candidates and policy makers, particularly conservatives: How can a modern political party or candidate be credibly "pro-family" and support "family values" in a way that avoids sounding like a relic from a bygone era? How can a policy maker strengthen American families in ways that don't involve narrowing the definition or penalizing those who choose a nontraditional path?

Today's Republican Party is in quite a difficult position. Even Republicans who shy away from talking about "social issues" can be easily painted as out of touch and intolerant by the party brand. Take same-sex marriage and Mitt Romney. While Mitt Romney was no supporter of same-sex marriage, he did not raise it frequently as a topic on the campaign trail. In a dramatic reversal from the 2004 election, where the presence of gay marriage ballot initiatives was pointed to as a possible boost for President Bush's reelection chances in swing states like Ohio,[26] by 2012 the consensus on the issue had shifted so much that it presented more downside than upside for the Republicans. Nonetheless, one of the young swing voters I spoke to in Orlando noted his biggest problem with Mitt Romney was that "he was more worried about the gays, gay marriage being legal, and he was more worried about the things that are really not our problems right now. Our problems are financial, and until we get that figured out, we really need to quit worrying about what's going on in people's houses."

In focus group after focus group, young voters told me that they viewed gay marriage as a "deal-breaker" issue, and that even if the Republican Party's economic policies sounded appealing, they'd have a hard time casting a ballot for someone associated with the GOP. To get a sense for how widespread this "deal-breaker" sentiment spread, I conducted a small experiment.

In survey research I conducted for the College Republican National Committee, we asked young voters for their positions on a variety of issues, including taxes, defense, and immigration. We also asked for their positions on gay marriage. Later in the survey, we presented them with a hypothetical "ideal candidate," essentially feeding the respondents back the policy positions they'd taken earlier, with one exception: those on marriage. For all respondents, the "ideal candidate" was also presented as one opposed to same-sex marriage. Among the 44 percent of young voters who favored legal same-sex marriage, about half said that they would probably or definitely not vote for an anti–gay-marriage candidate, *even if that candidate agreed with them on all of the other issues mentioned.*[27]

While there are many high-profile figures in the GOP who support same-sex marriage, ranging from Dick Cheney to Ohio senator Rob Portman, most either oppose same-sex marriage or have tried to promote a "Let the states decide" middle path while still asserting that marriage is between a man and a woman. I think it is inevitable that the Republican Party's position on this issue will change one day. And I hope that day comes sooner rather than later. But the trouble that the GOP has had as of late is not just a result of a disconnect on the issue of gay marriage. If the Republican Party were to change its platform tomorrow to wholeheartedly embrace same-sex marriage, this would still not fully address the other issues—the decline in marriage over-all, the separation between marriage and children, and the emerging role of moms as breadwinners—on which at times Republicans can seem tone-deaf or trapped in a time warp.

Any savvy political figure or party who wants to be credibly "pro-family" and still in tune with the American electorate should focus far less on creating or promoting a particular *definition* of family and instead should focus on promoting policies that make it easier for families of all types to be strong and happy.

With more moms in the workforce, it behooves Republicans to emphasize policies that offer workers of both genders more of what they want: flexibility, good wages, and the ability to spend time with their kids. Republicans have often gotten tripped up by their criticism of policies that would mandate paid maternity leave or would more strictly enforce pay equity. And it's certainly the case that the left's proposed solutions don't always bear the fruit they promise. Take, for instance, the Lilly Ledbetter Fair Pay Act, which did nothing to lower the "pay gap" but make it easier to sue your employer. As of 2013, the pay gap had barely budged during President Obama's time in office. (In fact, some of the most significant progress in closing the pay gap came during the presidencies of Ronald Reagan and George H. W. Bush; it turns out that a booming economy is pretty great for women.)[28]

During 2014, Nebraska Republican senator Deb Fischer wrote in *POLITICO:* "Republicans fully agree that gender-based pay discrimi-

nation in the modern workplace is unacceptable—we just have different ideas from some of our colleagues about how to best combat it."[29]
Fischer and four female Republican colleagues put forward legislation on the subject, as did Washington State representative Cathy
McMorris Rodgers in the House, focused on protecting employees
from retaliation if they inquire about what others in their workplace
are paid and on offering workers more flexibility to do things like con-
vert overtime into time off work. Want to be pro-family? Be the party
that wants to make it easier to go to your kid's soccer game.

There's also the question of what to do about maternity leave, given
that the U.S. has no laws on the books requiring employers to offer
paid maternity leave whatsoever. The concern of some conservatives, of
course, is that a maternity-leave requirement would create perverse incentives: instead of making things better for women, every female job
applicant of childbearing age would look like a potentially expensive
liability to an employer. And it *is* the case that when women leave the
workforce for long periods of time to take full advantage of generous
leave policies, they find they're set back when they return to work. "In
fact, generous maternity-leave policies have a tendency to harden a
country's glass ceiling, and women in the Nordic countries [with generous leave] are actually *less* likely to reach career heights than women
in the U.S.," writes Kay Hymowitz of the Manhattan Institute for
Policy Research.[30] Even policies that are well-intentioned can always
have negative consequences.

So what to do? The *Economist* has cheered the policies of Sweden
that offer families parental leave but let the parents divide it up as
they choose and incentivize fathers to take at least a reasonable chunk,
noting: "Since Swedish men started to take more responsibility for
child rearing, women have seen both their incomes and levels of self-
reported happiness increase. Paying dads to change nappies and hang
out at playgrounds, in other words, seems to benefit the whole family."[31]
And while you're unlikely to see conservatives calling for policies that

more closely resemble those of a notoriously generous welfare state like Sweden, as they navigate the debate over the most appropriate policies to support working parents, a truly modern approach will remember that it isn't just moms taking care of the babies anymore.

There's also the financial burden of being a parent. Senator Mike Lee of Utah proposed changes to the tax code that were hailed by *National Review* as a "conservative tax-reform plan that aims to improve opportunity and reduce the bias against families inherent in the U.S. tax code," simplifying tax brackets and creating a $2,500 per child tax credit—something that would provide more tax relief for most married couples than the current system of deductions and taxes.[32] The plan would also address the "marriage penalty," whereby some couples get hit with a higher tax bill after tying the knot, particularly if both partners are contributing about the same amount to the family's bottom line.

It's not hard to see how addressing the problems of the marriage penalty would be a huge boon to the increasing number of married couples where wives are making as much or more than their husbands—a thoroughly conservative solution to a thoroughly modern problem. Not to mention, increasing the child tax credit would give a boost to moms and dads regardless of their marital status, appealing to waitress moms and CEO moms alike.

W. Bradford Wilcox—one of the coauthors of the aforementioned *Knot Yet* report—and Andrew J. Cherlin, a professor at Johns Hopkins University, collaborated on a report for the Brookings Institution called "The Marginalization of Marriage in Middle America," which suggests a number of policy prescriptions that would improve the prospects of the institution of marriage in America. In addition to also supporting eliminating the "marriage penalty" and expanding the child tax credit, they propose increased training for middle-skill jobs as a way to particularly help families in the working class. Particularly by helping young men find training for suitable jobs given the difficult labor market they face, not only could policy makers improve the nation's human capital, but it could also provide young men (and women) with a greater ability to feel financially secure and able to take the leap into the commitment of marriage. Wilcox and Cherlin also suggest that focusing on improving preschool education for disadvantaged children is another way to create longer-term gains in human capital, though a side benefit that is not noted in their report is that providing disadvantaged children with better early education might also address, in part, the child care burden that many lower-income or "Middle American" single moms are facing.[33]

Helping families manage the increasingly expensive burden of child care is another way that conservatives can be solidly pro-family. Currently, a family where there is no stay-at-home parent (whether a single mom or a two-income married couple) can use up to $3,000 of child-care expenses for one child or $6,000 for multiple children toward figuring the child and dependent care credit. However, the average child-care expenses far outstrip these amounts, with the average cost of full-time child care for a 4-year-old varying greatly from state to state but still averaging $3,900 in Mississippi, the least expensive of the states.[34] Not to mention, as the IRS cheerfully notes, "if you pay someone to come to your home and care for your dependent . . . you may be a household employer and may have to withhold and pay social security and Medicare tax and pay Federal unemployment tax. See Publication 926, Household Employer's Tax Guide."[35] The difficulty and expense associated with taxes around in-home child care leads many families to simply ignore the IRS and hire someone "off the books."[36] Expanding the child-care tax credit to more effectively keep up with the rising cost of childcare—as well as making it easier for parents to stay on the right side of the law when looking for in-home help with child care—are both pro-family ideas that would fit nicely into a low-tax, reduced-regulation policy maker's agenda.

As the image of the American family changes, politicians or politi-

cal parties who focus primarily on establishing or narrowing a particular definition of the family will find themselves increasingly viewed
as out of touch and irrelevant to the lives of those who have chosen a
new path. The new way to be pro-family in American politics is not to
define family but to empower it.

FOUR

Taking Uber to Whole Foods:
Density and the Rise of Open Data

Natasha is one of my best friends, and has been since I was a teenager. She's been my faithful sidekick and loyal companion when I've needed her most. She's gone on countless adventures with me. When I first came to Washington for an internship, she was right there, too, braving the cold even though neither of us was really made for snowy weather. From my highest highs to my lowest lows, Natasha has always been by my side. She's witnessed me singing along with songs on the radio more times than I care to admit. She was a best friend to me, especially during that time of transition between high school and college. And when I moved away to Washington for good while she stayed behind in Florida, I was devastated that we couldn't hang out anymore. She is a piece of my heart.

I suppose I should clarify that Natasha is not a person.

Natasha is a car. Not just any car, of course, considering my deep emotional attachment to her. Natasha is a bright red Ford Mustang who came into my life the summer before I headed off to college. She arrived after the demise of the transmission of my previous car, a late-1980s Integra. The Integra, wonderful in its own "retro" way and with headlights that flipped up from the hood when they were turned on, had enjoyed a long life as a member of the Soltis household. However, after the Integra's transmission gave out on me while I was driving up I-4 in the blistering Orlando summer heat, that was the end. The Integra had been handed down to me when I first got my license, which I did promptly upon turning 16 years old and not a day later, because driving was a *big, big, big* deal. It meant freedom. It meant autonomy. It meant independence.

Apparently, young adults today hate freedom and independence. I kid, of course, but the data indicates that the allure of driving seems to have worn off for today's teenagers. The University of Michigan has studied trends in young adult driving for decades; back in 1983, when pop-up headlamps were in vogue, some 69 percent of 17-year-olds had a driver's license. By 2010, that had fallen to less than half. Even at age 18, only 54 percent of young adults have a license these days.[1]

What to me had been an essential rite of passage, a crucial moment in growing up, is now something that only about half of people have done when they reach adulthood. In the classic 1990s film *Clueless*, when the blond, popular girl protagonist Cher fails her driver's test, it is the end of her world. "You're a virgin who can't drive" is lobbed at her as the ultimate high school insult; today such a status would be uncontroversial. The causes of the decline in young adult driving are debatable, with researchers pegging it to everything from youth unemployment, a preference for biking or mass transit, busy schedules, and increased Internet use. "A few other factors explain the trend: There's the growth of bike share programs in some major cities; many young adults have ditched the suburbs for urban areas with public transportation, according to the survey," wrote *Fortune* magazine.[2]

And though I had eagerly earned my driver's license back in my teen years, loved driving, and felt deeply emotionally attached to my car, I, too, handed over the keys and walked away from driving. After college, I found myself on the cusp of an exciting career in Washington, a city where parking would be expensive or nonexistent, where the cost of maintaining and insuring my car would be astronomical, where most everything I'd need would be accessible by DC's Metro system. Despite my completely happy and fortunate suburban upbringing, I was chock full of young adult angst about living in the suburbs and was eager to get away from sprawl and strip malls.

And so it came to pass that I said good-bye to Natasha and moved to the city. I bought a Metro card and took the subway to work. When I needed a vehicle to drive out to the nearest Ikea, I used Zipcar, a car-sharing service, to rent a car by the hour so that I could transport my assembly-required Swedish furnishings to my humble apartment. I'd walk to the grocery store up the road, but if it was icy out on the sidewalks, I could indulge in the luxury of Peapod, a reasonably affordable grocery delivery service that could drop off much more than an armload of groceries right at my door step for a modest fee. While my relationship with my anthropomorphized car may have been somewhat unusual, my choices were not: I was but a single data point in a number of much, much larger trends about where young Americans want to live and how they want to get there.

Some of this move away from the "white picket fence" lifestyle is being driven by the difficulty young people have in earning or saving up enough to buy a home in the first place. Years after the technical end of the "Great Recession," homeownership is still in a state of decline in the U.S. Peaking in the mid-2000s and turning lower around 2007 before the onset of the financial crisis, homeownership in America today is now as low as it was twenty years ago, with fewer than two-thirds of Americans owning homes. While other economic indicators such as the stock market and unemployment rate rebounded after the recession, as of 2014 the trend lines on homeownership still point downward.

Older Americans have always been more likely to be homeowners than young people, for a variety of obvious reasons: older age means you've had more time to save up to make that purchase; you probably have a spouse or kids to care for; perhaps you're more settled. Even during the homeowner heyday of 2004 or 2005, about 80 percent of those age 55 and older owned their own homes, compared with only about 43 percent of those under age 35. Fast-forward ten years, and there have been declines in homeownership among all age groups, with the exception of those over the age of 65, who still own homes at rates about the same as those of pre–housing bubble seniors. The biggest declines have come among young adults; homeownership among those under age 35 has continued to decline even years after the burst of the housing bubble and is at twenty-year lows. Meanwhile, the situation is even more serious for those in the "Generation X" age range, among whom the homeownership rate has cratered.[3] The National Association of Realtors noted that the percentage of first-time home buyers has fallen to a twenty-seven-year low.[4]

Some in the real estate industry have argued that adjusting for things like delayed family formation make the drop in young adult homeownership less serious, but that's precisely the point: for both economic *and* cultural reasons, homeownership has fallen out of fashion, and unless the real estate industry has a secret plan to encourage young adults to start families, the drift away from homeownership may continue. In fact, a study in 2009 showed that not only has homeownership among the young been on the decline since the 1980s, but also that declines in family formation *and* increased financial uncertainty are significant factors that have driven young people away from the housing market.[5] Many young adults continue to live at home with their parents for a little while for financial reasons.[6] Even if they want to buy homes—and the data is mixed on that front—many just can't.

There's also the fact that student loan debt is completely eating away at many young people's ability to save up for a down payment in the first place, and that the economy continues to stymie young adults' economic aspirations. Nowadays, young adults are more likely to have student loan debt than a mortgage.[7] Three out of four Americans think that it would be challenging for a young adult entering the labor force in their community to become a homeowner, and young adults are the most likely to think that we are still in the midst of a housing crisis. Huge majorities of Americans think that it is harder today than it was twenty or thirty years ago to build wealth through homeownership, and two-thirds of young adults think you can be a renter and still achieve "the American Dream."[8]

"Before the Great Recession, we spread apart—out of cities and into the suburbs and single-family homes. After the Great Recession, we came together. A quarter of young adults have moved back in with their parents for a significant period of time. More have shacked up in apartments and tripled up on roommates to split the costs," writes Derek Thompson at the *Atlantic*.[9] It's not so much that young people don't *want* to buy homes, it's that they can't, and when they do, they aren't as likely to buy the nice house in the suburbs with the lawn that needs mowing and the driveway that fits four cars. And if they're going to rent, they at least would like to be able to live near work, stores, and places where they can socialize.

The shift of young Americans into more dense areas hasn't necessarily meant flocking just to "legacy cities" like Chicago or places like San Francisco, where housing remains exorbitant; instead, many are moving to the more urban parts of relatively affordable metropolitan areas. A Brookings Institution study in 2012 found that after the housing market crash, while homes in the outer suburbs lost a great deal of their value, homes in denser and close-in areas held up better, adding that "emerging evidence points to a preference for mixed-use, compact, amenity-rich, transit-accessible neighborhoods or walkable places."[10] So many people want to live this transit-accessible, walkable life that the sorts of places in many "legacy" cities that offer such a lifestyle wind up being in extreme demand and are priced far too high for today's young adults; those looking for the walkable, diverse, urban-ish experience without the price tag are certainly hunting for and finding places to live that lifestyle.

Places like Houston, Nashville, Denver, and Austin have seen huge booms in the number of college-educated young adults who are coming to town, and the number of young people who have moved within three miles of a major city center has increased dramatically in the last decade and a half.[11] "When big cities like New York and San Francisco become unaffordable for young people to live, they increasingly choose smaller cities like Baltimore and Portland over the suburbs that many in their parents' generation chose," writes Claire Cain Miller at the *New York Times* blog "The Upshot." It may have been relatively unthinkable a decade ago for a real estate listing to note public transit accessibility as a key feature; nowadays, millions of potential home buyers check out a listing's "walk score" as a vital indicator of whether or not that property will require you to hop in the car every time you need to run out to grab a gallon of milk.[12]

Republicans should take notice: the GOP may win in rural America and do reasonably well in the suburbs, but they are soundly defeated among voters in urban areas. Even in the suburbs, as development occurs and more people move into denser areas, that greater density often leads to more Democratic-leaning politics. The closer you live to your neighbors physically, the more likely it is that you vote Democratic. Urban living brings with it a very different set of experiences, preferences, and needs, and Republicans have not always succeeded when fighting on city turf. With fewer and fewer young people buying big SUVs and the home with the white picket fence, what are the political and policy ideas for conservatives who want to win votes—and young voters—in the growing, dense, more urban areas of America?

☆

The restaurants in your neighborhood say a lot about how you probably vote, according to *Cook Political Report* analyst Dave Wasserman. Wasserman, a rock star in the world of election analysis, dove into the data to see what our consumer preferences had to say about our political leanings and found that the phrase "You are what you eat" applies to voting as well. His proxy for right and left? Cracker Barrel and Whole Foods.

Cracker Barrel, for the uninitiated, is a chain of restaurants that offers huge portions of hearty American fare like biscuits and gravy and all things fried. While you wait for your table to be ready, relax on the quaint porch full of rocking chairs that sits in front of each store, or browse the "Old Country Store" area of the establishment, where rock candy, toys, and all manner of Americana are available for purchase. Cracker Barrel says "nostalgia," "family friendly," and "homemade authenticity" are key brand attributes of the chain. They sell comfort and cholesterol, and they do it well.[13]

Whole Foods also aims to cultivate something like "homemade authenticity," but does so with perhaps less gravy. If you get your Thanksgiving turkey from Whole Foods, there's a scale that essentially rates how happy that bird's life was before it wound up in your oven. The point of origin of the meats and cheeses and produce are all proudly displayed, and all manner of vegan or vegetarian or organic food options are available—for a price. While a typical Cracker Barrel customer might be out for breakfast after Sunday church, a Whole Foods customer is more likely picking up pita chips and hummus on her way home from Sunday afternoon yoga.

Given these descriptions, the right-left divide between customer bases might not be a surprise, but neither is it just a theory loosely based on stereotyping.

"Pollsters and corporate marketers increasingly think alike. The expansion of Whole Foods and Cracker Barrel in the 1990s coincided with a marketing craze that divided America into small, targetable groups of like-minded people," wrote Wasserman in the *Washington Post*.[14] "Whether you're selling kale or a political candidate, the strategy is the same: Divide and conquer."

Nobody of my generation knows American politics as well as Dave Wasserman. As a college student at the University of Virginia studying under famed political science professor Larry Sabato, Wasserman wrote a thesis in which he studied redistricting across the country and would go on to accurately predict precisely the results of the 2006 election (a Democratic gain in the House of twenty-nine seats), which was in the same year he graduated from college. Ask Wasserman to give you a rundown of the demographic and political changes happening in just about any county in America and he can give you a detailed response, drawing upon the encyclopedic knowledge of American political geography that he has developed in the last decade.

In 2011 he mapped out every Whole Foods and every Cracker Barrel and looked at the political leanings of the counties that contained one or the other. He noted that Democrats do better in the sorts of counties that have Whole Foods markets while Republicans win in most places with a Cracker Barrel. However, he also noted that the gap in political behavior between the Cracker Barrel counties and the Whole Foods counties had grown significantly in the last few decades and was still widening, and that the very few places with both a Whole Foods and a Cracker Barrel represented picture perfect examples of "swing areas" that politicians try hard to win. In 2012 the "culture gap" defined by these two establishments had grown even further, with President Obama winning fewer than three out of ten counties featuring a Cracker Barrel.[15]

A map of where these two establishments have set up shop highlights a key element of the divide, with Whole Foods stores packed into more urban and upscale areas and with Cracker Barrels in more sprawling locations. You can take the subway to many a Whole Foods but it is doubtful that there are many Cracker Barrels as accessible by public transit. And it is this widening urban versus rural split that is at the heart of much of our modern political divide.

Going back to the 1950s, Republicans have done slightly better with rural voters than voters elsewhere, but it was in the 2000s that the gap began to open widely.[16] In 2006, political scientists James Gimpel and Kimberly Karnes wrote: "Party strategists are alarmed by this gap, particularly on the Democratic side. Although on their own, the nation's tiniest burgs do not amount to much, collectively they do cast enough votes to anchor the Electoral College to the Republican candidate in many states." Of course, rural voters nowadays tend to have a number of those characteristics that align with Republican voting behavior: they tend to be white, more religious, with traditional family structures. Gimpel and Karnes also propose economic reasons for a rural rightward lean, in part because rural voters "see themselves as independent businesspersons rather than on-the-clock wage slaves" and also because rural areas have less income inequality that residents might feel needs addressed through policy.[17]

In the 2004 election, George W. Bush won voters who lived in rural areas by a 15-point margin, while losing the voters who live in urban areas by only nine points.[18] By 2012 the proportion of voters in cities had ticked up slightly and Democrats were winning those urban voters by huge margins. Republicans, meanwhile, won rural voters by 20 points, but fewer voters were from those rural areas. The gap between the urban and rural voter had gone from a 24-point difference in 2004 to a massive 46-point gap by 2012, and it was the cities that were growing in electoral importance.[19]

Indeed, the denser the area, the bluer it is on the map. "The difference is no longer about *where* people live, it's about *how* people live: in spread-out, open, low-density privacy—or amid rough-and-tumble, in-your-face population density and diverse communities that enforce a lower-common denominator of tolerance among inhabitants," wrote Josh Kron for the *Atlantic*. And while the big cities have long been a Democratic stronghold, the big shift from 2004 to 2012 was not coming primarily from those "big cities" like New York City and Chicago. In fact, voters in "big cities" of over half a million people actually made up a *slightly smaller* chunk of the voting public in the 2012 presidential election. Instead, it was areas that count as "urban" in the exit polls and are somewhere between the suburbs and major metropolises—"mature suburbs" or "smaller cities" with 50,000 to 500,000 people—that made a big difference, increasing as a proportion of the electorate and breaking for Obama by a 58–40 margin. President Bush had tied Kerry in these "smaller cities" in his own reelection.

"The population of mature suburbs in the U.S. grew to about 60 million in 2010 from about 51 million a decade earlier, according to a Wall Street Journal analysis of census data," wrote Elizabeth Williamson and Dante Chinni in the *Wall Street Journal*. "The newer residents look, shop and vote more like urban dwellers than suburbanites of the past . . . Politically, Democrats see opportunity; Republicans see a challenge."[20] Democrats win the urban areas, Republicans win the rural areas, and they duke it out in the suburbs, but growing suburbs these days look less like the sprawl of the past and more like smaller cousins of the bigger cities. And with more urban lifestyle habits come more urban voting patterns. "The voting data suggest that people don't make cities liberal—cities make people liberal," wrote Kron, pointing out that, even in Republican states, cities like Houston and Indianapolis voted for Obama.[21]

On the other hand, correlation is not necessarily causation, and it is possible that people with more liberal views just happen to like living in more densely populated areas. The Pew Research Center has looked at how political attitudes match up with preferences about living and getting around. Among voters who are consistently or mostly liberal, there is a strong preference for "a community where the houses are smaller and closer to each other, but schools, stores, and restaurants are within walking distance," while conservatives overwhelmingly prefer "a community where the houses are larger and farther apart, but schools, stores, and restaurants are several miles away."[22] While there is almost no ideological correlation when it comes to questions about the importance of living near one's extended family or having access to the outdoors, more liberal people have a strong preference for living in diverse communities and having access to museums and theaters.

There are clear political attitudes that align with where people live. Your zip code tells a political campaign an awful lot about how you might lean. In the short run, Democrats' struggles in rural areas have made it hard for them to hang on to seats in Congress from places with more spread-out populations. But a look at the longer-term trends might suggest it is Republicans who should be nervous. People under the age of 30 are overwhelmingly more interested in living in denser areas: only 14 percent feel the call of wide-open spaces, while 38 percent want to live in a city. In response to Pew's question about whether they'd rather live somewhere more widely spaced and with bigger houses or somewhere with smaller houses and more "walkable" communities, a majority of young people say they'd prefer to live where people are closer together.[23] As more and more people flock to dense communities, they may find themselves walking to Whole Foods and maybe, just maybe, voting a little more often for the Democrats.

☆

When I moved to DC and left my car, Natasha, behind, I also got to learn to adjust to relying on another mode of transportation: taxicabs. In the mid-2000s, the Washington area's cab system did not require metered cabs but instead operated on a system of zones: a yellowed map of Washington pasted to the back of the driver's seat would indicate various zones in the city and fare was calculated based on how many "zone lines" the cab crossed on its journey. Driver and passenger might not always agree on the location of the pickup spot on the map at the journey's end, or might disagree over what zone lines had been crossed. Changes in fare would be indicated by stickers posted on cab windows. If you wanted to drive outside of the District of Columbia itself and, say, take a cab to Arlington, beyond the jurisdiction of the zone lines, things got even more complicated and unclear. It was a total, miserable mess.

But at least you could usually *get* a cab in DC. If you hopped across the Potomac River to Virginia to call for a cab, in the "dense suburbs" instead of the city itself, based on my limited experience, you had about a 60 percent chance that the cab would show up at all. Even if it did, you'd usually have to wait a significant amount of time for your ride to arrive. After thirty or forty minutes passed, you could get back on the phone with Dispatch and would get a generic assurance that "your driver is on the way," which meant little. And, of course, once you got *into* a cab, even if there was a meter, there was no guarantee your experience would be a pleasant one or would be fairly priced.

Enter Uber. For the uninitiated, Uber began as an app that connected passengers with off-duty car service drivers in major cities like New York and San Francisco. These drivers would have scheduled pickups, driving VIPs to events and such, but during their downtime they were parked or idling, waiting for their next appointment. Uber figured out that there was a way to turn that inefficiency into cash, and soon reasonably well-to-do young professionals in big cities were shelling out about twice the rate a cab would charge in order to be shuttled to their next party or dinner in a black car.[24]

But the benefit of Uber wasn't the black cars. It was the ways that the app dramatically improved the customer experience. Disagreements over the fare or route? Nope! The whole trip was tracked by GPS, minimizing potential conflict or disputes after the fact. Were you waiting and waiting endlessly, wondering if and when your cab would arrive? Nope! You could watch your driver on the map as soon as they agreed to pick you up, and even give them a call directly if you had a question about their ETA. A less-than-pleasant in-car experience? Nope! You got to rate your driver when you got to your destination, and if they were rude or insisted on an extreme temperature or had a dirty backseat, you could note it, warning Uber and other potential passengers. Were you out of cash or unsure what to tip? No problem! Uber handled the payment and billed your credit card. Nearly every major problem that the typical taxicab customer might experience upon rolling the dice and flagging down the next passing taxi was addressed and usually eliminated through the wonder of technology.

And while, at first, using Uber meant indulging in a little luxury and traveling by town car, the company soon expanded their offerings. There was Uber Taxi, where independent cab drivers partnered with Uber and would transport passengers for a fare comparable to that charged on the meter. And then came UberX, where pretty much anyone with a good driving history and an insured automobile could get into the game, offering dirt-cheap rides with all of the upside of the Uber app. Other companies, like Lyft, operate on a similar model. Someone like me who previously would have only taken Uber for special occasions could now get a ride to the airport in some nice stranger's Prius for a couple of bucks.

Remember when you were a kid and your parents told you not to get into cars with strangers? It was good advice at the time, but major start-ups have now been built around the idea that, as an adult, getting into a stranger's car can actually be a cheap, efficient way to get somewhere, provided that stranger has been adequately vetted by other passengers too.

There was a market for the idea, in a big way. In June of 2014, Uber was valued at a cool $18 billion.[25] Just six months later, a round of funding valued the company at $40 billion—more than major car rental company Hertz.[26]

Suffice to say, cabs *hate* Uber, as well as Lyft and other "ride-sharing" companies, as they came to be known. Ride-sharing companies are absolutely eating the cab industry's lunch. Almost nothing about the existing taxicab system in most major cities resembles a free market, and the results are exactly what you'd expect. In a properly regulated free market, customers can make informed decisions about whether or not to engage someone in services for hire. They can vote with their wallets, choosing between a variety of competitors to patronize only quality vendors with good pricing, and those who offer poor service wind up failing.

The cab market in most cities is the opposite of this in nearly every way. When I'm standing on a street corner in a city, trying to hail a cab, I'm not choosing between quality drivers; I'm hopping in whatever cab pulls up and hoping for the best. I'll pay the same rate whether the driver is kind and funny and highly competent (as many drivers are!) or reeks of cigarette smoke and blasts the heat in July and drives like they're running away from the cops. There's no choice or competition, on price *or* quality. The lack of market forces makes the taxicab industry in many cities function like something out of the Soviet era: inadequate supply and mediocre quality.

Ride-sharing companies add competition, and there's nothing an existing cartel hates quite like competition. In cities across the U.S., ride-sharing companies entered into battle with local regulators and taxicab unions, with the regulators and unions trying to keep the newcomers out of the market. In DC, for instance, cab protests have involved drivers swarming particular major thoroughfares and loudly honking their horns to draw attention to their plight (likely perturbing their intended audience in the process). But it wasn't just free-market types and libertarians championing the cause of ride-sharing companies: I remember being amused at the many left-of-center writers I saw dropping their pro-union and pro-regulation posture when the unions and regulations were going to keep them from being able to get a cheap, quality ride home from work or happy hour (or perhaps Whole Foods!). The ride-sharing battle in many cities pitted entrenched interests against an upstart. Overwhelmingly, the young—moving to denser areas, eschewing cars when they can—were on the side of the upstart. And the battle over ride-sharing companies and regulations created a near picture-perfect example of the power of the oft-maligned free market to do great things, to encourage innovation, and to improve people's quality of life.

Some Republicans pounced on the opportunity. Senator Marco Rubio visited Uber headquarters and spoke out against regulations that were keeping the growing tech company from expanding in certain markets.[27] Then, during the late summer of 2014, the Republican National Committee put out an online petition asking people to sign up to "stand with Uber" in the fight against unions and regulation. (Of course, the ride-sharing companies say they endeavor to be nonpartisan; Uber brought on board Obama campaign guru David Plouffe—hardly a Republican hire—to lead its strategic communications and policy efforts.) It may have been an unsolicited and nakedly political move on the part of the RNC, but it was a smart one. "Car-hailing and ride-sharing services like Uber, Lyft, Sidecar and others are wildly popular among wealthy, young, tech-savvy urbanites—precisely the kind of voters that the Republican Party needs to win over to remain competitive in the long run," wrote *POLITICO.*[28]

For all that Republicans go to great lengths to talk about how regulation stifles innovation—how the free market leads to better consumer choice and lower costs—they often struggle to put that in concrete terms; here, Republicans could say to young, urban voters, *Look at who is trying to stop you from being able to take an Uber.* Indeed, the RNC's pitch made no mistake about the enemy and the costs. "Enough is enough. We don't need the intrusive government implementing any more strangling regulations, limiting consumer choices or interfering in the free market," wrote the RNC's finance director in a fund-raising e-mail to potential supporters.[29]

There's huge risk in any political candidate or party affiliating closely with a particular company. Uber has come under fire for, among other things, trying to muscle its own competitors out of the market and for using customer data in questionable ways. There have been a small handful of isolated but nonetheless awful cases where drivers were accused of sexually assaulting passengers. And while many regulations proposed in the name of "passenger safety" are just intended to protect existing firms and block competition, there's certainly room for policies that do protect passengers without unduly burdening drivers. But, on the whole, the controversy around the ride-sharing industry offers a huge opportunity for Republicans to make a case about the perils of regulation and the power of the market.

Young people are reluctant to be car dependent and are moving to denser areas. Particularly in those "mature suburb" areas or emerging cities where young adults are flocking, where there isn't great public transit or a regular stream of taxis on the street, ride-sharing is the market meeting a major transportation need.

It isn't just young, well-off hipsters using services like Uber who have relied on the market—not government—to meet their transit needs. In New York City, for instance, the commuter van industry emerged following public transit strikes decades ago. The industry offered drivers, usually immigrants to New York, an opportunity to earn money while providing transportation options to those in the low-income areas that were not being served well by public transit. In the early 1990s, the union for the public transit workers fought to crack down on the vans because they presented competition; today, unnecessarily heavy regulation and fees cost drivers thousands of dollars to become licensed operators, leading many drivers to simply operate illegally.[30] The vans are not even allowed to take similar routes to the buses'. Where government was failing low-income people, the market stepped in to solve the problem and to offer economic opportunity. To the entrenched interests, this could not stand.

In cities across the country, it is frequently entrenched and sometimes corrupt interests—often including unions and regulators—that are reducing economic opportunity and transportation options for residents. City dwellers may lean leftward politically, but they're also among those most harmed by ineffective public monopolies and squashed competition. Meanwhile, it has been entrepreneurs who have created services to fill in the gaps and meet the needs of people across the income spectrum. Republicans can look to some of our nation's cities to find plentiful examples of big government, union power, and overregulation gone terribly awry, where young residents are looking for choices, efficiency, and technology to solve the problems they face.

☆

There's an app that can tell you if the restaurant where you're about to eat has a number of city health code violations. There's an app that can tell, as you're driving, if and when you've hit a pothole and can send that data to the city government to alert them that the road needs fixing.[31] There are apps you can check to see when the next bus or subway train is coming. If you live in Chicago, when it snows, you can see where the snowplows are and track which streets have been cleared by visiting ClearStreets.org. You can find out if there's sewage in the Chicago River if you head to the appropriately named IsThereSewage intheChicagoRiver.com. (Whether you find that horrifying or useful depends on your perspective.)

When we think of tech start-ups and innovation, companies like Uber and Twitter come to mind. But it isn't just hip new companies where technology is being used to improve the quality of life for people living in America's cities. Nowadays, smart city governments are trying to catch up and behave a little more like innovative start-ups themselves. Tracking sewage is less sexy than black-car service on demand, but it is no less important. Just as young people expect to be able to use an app like Yelp to check on (or rate) the quality of a restaurant, nowadays the expectation that information—and accountability—is just a click away extends to our government. The "open data" revolution is here and has the potential to dramatically improve how our cities—and governments—operate.

To use perhaps a silly example to describe the power of open data, consider the classic computer game *SimCity*. In the game, you play as the mayor of a fictional town and are tasked with growing the city and keeping residents happy. You set tax levels and city ordinances, decide how the city will spend its money, and are able to monitor everything from air pollution to the number of books checked out of the city library system. Traffic problems, brownouts, water shortages, property values, and crime statistics are all just a click away, and you as the mayor can use this data to optimize your city and make your digital "citizens" happy. (It is possible that my childhood pursuit of a high job approval rating in *SimCity*, the game's primary metric of success, is related to why I became a pollster who studies approval ratings.)

Running a real city is quite a bit more complicated than my beloved *SimCity*, to be sure. But nowadays many of the same sorts of real-time monitoring capabilities—detailed information on crime, utilities, traffic, pollution, and commerce—are available for actual policy makers and citizens to use to improve how their cities run. (Developers at Open City, a group that promotes open data projects particularly in Chicago, even has an app called 2nd City Zoning that lets you see the zoning rules projected on a map of the city, and was inspired by the interface of *SimCity 2000*.) Governments embracing open data make information about public services easily available and usable, and also enable software application developers to take a stab at creating tools and dashboards that use the data. The benefits of open data are both in transparency and utility: people can see more about how government is performing and can also work to make things run better. By taking existing information, whether it is data about how the government spends money or data about how certain city services are functioning, techies can build tools that help make cities a better place to live.

It isn't *only* cities that are exploring open data projects. States and the federal government have their own initiatives, and states like Hawaii, Illinois, Maryland, New York, Oklahoma, and Utah (hardly a uniformly partisan group of states!) have been praised for their "open data" projects.[32] However, it is in denser metropolitan areas where many projects are taking off and where some of the best examples of open data at work have emerged. Code for America, a nonprofit that places thousands of volunteers in roles to build open source tools to make government run better, focuses its efforts on cities with partnerships in places like Indianapolis, Miami, and Albuquerque.[33]

"Open city data can help app developers, urban planners, and others understand a city's problems and manage city services in ways that improve the quality of life and business prospects for its residents," says Joel Gurin of New York University's Governance Lab, writing in *Forbes*.[34] Across the country, in cities big and small, places run by Democrats and by Republicans, the push is on to use available data about government in order to be more transparent and more effective.

Take San Diego, America's largest city currently run by a Republican mayor, Kevin Faulconer, who ran on a promise to push "open government" and hired the city's first "chief data officer" tasked with making it easier for citizens to gain access to information about city government.[35] Or South Bend, Indiana, where one of America's youngest mayors, Peter Buttigieg, has championed data and technology in order to find efficiency in government, such as improving the sewer system and city services helplines. Buttigieg is a Democrat, but his efforts to bring in Code for America to develop apps that connect citizens to city services more effectively are decidedly nonideological.[36]

Open data initiatives are a nonpartisan good government idea. Policy makers from both parties can and should pursue them. However, there's a particularly strong case for Republicans to make open data a key priority, especially when governing at the local level. Consider who might stand most *opposed* to open data projects: agencies with an interest in the public not really knowing about their performance or how they spend their budgets; contractors who are being overpaid to underperform; bureaucrats who are averse to accountability and don't feel like catching up to the twenty-first century. None of those are groups that conservatives should try to protect.

One of the biggest challenges in implementing open data projects is in getting data in an organized, useful format that is machine readable (meaning computers can interpret it). This process certainly takes time and sometimes requires funding. This shouldn't be a reason why Republicans balk at open data initiatives. The end result is more ways to hold government agencies accountable and more ways to spot waste and inefficiency. Even better, because of the "open" element of open data, it isn't left just to government to police itself: citizens outside of government can build their own tools instead of relying on bureaucracy to provide them. It gives people the opportunity to try to solve problems for themselves rather than waiting for the government to come down from on high with a single solution. If you're a conservative who loathes government waste and inefficiency, open data should be your new best friend. Furthermore, if you're a conservative who would rather see problems tackled locally, not by federal government agencies, effective local governance is an important goal.

In addition to being good policy, the politics couldn't be better for Republicans. Republicans have taken hits in recent years for not being the "tech-savvy" party. Focus group after focus group of young voters have told me they think of Republicans as the "old" party. Yes, "open data" covers all the key issues that Republicans already talk about, including efficiency, accountability, and reduction of waste in government. But it also opens the door for new areas that Republicans ought to champion—areas that buck the typical old-school Republican stereotype. At the same time that Republicans try to improve the technological side of *campaigning*, they ought to make the technological side of *governing* a key piece of their agenda. It is a bit of an oversimplification, but young people today expect to be able to do pretty much everything online, usually from an app on their phone. That includes dealing with their government, getting information about public services, and holding officials accountable.

And as young Americans move to denser areas, Republicans have an incredible opportunity to demonstrate to these young voters that the GOP is the party of innovative good governance rather than the status quo.

FIVE

Start-Ups and Stock Markets: How Young Workers View Their Careers (and Their Retirements)

During its three decades on the air, MTV has augmented its standard lineup of music videos and reality TV programming by dabbling in the world of political news coverage. In the early 1990s it was MTV that famously asked Bill Clinton "Boxers or briefs?" and over the years the network has interviewed political candidates from both parties as they vied for the highest office in the land.[1]

In 2012, only one of the candidates for president agreed to be interviewed on MTV: Barack Obama. (One can reasonably assume the Romney team saw little upside in putting their candidate on the same network as Snooki.) The late-October interview was not the Obama campaign's first interaction with MTV during the election cycle. That June the campaign had debuted a campaign ad starring Sarah Jessica Parker during the network's MTV Movie Awards, along with a fundraiser contest offering up a seat at Parker's home at a dinner hosting the president himself. (The choice of Parker came as a result of a data-driven analysis about the appeal of various celebrities, and Carrie Bradshaw devotees were evidently a target for the Obama campaign.)[2]

But just two weeks before the election, sitting in the White House, MTV personality Sway Calloway asked the president to make his pitch to young people. One question in particular stuck out:

"Our audience, they like entrepreneurs, like Mark Zuckerberg and the people who created Twitter, Instagram, Tumblr, that sort of thing. If you're reelected, how will you open new pathways for aspiring entrepreneurs?"

Interesting. Republicans would surely claim they'd been making the stronger "pro-entrepreneur" argument, lauding "job creators" and taking the president to task over comments construed to mean that people who start their own companies "didn't build that."

The president's response to Calloway's question was perfect.

"One of the things that we've already done is we've passed something called the JOBS Act that is making it easier for young entrepreneurs to raise money through the Internet—you know, something called crowdfunding. Historically there were a lot of rules that said if you wanted to raise money from investors, you had to go through all the hoops of the SEC, hire all kinds of lawyers. It was a huge, expensive proposition. But there are a lot of young entrepreneurs, they may just need to raise a couple hundred thousand dollars to get started on that idea, or maybe half a million dollars, and they can't just put it on a credit card. But they can now access others who might be interested in that idea, in a way that still protects investors, but also allows them to move forward."[3]

In an election happening in the shadow of the financial crisis and the Occupy Wall Street movement, the president went on the air to a friendly, young audience and made a case for repealing financial regulation.

It was masterful. And it was a Republican idea.

Perhaps that's a bit unfair. The JOBS Act, or "Jump-start Our Business Start-ups," was cobbled together out of a variety of bills proposed by both Democrats and Republicans. In a Congress that was able to get little if anything done during the year 2012, the bill—officially sponsored by a Republican—passed easily with 390 votes in the House and 73 votes in the Senate.[4] Not a single one of the no votes came from a Republican; all opposition, in the House and Senate, came from the president's own allies in Congress.[5]

And here, on national TV, the president was touting the idea as something he'd done to help young entrepreneurs. He did sign the bill, and kudos to him for doing so. But the arguments for the bill seem to align naturally with a conservative attitude toward regulation and markets. Would it have been so difficult for a center-right candidate to go out on the trail and talk about how there are areas where government regulations—presumably intended to protect Americans—wind up just entrenching the status quo and preventing ordinary people from doing extraordinary things?

Republicans often talk about how regulation stifles innovation, but they do so with broad platitudes. Here was a perfect example of how a conservative policy could help young people start their own businesses, of how outdated regulation is out of sync with the way many young people want to build their careers. A large proportion of young people say they hope to one day start their own businesses.[6] For all that the GOP loves to condemn the scourge of excessive regulation, here was a tailor-made example of smart policy that would give people more control over their own money and help young people pursue their dreams.

It was left to the president to talk about this idea to America's young people, representing a huge missed opportunity for Republicans to showcase how they understand the way the workforce and economy are changing for millennials. At a time when young Americans were facing double-digit unemployment, underemployment, and difficulty finding jobs that offered opportunities for growth, there was a hunger for leaders to offer solutions and reforms that would make sense given the changing career paths people were taking.

America's workforce is undergoing a transformation. Today's young people will start different businesses and build different careers from those of their parents' generation. They prioritize things like personal fulfillment and flexibility over wages in the workplace, and they aren't joining unions. They can expect their retirements to look quite different from those of their parents and grandparents, and know that they're going to be on the hook for quite a bit of retirement spending in the not-too-distant future. These trends offer enormous opportunities to political leaders and campaigns eager to demonstrate that they understand what the future of the economy can look like.

☆

My first job, at age 16, was working at the King Kong "Kongfrontation" ride at Universal Studios in Orlando. I took the job in order to partially finance my high school debate habit, and also because my friend Shayne, who worked on the "Jaws" ride, made it sound like a pretty fun gig. The concept of the ride was that the guests were being evacuated from the path of King Kong via the Roosevelt Island Tramway, where, obviously, things go horribly awry. The smell of bananas and propane fill the air. Chaos ensues. My job entailed dressing up like a New York City transit police officer and performing a five-minute script's worth of material for riders a few times every hour, leading them into the clutches of King Kong and, ultimately, to safety. *"Everybody hold on . . . HE'S DROPPING THE TRAAAAAM!!!"*

I loved that job.

The beauty of it all, in addition to the fact that I sometimes got to use a walkie-talkie and was being compensated for hammy acting, was that the hours were perfect for a student. I could be scheduled solely during summers, weekends, and holiday breaks—exactly the times when Orlando theme parks could use a few extra staff members on hand. I stayed with Kongfrontation until the ride's closing in 2002, and though I was briefly transferred to the park's "Earthquake: The Big One" attraction, I soon ended my illustrious four-year part-time career as a theme park employee.

It's not entirely clear how the Bureau of Labor Statistics (BLS) would count my time as a ride attendant at Universal. "For example, if an individual worked in a retail establishment during the summer, quit at the end of summer to return to school, and then resumed working for the same employer the following spring, this sequence would count as two jobs, rather than one," notes the BLS in their analysis of the results of the National Longitudinal Survey of Youth 1979, a project that studied the lifetime careers of nearly ten thousand people born in the late baby boom years of 1957 through 1964.[7] (I never technically quit at the end of the summer or holiday seasons, so I assume the BLS would let me count it as one long period of employment.) Therefore, by the time I'd turned 24, I'd held two jobs, each for a rather lengthy period of time: the theme park job and my first job in political polling. I'd stay in that first polling job for roughly nine years.

I am *exceedingly* abnormal in this regard.

Most research finds that people churn through jobs at a young age, and that such a phenomenon is not particularly new. The aforementioned BLS study of late baby boomers—fascinating because it interviews the same group of people over and over at certain intervals (also known as a "panel study")—found that between the ages of 18 and 46, the average late boomer had held 11.3 jobs. Half of those jobs had been held before the respondent was aged 24. As respondents aged, the length of time they worked for each employer grew.

In 1982, Stanford economist Robert E. Hall examined the prevalence of long-term jobs in the American economy. "The typical pattern is to hold a number of brief jobs in the first few years after leaving school," he wrote. He went on to note that "eventually one job turns out to be a good match and lasts several years" and that once someone had been in a job for five years, they were quite likely to be there for twenty years.[8]

Twenty-five years later, the job market had changed. Princeton economist Henry Farber tackled the subject in a paper called "Is the Company Man an Anachronism?" Published September of 2007, roughly the eve of the financial crisis and "Great Recession," Farber found that "young workers entering the labor force in recent years and in the future will face a very different type of career than did earlier cohorts." Farber pointed to a variety of factors, including the decline in manufacturing jobs and employers increasingly turning to contract and part-time workers as possible influences. Analyzing over forty years of employment data, he concluded: "What is clear is that young workers today should not look forward to the same type of career with one firm experienced by their parents."[9]

My father has worked for the same company since he started his career after graduating from college. *He's been there longer than I've been alive.* People of my generation are unlikely to have the same sort of career path. Nowadays, companies aren't hiring young workers with the expectation that they will stay around for a few decades, from graduation to retirement.

But it isn't just the possibility of job tenure that has changed for young workers. What young workers want out of their careers and what they expect from employers is changing, and companies have to evolve in order to recruit talent.

"The companies that have already been the most successful in attracting talented millennials—Google and Apple among them—are naturally innovative employers who are never restrained by 'how things used to be done,'" said the researchers at PricewaterhouseCoopers.[10]

And yet there is still one part of the American economy that looks today very much like it did fifty years ago: the government and public sector, where heavy unionization and long careers in the same place are the norm, and where workers are less likely to be rewarded for their performance. Young people today aren't necessarily thrilled about signing up for the public sector workforce, joining a union, and working for the government for a few decades.

They'd rather work at Google.

At the most prestigious levels, the public sector doesn't stand a chance of recruiting top talent. At places like Harvard, where big consulting firms and tech giants swoop onto campus and snap up the best and the brightest with the promise of prestige and fat paychecks, not all students are clamoring to become America's Next Top Civil Servant. Even at the Kennedy School of Government, where students specifically go to learn about things like public policy and administration, less than a third (31.6 percent) of graduates in 2013 went into national, state, or local government positions—fewer than the 36.8 percent who headed to work in the private sector. (By comparison, in the year 2001, 41 percent of graduates went into national, state, or local government positions, and 29.8 percent went into the private sector).[11]

Yet, although public sector jobs struggle to compete with the McKinseys and J.P. Morgans for the top-tier hires, that's a small sliver of the workforce. In the aggregate, the public sector's recruiting problem isn't so much that the private sector is beating them on average pay; in late 2014, the Bureau of Labor Statistics estimated that, while the average private sector employer paid about $30 an hour in wages and benefits, the average state and local employer paid out $43 an hour.[12] What, then, are young workers looking for that the public sector just isn't delivering?

A Pew Charitable Trusts report on state governments struggling to attract young workers suggests that making public sector employment look more like private sector employment could be a start. In the report, state HR directors noted things like high levels of mobility and job hopping and the declining attractiveness of traditional pensions making recruiting and hiring more of a challenge, and indicated that what new applicants are looking for are things like flexibility in their careers and in their retirement planning (preferring, for instance, defined contribution retirement programs over the old models).[13]

Furthermore, young people want to be able to move up and be rewarded for what they do, something that is perhaps harder to do in a work environment where seniority is overvalued and rewards and promotions based on performance are slow in coming. Studies of young workers suggest that opportunities for career advancement are a top priority.[14] A survey conducted by the online professional social network LinkedIn found that while compensation and benefits are the most important features that both current professionals and students look for in a job, students are very focused on finding careers that offer a strong career path, and are far more likely to name that factor as important than were older, currently employed workers.[15]

A PricewaterhouseCoopers study of over four thousand millennials around the world found the same, noting: "Historically, career advancement was built upon seniority and time of service. Millennials don't think that way. They value results over tenure and are sometimes frustrated with the amount of time it takes to work their way up the career ladder. They want career advancement much quicker than older generations are accustomed to."[16]

Millennials want to work hard and get rewarded for it right away. Yet many government positions offer one primary path to advancement: Wait your turn. The federal government itself, to its credit, surveyed the 16 percent of its workforce that falls into the millennial generation, finding "only 1 in 3 Federal millennials said that creativity and innovation are rewarded in their organizations; and only 34 percent were satisfied with the opportunities they have for career advancement."[17] For federal workers on the whole, while most are satisfied with the work they do, only 32 percent say that promotions in their work unit are based on merit, or that differences in performance are recognized in a meaningful way.[18]

If you're looking to see hard work rewarded with a move up the career ladder, working for the government doesn't seem like the optimal path forward. And frequently, even when the government tries to adapt, it comes under fire from public sector employee unions. In 2000, the American Federation of Teachers passed a resolution saying flat out that "pay for performance in the public sector is incompatible with quality services that depend on taxpayer money," not restricting the remark to teachers alone.[19]

One of the biggest areas where the public and private sectors have diverged in the last few decades is unionization. Public sector unions enjoy relatively high membership rates, yet less than 7 percent of private sector workers were members of unions in 2013.[20] While in the mid-1970s there was little difference in the age of the workers in the public versus private sector, the age gap has widened in the decades since then, so that the public sector now has a much older workforce than the private sector.[21]

The fact that the public sector has an older workforce and is where union membership is high, then, makes it unsurprising that young people are less likely to be union members. The Bureau of Labor Statistics estimated that while 11.4 percent of workers were members of unions in 2013, only 4.2 percent of workers between the ages of 16 and 24 were members. Even setting aside the question of actively joining, only 11 percent of millennials are represented by a union in their workplace.

This is not to say that young people think poorly of unions; some 61 percent of adults under the age of 30 say they look favorably on unions, according to the Pew Research Center—a slight decline from unions' standing pre-recession, but still high nonetheless.[22] Young Americans aren't hostile to unions; they're just not joining them. And in some cases, policies supported by unions, such as "Last in, first out" (or "LIFO") hiring and firing policies make it so that talented young workers are the first on the chopping block if layoffs are needed.

("LIFO" is opposed by voters even in a more heavily unionized state like New York.)[23]

For a party that is so often labeled as old-fashioned and stuck in the past, remember that it's not the GOP that usually fights against efforts to modernize or improve how we manage our public sector workforce. For instance, in 2006 the Bush administration supported a bill proposed by Republican senator George Voinovich that would "deny pay raises to federal employees who get poor job evaluations."[24] Seems like a no-brainer, right? Not so fast. Under opposition from unions, the bill was referred to committee and never saw the light of day. Around the same time, the TSA, fighting employee turnover and dissatisfaction, tried to create opportunities for career growth by offering employees new career paths guided by a pay-for-performance system, but such efforts were fought by employee unions, and the Democratic Congress opposed funding the new systems.[25]

Paying people based on how well they do their job shouldn't be partisan, and it's exactly what millennials expect out of the workplace. Careers that offer advancement, flexibility, mobility, retirement savings plans that are portable—this is where the private sector is heading; and yet when attempts are made to reform the public sector, unions and many Democrats push back. Even if you think that things government does should be few, that doesn't mean they should be done ineffectively. The Pew Charitable Trusts report on the problems that the public sector has with their talent pool found that many state agency personnel directors must deal with "lackluster workers" who are dissatisfied with their jobs, yet still stick around to secure maximum pension benefits.[26] Even if—in fact, *particularly if*—you think limited, effective government is a good thing, figuring out how to get bright, enthusiastic young people into public sector careers and then reforming the way that workforce is structured ought to be a noble priority.

The idea isn't exclusively or even primarily about making millennials want to work for government; it's about making a government that works better for them. At every level, the government operates in ways businesses today wouldn't dream of, and for the most part it makes taxpayers worse off, paying more for less in results. If it is young people who have the attitude that output, not tenure, should be the criterion on which they are judged as employees, and want to see flexibility rather than stagnation, then there's room to reach younger workers by pushing for reforms that bring these principles to our public sector.

Republicans may be thought of as the party of all things old-fashioned, but in the battle to bring our government agencies and public sector workforce into the twenty-first century, it's typically Republicans fighting for reforms that will deal with unsustainable public pension schemes, job tenure, and seniority rules. In public sector workforce and pension reform, Republicans can save tax dollars with policies that make sense for young Americans. Instead of always being the party that talks about how awful government is, Republicans have an incredible opportunity to be the party that can make limited government work more effectively and more like the best parts of the private sector, rewarding hard work, promoting efficiency, and embracing modernization.

☆

If there's anything about the way the public sector workplace functions that truly is a blast out of the past, it is the defined benefit pension programs that are threatening to sink the budgets of cities and states around the nation. The history of pensions for civilian workers in the United States goes back to the mid-nineteenth century, and in 1920 the Civil Service Retirement Act provided pensions to federal public sector workers who put in at least fifteen years of service.[27] Private sector pension coverage became widespread somewhat later, in part as a response to wage controls in the 1940s that encouraged employers to seek alternate means of providing compensation, and in the mid-twentieth century the norm in private pensions was also the fifteen-year service requirement. In the 1970s, federal law regarding private pensions led to reduction in the required length of service for benefits to vest, and by the nineties most private pensions required five or fewer years of service.[28]

In the last few decades, the nature of America's private sector retirement benefits have changed significantly. In 1981, over 80 percent of private sector workers at large firms participated in a "defined benefit" pension plan, whereby benefits are determined by some combination of years of service and salary during one's working years. By 1997 the number of private sector workers at large firms who participated in a defined benefit plan had fallen to only half. Meanwhile, looking at private sector firms of all sizes, while 35 percent of workers participated in a defined benefit plan in the early 1990s, it had fallen to only 18 percent by 2011. Many of those private firms that still do have some workers participating in defined benefit plans have "frozen" their plans, not offering them as an option to new employees.[29]

The private sector has realized that the old model of defined benefit retirement funding is unsustainable and, for a younger and more mobile workforce, much less appealing compared with a more flexible and portable "defined contribution" plan, where employers make a contribution toward the employee's retirement and then employees can manage their funds as they choose. At a Wharton School conference in the summer of 2014 featuring many of the nation's top experts on retirement and pensions, Honeywell vice president Kevin Covert noted: "I don't know of any major corporation that would start a [defined benefit] plan today."[30]

But while the private sector has walked away from defined benefit pensions, the public sector is stuck in the 1920s. By 2005, when only a third of private sector workers were still in defined benefit plans, 92 percent of public sector workers had defined benefit pension coverage.

Researchers at Boston College suggest a number of factors that have led to the wide divergence in retirement plans, including the fact that public sector workers have longer tenure in their jobs, are more risk averse, and are much more likely to be in a union. Additionally, while some companies come and go, "no such 'organizational churn' exists in the public sector, as most governmental units exist in perpetuity," and "the perpetual nature of state and local governments also leads to higher levels of unionization, further strengthening support for defined benefit plans."[31]

Many public sector pensions are a mess these days or, at a minimum, are ticking time bombs. "States have made promises that far exceed the assets they have set aside to cover them, and at some point, taxpayers will have to pay an exceedingly large bill to settle those promises," wrote fiscal policy analyst Josh Barro in *National Affairs* in 2012.[32] Through actuarial estimates that underestimated how long people would live to collect benefits and through many states' failure to set aside adequate funding to pay out benefits, fiscal train wrecks are pending or occurring across the country.

Illinois is staring down a $100 billion shortfall in its underfunded pension system, and the state's credit rating has taken multiple hits as a result of the state government's historical pattern of fiscal ineptitude; meanwhile, reforms to address the shortfall were challenged in court by state employee unions.[33] Rhode Island, too, faced billions in unfunded pension liabilities, and controversial reforms there that would go halfway to addressing the funding gap have also landed in court.[34] In Wisconsin and New Jersey, Republican governors Scott Walker and Chris Christie each faced strong resistance in their efforts to tackle state employee pension problems and the unsustainable benefits that had previously been negotiated by powerful public employee unions.

States are not alone: many municipalities are facing similarly insurmountable challenges. Take San Jose, California, where eleven different city employee unions have squared off with the city council and voters over changes to unsustainable pension programs. For instance, at present, firefighters in San Jose can retire when they reach age 50 and be guaranteed nearly a full salary through retirement; a push by the city council to change the rules only for new hires, to raise the retirement age to 60 and to make the defined benefit pension worth two-thirds of their salary, was met with opposition by the firefighters' union.[35] This wasn't about reducing what *current* employees receive; this was about making more sustainable choices in the future. Nonetheless, it was fought by the unions.

Promises have been made to many public sector employees—often the very same ones doing important work educating our children, fighting our fires, keeping our streets safe and clean—that, in many cases, simply cannot be kept without pushing serious pain onto taxpayers and the next generation. It seems grimly inevitable at this point that if some reforms are not made today, these problems will only snowball, leaving the next generation to clash with unions as they seek a way to clean up the mess.

It is thus far primarily conservatives who have championed efforts to update how the public sector handles retirement and benefits, and it is the next generation who should be most eager to hear what conservatives have to say on the matter. It is those young workers who are going to be on the hook as taxpayers when it comes time to deal with the consequences of unsustainable pensions. And it's one thing to argue that we should try to do right by those who paid into a system and were promised something, and quite another to argue that an unsustainable system ought to be perpetuated for new employees. Young people are, in general, not hungry to cut benefits for their elders, but they are eager to create smarter systems for people far from retirement age.

The tricky needle to thread here isn't just about public sector pensions. The entire way we handle retirement in America, including Social Security and Medicare, is ripe for reform. Young people don't want to depend on Social Security in their old age and most think it won't be around for them anyhow. Yet entitlement reform, though it would certainly benefit millennials down the road, is not actually a surefire way to win the hearts and minds of the youngest voters if they think changes will potentially harm their elders. They know that the system, as is, is far from perfect and that, frankly, they're probably on the losing end of the deal. But they don't get energized about fighting Grandma for their slice of the shrinking Social Security pie.

After the selection of Paul Ryan as the vice presidential nominee for the Republicans in 2012, I was frequently asked, "Well, surely his talk about making these entitlement programs sustainable long-term will resonate with the young, yes?" Yet, at the moment, young people in America aren't terribly worried about the fact that the proportion of the population that is in retirement is about to expand significantly. Pew found only 18 percent of young Americans think that the aging of America is a "major problem," while those aged 50 and older are nearly twice as likely to say the same.

Furthermore, young adults aren't calling for cuts in benefits for current seniors in order to protect their pocketbooks in the future. This is not a case of intergenerational fiscal warfare in the minds of millennials. Polls show that, given the choice between deficit reduction and "preserving Social Security and Medicare," slightly more young people choose preserving benefits for seniors over cutting the deficit. Only a slim majority think that if Social Security and Medicare benefits are kept at the same levels, this will put too great a burden on the young.[36]

The reaction of most young people, rather than to call for cuts in programs, has been to want to take their *own* retirements into their *own* hands. They don't trust that the government will take care of them when they're old, and aren't sure they think it is the government's responsibility to do so. Millennials, despite not having much confidence in Social Security, are more likely to think their income and assets will last them through retirement than are Generation Xers or baby boomers, and 86 percent of young adults think it would be great if younger workers could put retirement funds into personal accounts.[37] Furthermore, fewer than one out of four Americans thinks that the government holds the primary responsibility for ensuring senior citizens are comfortable in old age; nearly half of Americans place that responsibility on the seniors themselves.[38]

However, rehashing the privatization debate isn't necessarily a slam dunk, either. The libertarian Reason Foundation's research on the topic found that only half of young people want those personal accounts if they are told that such a move would mean cutting benefits to current seniors.[39] Furthermore, with trust in Wall Street at extraordinary lows, it is unlikely that young voters will be won over with an appeal that involves socking funds away in the stock market. The investment bank UBS did a study of millennial investors and found they have been scared away from the stock market and prefer to keep most of their long-term savings in cash, with less than a third of it invested in stocks.[40] The UBS study also noted that young people are as worried about their parents' retirement as they are about their own. Selling young voters on a plan that can be spun as sacrificing their parents' livelihoods to the stock market? Not a recipe for success.

Though government retirement programs—both public sector worker pensions and broader entitlements—are going to harm young people if changes aren't made, the way for conservatives to win over young people is not by aggressively championing cuts in benefits to those at or near retirement. Young people know that, one way or another, they're likely to be footing part of the bill for their parents' retirement. The notion that young voters will be won over with a message that blames their grandparents for generational theft is absurd and totally unsupported by any data.

At the same time, retirement and pension programs as they are currently structured make no sense, given the way young people look at their own retirements. Public sector defined-benefit pension programs are out of sync with how young workers prefer to handle their own retirement savings. On Social Security, there's surely a middle ground between shipping money off to Washington where it can never be touched—and will probably never be seen again—and putting one's entire retirement security at the mercy of the stock market. Personal control over their own situation, rather than a high return on investment, is what young people mostly want out of their retirement savings. Reforms that give individuals more power over when and how they retire are how conservatives ought to approach young voters.

☆

Zach Galifianakis is not Charlie Rose. He's not Tom Brokaw. He's not Barbara Walters. His launch to fame came in the bachelor party comedy *The Hangover*. On *Real Time with Bill Maher*, during a segment on legalizing marijuana, he pulled out a joint and appeared to smoke pot live on the air. He's played a political candidate before, opposite Will Ferrell in the crude political comedy *The Campaign*, but that's perhaps the closest he's come to the more serious world of politics.

When President Obama sat down for an "interview" at the White House for Galifianakis's "Between Two Ferns" video podcast, a spoof on traditional interview shows, people were stunned. On the six-minute show, Obama plays right along with the show's premise of parodying a serious interview program. Both men keep a straight face; Obama makes fun of the third installment of *The Hangover* trilogy, while Galifianakis asks Obama if he'll be building his presidential library in his "home country of Kenya." Halfway through the interview, we arrive at the point: the Affordable Care Act and the open enrollment period for the Healthcare.gov insurance exchanges.

"Have you heard of the Affordable Care Act?" asks Obama of his interviewer.

"Oh yeah, I heard about that, that's the thing that doesn't work,"

Galifianakis replied. "Why would you get the guy who created the Zune to make your website?"

During later briefings with the White House Press Corps, a reporter questioned if such an interview was appropriate for a sitting president. Surely, appearing in a Web video hosted by digital comedy hub Funny or Die was not at the level of the leader of the free world, yes? Press Secretary Jay Carney punched back: "I think what it says is gone are the days when your broadcasts or your broadcasts or yours can reach everybody we need to reach," Carney said to the assembled reporters, not-so-subtly needling the traditional news networks for their inability to reach young people.[41]

The Obama administration was trying hard to sign up young uninsured Americans by the enrollment deadline. Within days, millions had watched the president's interview, in which he calls for young people to visit the "fixed" Healthcare.gov to sign up for insurance that will cost as much as a cell phone bill. Funny or Die became a top referrer of Web traffic to Healthcare.gov.

From a communications perspective, the strategy was genius. Young voter trust in traditional media sources is incredibly low, while trust in comedic faux news programs like *The Daily Show* are sky-high. Toward the end of the run of Comedy Central's similar hit show *The Colbert Report*, as many online adults relied on that program for news as those who relied on more traditional sources like the *Wall Street Journal*, according to the Pew Research Center.[42] In my focus group research for the College Republicans, a significant number of young voters named *The Daily Show* and *The Colbert Report* top sources of news. Comedy, sarcasm, and parody are all potent ingredients for reaching young people with the news today.

And the White House needed young people, big-time. The Affordable Care Act, also known as Obamacare, created new rules for health insurance that would require insurers to allow people with preexisting conditions to get coverage (a provision called "guaranteed issue") and would limit insurers' ability to charge older enrollees significantly more than young enrollees. This made it necessary for lots of young and healthy people to sign up for coverage and pay more in premiums than they will generally get back in health care services, effectively subsidizing the care for the older and sicker enrollees.[43]

The push was on. Noted health care expert Katy Perry (ha!) re-tweeted a presidential call for young people to sign up for care at Healthcare.gov.[44] During the holidays, we saw Organizing for Action's "Pajama Boy" (maligned by some as an "insufferable man-child"), a young man in hipster glasses and red plaid flannel onesie pajamas, with the call to spend the holidays doing the following: "Wear pajamas. Drink hot chocolate. Talk about getting health insurance."[45] Democrats were adamant that by talking about how Obamacare offers birth control without a co-pay or allows children to stay on their parents' plan until the ripe age of 26, they would win over young people. They also hoped that the young would sign up and pay premiums of their own.

A year after the launch of Healthcare.gov, young voters were not enamored of President Obama or the Affordable Care Act. Only 37 percent of young voters told Harvard's Institute of Politics pollsters that they approved of how President Obama was handling the issue of health care, and only 39 percent said they approved of the Affordable Care Act.[46]

Nonetheless, young voters hadn't exactly embraced the Republicans' approach: only 25 percent said they trusted Republicans more than Democrats to handle the issue of health care.[47] In focus groups across the country, while I've heard plenty of frustration about the law from young voters who feel it has dramatically increased their health care costs or made them have to switch plans and doctors, I've heard others who were thankful that they were able to stay on their parents' plan after college graduation while they struggled to find a job.

Yet perhaps the most important impact that the Affordable Care Act could have for young people over the long haul has nothing to do with 26-year-olds staying on Mom's insurance plan. (Frankly, even if the Affordable Care Act is repealed or other pieces of the law are tossed out by the courts, it is hard to envision politicians of either party really rolling back such provisions.) It isn't even about the potential impact of rising premiums, reduced choice, diminished health care quality, or government expense. There are countless criticisms of Obamacare that conservatives are right to note will have an outsize negative effect on young people if and when they come to pass.

But there is one effect of the law that should intrigue conservatives and, if nothing else, shed light on what conservatives ought to pursue if they find themselves in a position to enact health care reforms of their own. That effect has to do with "job lock" and the way that reforms that improve the individual market could actually help the push toward a health care system that makes much more sense, given young people's preferences for more flexible, more mobile careers.

Employer-based health insurance benefits, like defined benefit pensions, are another leftover artifact of the World War II era, when employers had to find things besides wages to recruit workers. And while the pensions are being abandoned in favor of a more modern system, it is still the norm to get one's health insurance coverage through an employer.

If I leave my job to go work for another firm, or to freelance, or to work part-time, I don't lose my car insurance or homeowners' insurance. However, I have to worry about what will happen to me if I get hit by a bus (or get a bad fever, or discover that that mole is actually cancerous). Politicians on both sides of the aisle talk about how we ought not to put government or a boss between someone and their doctor, but the reality is that we already have when government and employers are the primary providers of health insurance.

For young people who move from job to job and want to have control and portability for their retirement benefits, the same makes a great deal of sense for health care. Prior to the passage of the Affordable Care

Act, it was possible for someone to pursue coverage on the individual market and to purchase a plan that covered the things they felt were important. That coverage would have no link at all to that person's employer. If all they wanted was coverage for "I got hit by a bus"–type traumas, rather than for routine doctor visits, they could get it and get it for cheap. The Affordable Care Act took away that flexibility, creating a "minimum coverage requirement" that mandated that all plans cover a whole host of things that young people might have no interest in being covered for. This eliminated many plans and made people in those plans have to spend more to stay covered. (When millions of Americans got letters saying that their old insurance plans were being cancelled and that their new plans would cost much, much more—the debunking of "If you like your plan, you can keep your plan"—this was largely what was occurring.)

And though the Affordable Care Act took away some of that flexibility, it has made it easier for some to walk away from the employer-based health care system and pursue individual coverage. Oddly enough, this was also at the heart of the maligned John McCain health care reform plan in the 2008 election, which would have let people get tax benefits if they got individual insurance. The conservative analysts at the Heritage Foundation praised it because it would begin to break down the link between one's employer and one's health care.[48] The Congressional Budget Office released a report that suggested the Affordable Care Act would lead to fewer hours worked, a finding that was pounced upon by conservatives as proof that Obamacare was killing jobs, but in the report, the cause of the drop wasn't solely jobs being cut—it was about people being comfortable retiring or going part-time and not fearing loss of coverage.

"Employment lock," as the report calls it, is responsible for lots of Americans staying in a job they'd rather leave because they can't afford to lose the health insurance benefits they have. This isn't just about able-bodied people who would rather quit their job, loaf on the couch, and soak up Obamacare benefits; this is about people who might like to work less (taking early retirement, staying at home with the kids, you name it) or freelance and could generally afford to do so, but wouldn't have had a good way to get health insurance for their families outside of an employer-based system. Travis Kalanick, the CEO of the ride-sharing company Uber, went so far as to praise the Affordable Care Act precisely because the expanded individual market made it easier for drivers to leave their old jobs or networks of drivers and gave them the freedom to be freelancers who contract with Uber.[49]

Conservatives should be all for a system that puts people more in charge of their own health care and makes insurance a person's individual responsibility. And, given the career paths and benefits preferences of young people, making health insurance more portable and less linked to a particular employer is an obvious step. The optimal answer isn't to put insurance even further into the hands of the government. The Affordable Care Act expanded government regulation and imposed a system that will wind up costing a lot of young people a lot of money in health insurance benefits they don't want (or in tax penalties they'd rather not pay). And it did so by eliminating some of the flexibility and options that had existed in the old individual market. This is regrettable, and Republicans are right to want to pull back on those changes.

But going back entirely to the pre–Affordable Care Act health care system isn't the optimal outcome, either—not without some major reforms that further strengthen the individual market to stand in its place. Republicans have a strong message to send to young people on the problems with the Affordable Care Act, but should remain cognizant of the ways that reducing "employment lock" and creating a stronger individual insurance market is an important goal for making health care more accessible to the young.

Young Americans want to be in control of their own careers and their own finances. They want to be able to start small businesses. They want to be able to move up and be rewarded for what they achieve. They want to be able to change jobs along the way and not have to worry about losing their health insurance or retirement account if they do. Many of the old systems that govern careers and benefits are ripe for reform, and smart conservatives will take the lead on reaching out to young Americans with forward-looking ideas that address the changes that need to be made.

SIX

Coding Our Way out of Student Debt: How to Refresh Higher Education

Sanders Theatre at Harvard University is a breathtaking space. Rich wood beams, stained glass windows, and a massive chandelier all give the room—one of the largest available lecture halls at Harvard—a majestic, historic feel. It was built as part of Memorial Hall, the monument on Harvard's campus erected to honor the college's students who had died fighting for the Union during the Civil War. The hallway just outside the theater is inscribed with the names of the dead. Marble statues stand along the sides of the stage. The room's acoustics make it an ideal place to come catch a performance by the Boston Conservatory's orchestra. It feels more like a place where you'd see a coronation than take a college course.

All of which makes the pounding dubstep music blasting from the speakers totally incongruous and highly amusing.

I've just walked into Sanders Theatre, and instead of feeling like I've just arrived for a lecture, I feel like I'm walking into a Las Vegas nightclub or a spin class. Onstage, a young man named Colton is further enhancing the nightclub-at-noon effect by donning sunglasses indoors and deejaying live. The glow from at least a hundred laptops illuminates the faces of the students in attendance; hundreds more are watching the lecture online instead of attending this class-slash-party in person. I find a seat near the front and can't help but nod along with the beat as I do. At the appointed time, the music stops and the students stop milling about.

"This. Is. CS50."

The course's instructor, David Malan, pauses briefly between each word of the phrase as he takes center stage. Young and energetic, clad in jeans and a simple sweater, Malan helms CS50, Harvard's introductory computer science course. As a part of my fellowship at the Institute of Politics at Harvard, I was encouraged to take some courses with the undergraduates, and it is immediately clear I've made an entertaining choice. My husband, Chris, a software engineer who makes iPhone apps, made a career change out of politics and into programming in part because he watched videos of Malan's course online; Chris assured me that, not only would I walk away from CS50 with useful insights about computing, but I'd also have a lot of fun taking it. On that front, at least, he appears to be correct.

In the very first lecture, Malan tells students about his time taking CS50 while an undergraduate student at Harvard in the 1990s. He notes that he did not initially major in computer science nor had he really ever coded before his arrival in Cambridge, and he reminds students that the vast majority of their classmates have never coded before in their lives. The course is not designed as a "weed-out" class intended to scare away unqualified students from the discipline; on the contrary, CS50 is designed to impart the problem-solving and technological skills that students of all disciplines can use in their lives and careers. Make no mistake: CS50 is *hard*. But Malan's approach has led CS50 to become the course with the highest enrollment among undergraduates at Harvard, ousting introductory economics from the top spot.

What would compel roughly eight hundred Harvard undergraduates, most of whom are not computer science majors, to take a tough class about coding? *Being* a computer scientist, of course, is a pretty smart career choice these days: the Bureau of Labor Statistics not only expects job growth in the field to significantly outpace job growth overall but also estimates the average salary in the field to be over $100,000.[1] But nowadays it isn't just software engineers who need a solid working knowledge of computers. From advances in everything from medical technology to auto repair, jobs in the American economy increasingly require at least a basic level of competency in the technical space. The Harvard kids who want to go work for Google know that even if they want to work in business strategy or marketing, they had better be able to demonstrate that they know what they're talking about in tech.

I'll probably never write another line of code in C or PHP in my life, but knowing the basics of programming and how computers solve problems will certainly help me in my career as a researcher. The same can be said of nearly anyone who takes the plunge and completes a class like CS50. But with STEM fields—science, technology, engineering, and math—in high demand, and with employers often struggling to find qualified applicants, gaining some basic tech skills is a no-brainer for any smart student who wants to minimize the risk of graduating with a bachelor's degree and having no quality job prospects.[2] Unemployment for young Americans remains painfully high even as unemployment has fallen for the population overall. In November 2014 the unemployment rate for those aged 20 to 24 was nearly 11 percent, significantly higher than the overall unemployment rate that month of 5.8 percent.[3]

This alone is not necessarily cause for alarm, as young people typically face higher unemployment rates. But the overall youth unemployment rate masks the serious economic challenges that young Americans are facing. What is more troubling is that, for young people *without* a college degree, the employment situation is extraordinarily challenging, and for those *with* a degree, the jobs they are finding often don't pay well or offer opportunities for advancement. Young people with a degree can't find good jobs; young people without a degree can't find jobs *at all*.[4] Add to that the enormous amount of student loan debt resting on the shoulders of the millennial generation, and you have a serious recipe for economic turmoil.

In our economy today, we have employers trying hard to fill open positions in the STEM fields, and we have a tech-savvy generation of young adults looking for a fulfilling career that isn't just a dead end with low pay. The demand for an education such as one might get in Malan's CS50 class is high—so high, in fact, that even rival university Yale is literally importing Harvard's course for fall 2015 in order to keep up with the number of students interested in studying the discipline. (Yalies wishing to take CS50 for credit in New Haven will watch Malan's entertaining lectures via streaming video, with their own on-campus teaching fellows for support.)[5] It's not just Ivy League Zuckerberg wannabes who are hungry for these skills, either: approximately 160,000 people worldwide have signed up for CS50x, an online version of the same material taught at Harvard. CS50x is available via edX, a resource that makes courses from prestigious universities available to anyone who wishes to sign up and learn.

It's not just CS50—or edX—that is coming up with innovative methods to get useful knowledge and skills into the hands and minds of interested students around the world. As the "knowledge economy" demands more and more brainpower from workers of all types, new models of higher education have evolved to challenge the traditional four-year residential bachelor's degree model. In fact, "four-year" is a somewhat outdated label, given that less than half of all students pursuing a bachelor's degree actually complete it within four years these days.[6] From online degrees to competency-based education and certification, new "nontraditional" models of getting education beyond high school are popping up to meet the needs of nontraditional college students. Even traditional institutions themselves have had to adjust to the demands of a new generation of students and the needs of today's economy.

And it isn't just college kids who are experiencing a flood of new models and methods for helping them grow in knowledge. America's kindergarten-through-twelfth-grade (K–12) education system is in serious need of modernization and improvement. Too often, students are leaving the K–12 system inadequately prepared for college and careers. From charter schools to new approaches to teaching, students of all ages and from all socioeconomic backgrounds have a chance to learn in new ways. Reformers from both parties have pushed changes that challenge the status quo in education policy and are aimed at making sure American students have the skills and knowledge to succeed.

But change is hard, and both our K–12 and higher education systems are massive institutions with decades of history informing "the way things are done." Particularly in K–12 education, the path to reform is littered with the failed ideas, fads, and flops that have come before and have made it even harder today to implement real changes that will help kids.

Furthermore, neither party has particularly stepped up as a champion of reform for K–12 or higher education. Within the Democratic coalition, colleges and universities themselves hold great influence, and teachers' unions are among the biggest donors to the Democratic cause; meanwhile, civil rights groups and business-minded Democrats pushing bold education reforms often find themselves at odds with their own party brethren. On the right, business conservatives may call for more accountability in regard to how federal dollars get spent on education, but will stand in opposition to grassroots conservatives who call for fewer dollars spent, period.

Young people are the closest to the education system: many of them are either currently students or recently were. They're the ones bearing the burden of student loan debt, and they're the ones facing economic challenges that are deeply linked to education. Opportunity and prosperity both flow from our education, and today's system offers ample opportunities for improvement and reform.

It's no surprise, then, that young voters are also more likely to focus on the issue of education and to support a variety of reforms. For instance, Harvard's research on young voters has shown they are about as likely to say that charter schools can create equality in America as they are to say that a higher minimum wage would do the same.[7] It is younger teachers who tend to be more supportive of K–12 education reforms like pay for performance.[8] There's also a critical intersection of young voter attitudes and those of voters from minority communities. More Latino voters name education as an "extremely important" issue to them personally than any other issue: economy, health care, and immigration.[9] Young voters, African-Americans, and Latinos are among the most enthusiastic about ideas like education savings accounts, voucher programs, and school choice "tax-scholarship" policies.[10] Young African-American and Hispanic voters are even more likely than their white counterparts to name "lowering the cost of college" as a top priority.[11]

Young people are looking for increased opportunity and are open to big changes in how we provide education in order to get there. They want to figure out how we can ensure that people get a good education so they can lead prosperous and self-sufficient lives. They want to make sure that education is accessible to all, rich or poor, and doesn't saddle people with an unmanageable debt burden after the fact. They want to see changes from the way things have always been done.

Republicans should get in the game.

☆

Americans owe over a trillion dollars in student loan debt—more than is owed on credit cards or auto loans. Student loans are not new, but the volume of debt certainly is. At the same time that the economic prospects for those without a college degree have grown dimmer, the cost of a college education has skyrocketed, leaving young people in a tough bind: eschew college and struggle to find a job, or get a degree and wind up with debt that still makes it hard to make ends meet.

Even when controlling for inflation, the cost of attending a four-year college is 2.3 times higher today than it was thirty years ago, and for a private college the increase has been *six times* higher.[12] In 2008, it was estimated that as many as two-thirds of undergraduate students borrowed money to finance their education, with an average of nearly $25,000 in debt.[13] Nearly four out of ten young adult households have student loan debt, with an average debt load of $13,000, according to the Pew Research Center, and those households with debt typically have a net worth far, far lower than that of households without student debt due to reliance on credit cards and other borrowing to make ends meet.[14]

Worse, nowadays millions are winding up with the worst of both worlds, paying tuition but not making it all the way to a degree or a credential, being saddled with the economic costs of school but none of the benefits.[15] Some 40 percent of students who begin college do not finish it, and there are huge gaps between the number of low-income students and high-income students who do not complete a degree by age 24.[16]

Why has student debt ballooned in recent years, now totaling over a trillion dollars in the U.S.? "[It has] been enabled by a basic economic dynamic: an insatiable demand for a college education, at almost any price, and plenty of easy-to-secure loans, primarily from the federal government," writes the *New York Times*.[17] It's certainly true that demand for college has gone through the roof. It is often said that "the bachelor's degree is the new high school diploma," and the unemployment data underscores the different economic outcomes people can expect with or without a college degree.

As more people have decided they want a degree, they have been able to get loans to pay for school quite easily. In general, we as a society think it is good that people can get financing for school, and that all debt is not equal: borrowing money for something like a sensible home or an education is "good debt," while borrowing money for a flashy new car or to put a shopping spree on a credit card is "bad debt." Student loan debt is arguably financing the most important investment of all, and with the best of intentions, we've created a system in which getting loan funding from the government is easy.

When someone buys a home or a car, the amount they can borrow and the interest rate they'll pay are a factor of their creditworthiness and how likely they are to pay back the loan; when this falls apart systemically, you wind up with the housing bubble. Nowadays, people talk about a coming "student loan bubble." For college lending, the student seeking a small loan to cover costs of, say, a bachelor's in accounting from a reasonably priced school gets the same deal as the borrower seeking huge sums to pursue a gender studies degree from a pricey school. The question isn't *How likely are you to pay it back?* or *Can you afford the payments?* but instead *How much do you want?* Precisely because there's no collateral—a bank can take your car or house if you fail to pay, but they can't take your *brain*—the rules make federal student loans easy to get but impossible to discharge, with student loan debt hanging on even after a borrower declares bankruptcy.

Democratic plans to deal with the student loan crisis in America often focus on making the loans more highly subsidized and easier to get. Student loan rates were slashed "well below commercial rates" a few years ago, and Democratic senator Elizabeth Warren championed a plan that would offer further subsidies to those who took out loans before the rate cut.[18] It makes for a nice talking point, but subsidized, easy loans are *fueling* the problem of rising college costs by reducing cost pressure on colleges. The other proposal championed by the left involves eliminating debt entirely, forgiving loans, and wiping the slate clean. The trouble is that, as always, nothing is free, and leaving taxpayers with the tab just means the younger generation—including those who did not go to college or who paid back their own loans—will wind up bearing the burden of that accumulated debt as government debt instead.

Republicans, meanwhile, averse to additional subsidies, have focused on plans that would change how loans are repaid, linking a borrower's income after graduation to their repayment rate. Earning nothing? Pay nothing for now. This idea, originally pushed by Representative Tom Petri (R-WI) and made available as an option in 2007, would let student loan borrowers use an income-based repayment plan so that monthly payments theoretically will never get out of hand.[19] This idea was turned into bipartisan legislation in the Senate in 2014, backed by Republican Marco Rubio and Democrat Mark Warner; under the plan, student loan repayment would look a lot like income tax withholding, in that it would be automatic and adjusted based on how much a borrower is earning.[20] Rather than shifting payment responsibility to someone else, this policy balances holding borrowers responsible with enabling enough flexibility so that the odds of default are minimized.

Making student loan repayment more manageable is a laudable goal, particularly if it can be achieved with minimal cost to taxpayers. Republicans ought to be focused on this issue if they hope to reach the young Americans who owe Uncle Sam a hefty chunk of change. While Democrats may champion more subsidies, more government money, and solutions that over the long run will only worsen the problem while portraying the GOP as the party of Scrooge McDuck, Republicans have a great opportunity to propose reforms that can ensure more loans get paid back and that more young households can begin to build net worth.

But figuring out how to deal with the dollars and cents on the back end is managing the symptoms of the problem rather than curing it. The best ideas aren't just about making debt easier to repay; they're about making sure young people are less indebted in the first place. They're about finding lower-cost ways to provide a college education. And they're also about making sure that when people are spending money on education, they're getting an education that meets their needs.

When I attended the University of Florida for my undergraduate education, I had the "traditional" educational experience. I graduated from high school and went directly to college, living on campus for most of my time in Gainesville, taking classes full-time, and generally enjoying the classic residential American four-year college experience. That is considered the "traditional" college experience, but nowadays it is far from the norm. As many as a third of undergraduate students these days are over the age of 25, four out of ten are enrolled at a community college rather than a four-year institution, and nearly half are enrolled part-time.[21]

Of the new models of education that have popped up to cater to nontraditional students, perhaps the most high-profile examples are online universities. When many think of online universities, they think of names like the University of Phoenix or other for-profit institutions. Far fewer know the incredible, bipartisan success story of the not-for-profit Western Governors University (WGU).

In 1995, Utah governor Mike Leavitt, a Republican, first discussed the idea for an online institution that, through partnerships between states, could provide distance-learning programs. The bipartisan Western Governors Association shortly thereafter launched Western Governors University, and by 2011, Governors Mitch Daniels (R-IN), Christine Gregoire (D-WA), and Rick Perry (R-TX) had each established a WGU for their state.[22] As a nonprofit institution, not only does WGU offer affordable education and the credibility of official affiliation with the states, but it also offers a radically different model for learning: instead of receiving credit as credit hours, WGU offers "competency-based education," meaning students prove they have a particular set of skills or level of knowledge and move on accordingly, at their own pace, demonstrating mastery each step of the way rather than sitting through required lectures for a set period of time.[23]

Here's how WGU Washington describes their model:

"Designed to meet the needs of busy adults, WGU Washington's programs allow students to study, complete assignments, and take tests on schedules that fit their busy lives. Students move through courses at their own pace, advancing as soon as they're able to demonstrate they've mastered the material. Coursework and curriculum are developed in collaboration with academic and industry experts to help ensure that graduates are prepared for their careers. Terms at WGU Washington are six months long, and tuition is about $3,000 per term. Tuition is charged at a flat rate regardless of the number of courses completed, so students who have the time to accelerate through their program can finish faster, saving both time and money."[24]

The incentive structure of WGU encourages quicker completion rather than letting classes fall by the wayside, while also ensuring students are learning what they need. But WGU isn't just pumping out lectures and assignments to students online; it is providing the sort of support and mentoring that students also expect out of college. Gallup, conducting research in partnership with Purdue University, studied tens of thousands of college students across the country and found that WGU students were significantly more likely to say they felt supported and mentored. "WGU intentionally invests in one-to-one mentoring for each student from the time they enroll to the time they graduate. Being an online university doesn't prevent WGU from focusing on a core fundamental of human development like a mentorship," wrote Brandon Busteed of Gallup in an analysis of the research.[25] With thousands of students across the country getting the training they need to become teachers, nurses, and other in-demand professionals, WGU is a testament to creative thinking, technology, and *bipartisan* action, bringing innovative ideas to the market to help get people the skills they need for the jobs they want.

It's true that online education is still a relatively new arena, and despite the success of WGU, it has not yet proven itself to be an outright replacement for the traditional college education at a wide scale. WGU may be the right call for someone looking to get certified as a teacher, but might not be the path you'd take if you want to eventually get a doctorate in biomedical engineering. Emerging online education options like massive open online courses (MOOCs) may be growing and reaching millions, but they alone aren't spelling the end of the more traditional college education. Andrew P. Kelly of the American Enterprise Institute, one of the center-right's brightest minds on higher education policy, has pointed out that, in general, few students pursue online MOOC courses (like the aforementioned CS50x) for actual college credit in order to earn a degree.

However, Kelly believes that online education can be useful in helping address the aforementioned "skills gap" in technical fields. "In many industries, the gap between what colleges teach and what employers need is yawning. Four-year colleges often reject the notion that they should provide 'job training,' ceding a huge market to whatever entrepreneurs come along to fill it," notes Kelly. "An important question is whether the MOOC model can also teach the 'middle skills' that are critical for jobs in high-tech manufacturing, allied health professions, aerospace, and other growing industries. These middle-skill jobs require some training beyond high school but less than a four-year degree, and make up the largest swath of the economy. If MOOC-like models could provide online technical training at scale, they could create significant opportunities for American workers."[26]

Whether it is a single MOOC like CS50x or a full-fledged, credit-bearing degree program from WGU, technology has an incredible ability to offer people quality education and skills training at incredibly low cost. In particular, technology can help bring quality science, technology, engineering, and mathematics (STEM) instruction to students who might not otherwise have access to it. "Just a few decades ago, technological limitations meant that students could be taught only by a teacher who was physically present in their school. This was particularly limiting for rural or urban schools, which tend to have difficulty attracting enough talented STEM instructors," wrote researchers at the American Enterprise Institute. "Today, new technologies have made it possible to share expertise and instruction across great distances, making dramatic advances in STEM instruction possible everywhere."[27]

Republicans shouldn't be in the business of chasing every new education fad. If something doesn't work, whether it is a program of MOOCs or an online education initiative or a charter school with a unique approach, we should be comfortable saying so and focusing resources on what does. We should be results-driven. But we should absolutely be in the business of actively trying to find ways government—and our education system—can do things more effectively and at lower cost. We should be focused on giving people more choice and flexibility in how they build their skills. We should be eager to find ways to help people get skills to match job demands.

Young Americans are facing serious barriers to starting off satisfying careers that pay middle-class wages. They also rarely hear political leaders of either party offering any concrete plans for how they want to help young Americans get good jobs. Championing technology as a way to create greater choice, greater cost savings, and better learning in America is an obvious step Republicans can take to help young people, all the while shedding the image of being the party of the past.

SEVEN

Pot and the Pope:
How Young People Decide
What It Is to Be Good

The bells were ringing out from Westminster Cathedral in London, the largest Catholic church in England. It was around dusk on a chilly March evening, and I had just come out of the Victoria station of the London Underground, headed toward a small Indian restaurant in the area. I was in town for the International Democrat Union conference of young center-right leaders and was enjoying my final evening in the city, when I stumbled upon the commotion. The area was abuzz; a satellite truck had parked in front of the enormous brick church, and a small crowd of onlookers—some curious bystanders, some devoted faithful—waited eagerly on a piece of major news.

The bells. They must have chosen the next pope.

Dinner could wait.

Standing outside the cathedral, I knew no one, but it didn't matter; I remember feeling like I was connected to billions of people around the world through the shared spiritual experience of waiting for the biggest news in the world, standing around the reporter and the satellite truck, trying to find out who had been chosen. Here I was, in a foreign country on a business trip, far from home and anyone I really knew, standing on a strange sidewalk in a strange city with strange people outside a strange church. No matter: I heard the bells. I was invited to take part. Around the world, other Catholic churches were ringing their bells too.

Eventually, someone got word—through Twitter, of course, and before the reporter—and announced to the crowd.

"Bergoglio! The Argentinian!"

In March 2013, the College of Cardinals at the Vatican sent up a puff of white smoke and announced to the world the selection of the next head of the Catholic Church. Pope Francis, born Jorge Mario Bergoglio, an Argentinian Jesuit, would be the new leader of the world's second-largest religious faith. His predecessor, Pope Benedict, had taken the somewhat unusual step of abdicating, and the question loomed large: What would Francis mean for the Church?

"In choosing Francis, 76, who had been the archbishop of Buenos Aires, the cardinals sent a powerful message that the future of the church lies in the global south, home to the bulk of the world's Catholics," wrote the *New York Times* the day after Francis's election.[1] Indeed, while Europe and North America were home to seven out of ten Catholics worldwide in 1910, today that figure is only about one-third of Catholics worldwide, as growth in sub-Saharan Africa and Latin America has been enormous over the last century.[2] The Catholic Church is experiencing enormous demographic change, and had elected a leader that reflected the new face of the Church worldwide.

Yet, despite the growth of Catholicism in many regions of the world, horrible scandals like those involving covering up the sexual abuse of children have thrown the Church in crisis. In the U.S., the number of those in the priesthood is shrinking each year, and 91 percent of all nuns in the U.S. are over the age of 60.[3] The proportion of those U.S. Catholics who identify as "strong" Catholics has fallen to record lows.[4] Though John Paul II was an extremely popular pope upon his passing in 2005, Americans never quite warmed to Pope Benedict, and his abdication was viewed as a chance for an historic yet troubled institution to adapt to the demographic trends and energize a new generation of believers.[5]

I'm something of a newcomer to the Catholic faith. While I was baptized Catholic, I was raised and confirmed Methodist, went to an evangelical Southern Baptist church youth group for a time in high school, and only converted to Catholicism as an adult. My husband is also Catholic, but I began my classes—Rite of Christian Initiation of Adults, or RCIA—before I had even met him. There were a number of things that drew me back to the Catholic Church: its view of God not as a distant figure in the sky to whom we pray but a tactile, living presence in our world, and the universal communal experience of participating in sacraments being celebrated by people worldwide and back through the centuries. My RCIA classes were a wonderful, fulfilling experience, and my Catholic friends—even those who perhaps weren't the most regular attendees—warmly welcomed me into their faith family. I felt loved.

But there were certainly others who wondered what I was thinking, and were not shy about saying so. The rules of the Church—aren't they so outdated? So out of touch with the modern world? Whether on issues of gender or sexuality or reproduction, more than a few friends cast a bit of a side-eye at my decision to become Catholic. (Even most Catholics in the U.S. have qualms with Church teachings on these issues.) These criticisms aren't necessarily unique to Catholicism alone, but to put it in clinical marketingspeak, the Catholic Church has a bit of a *brand problem*.

So along comes Pope Francis with some very interesting things to say.

"The church sometimes has locked itself up in small things, in small-minded rules. The most important thing is the first proclamation: Jesus Christ has saved you. And the ministers of the church must be ministers of mercy above all," said Francis in an interview with the Catholic *America* magazine.[6] This, too: "If a person is gay and seeks God and has good will, who am I to judge?" he said in June of 2013, shortly after his election.[7]

The command to love, not judge, is not a new invention of Pope Francis's creation; it has always been there at the heart of the Christian faith. But it hasn't always been at the forefront of what the world—particularly the young—hears about Christianity. At World Youth Day on the beach in Rio de Janeiro, Pope Francis spoke to a crowd of around three million young people, where one attendee told the British newspaper the *Telegraph:* "He speaks in concrete terms—he talks about our lives, our needs . . . [Y]ou don't often get that from the Church."[8]

This pope *tweets*. He takes selfies with followers.

He's been on the cover of *Rolling Stone.*[9]

Yet, despite the social media savvy, enormous crowds, and hip magazine cover stories, Francis has remained notable for dressing in simple garments and leading a frugal lifestyle, sending a message that he's just one of us and that God expects us, above all, to love one another. He's a rock-star pope who chooses to live a life of anything but rock-star extravagance, because that is what he is called to do.

Granted, Pope Francis has not made sweeping changes to some pieces of Catholic doctrine; he's held firm on things like the religious definition of marriage and only ordaining men as priests. But his attention has been on a quite different set of matters, consistently putting the focus on things like the call to care for the poor and to love one another. He's also made clear that he intends to bring the Church in a new direction, controversially demoting an American cardinal who had been known for his more hard-line positions on issues such as providing communion to those who have divorced and remarried.[10] In October 2014 a report from the Vatican called for the Church "to welcome and accept gay people, unmarried couples and those who have divorced, as well as the children of these less traditional families," reported the *New York Times*. " . . . [I]t is the first signal that the institutional church may follow the direction Francis has set in the first 18 months of his papacy, away from condemnation of unconventional family situations and toward understanding, openness and mercy."[11] While not all Catholics are enamored of their new leader—some Catholics are upset over his position on things like conducting mass in Latin, and he's made remarks on climate change that have earned him both darts and laurels—a year into Francis's papacy, 68 percent of American Catholics and half of American non-Catholics said that they felt Pope Francis represented a change for the better for the Catholic Church.[12]

There are some relatively obvious implications and lessons to be learned from Pope Francis for those in politics—particularly Republicans. Republicans have faced many of the same "brand problems" as the Catholic Church: allegations that they are out of touch, too focused on strict rule following, and stuck in outmoded ways of thinking. And, quite frankly, while Republicans do quite well among religious voters, winning nearly six out of ten voters who attend church at least once a week, they struggle with those who attend less often. A majority of voters in the last four presidential elections have said they do *not* attend religious services at least weekly, and the proportion of voters who affiliate with *no* religion at all is increasing.[13] Ron Fournier at *National Journal* put it succinctly: "For top Republicans, Catholics in particular, the pontiff's headline-seizing efforts to reverse negative stereotypes of one of the world's oldest and most ossified institutions—almost exclusively through symbolic gestures—stands as an example for the GOP."[14] One often hears non-Catholics say they like what the new pope has to say, and his focus on elements of the faith that have universal appeal has the potential to draw the less religious to want to learn more.

But what if this isn't just about Francis tackling a "brand problem" and stereotypes? What if the appeal of Pope Francis isn't that he's putting a kinder, gentler face on the institution but rather that he's tapping into something for which people of all creeds are hungry? Sure, the humble attire and the tweeting and the calls for tolerance are wonderful. But if this was just about "brand," frankly, why would anyone else out there—particularly non-Catholics—even care? Why is it a big deal to people of all faiths—or no particular faith at all—that the leader of the Catholic Church seems eager to shift the emphasis to the "love one another"?

I think there's something deeper going on here than just "re-branding," and I think it has powerful implications for those who want to lead our nation. I think what we are seeing is a world so accustomed to celebrities and leaders who are lofty, disconnected, and self-aggrandizing that seeing a global leader living a humble life of service is uplifting. Pope Francis is a breath of fresh air. In a world where we are bombarded constantly with a message to pamper and worship ourselves, to look out for ourselves first and foremost, it is someone who puts front and center a call to serve *others*, to love *others*, who is the true iconoclast.

Pope Francis may be the leader of the Catholic Church, but you certainly don't have to be Catholic or even Christian or even a person who has any particular religious faith to think it is good to live a life of service, to be humble, to care for one another. These, of course, are not new ideas. That Pope Francis has come to represent "modernizing" the Catholic Church by extolling these qualities suggests that even as a new generation redefines morality, there are some things that are timeless: a craving for authenticity and the belief that we should love one another never go out of style.

We are seeing changes in how young people think about matters of right and wrong, how they decide what is or is not morally acceptable, how they decide what it means to live in a way that is good.

But not all of those changes mean today's young people are ready to throw out all the rules.

☆

You wouldn't know it from watching reality TV or tuning in to the local 11:00 news, but the kids these days are doing all right.

Teen birth rates are down significantly since the early 1990s.[15] Both young men and women are having sex for the first time at a slightly older age than in decades past.[16] Teen drinking, too, has fallen precipitously, and teenagers today are much more likely to think binge drinking is risky than did teenagers in the late 1970s. The juvenile arrest rate is down to about half of where it was in the mid-nineties.[17] Since 2001, trend lines that show the proportion of teenagers who use illicit drugs, apart from marijuana, have headed straight downward.[18] In fact, pretty much the only youth "vice" that has become more common in the last ten years *is* marijuana, which has corresponded with a significant drop in the proportion of teenagers who think smoking pot is dangerous. Even the *rebellion* is safe these days.[19]

It's not just teenagers who are generally making good choices. Take smoking: despite large increases during the 1990s in the percentage of young adults who smoked cigarettes, smoking has dramatically fallen out of fashion with young people, with fewer than one out of four college students in 2012 reporting that they'd smoked a cigarette in the last year.[20] In Vegas, while there's no shortage of young adults eager to get into the nightclubs, casinos are struggling to attract young visitors to the gambling tables.[21] Broader trends toward temperance aren't confined to America, either: countries across western Europe have seen similar declines in youth drinking, smoking, and sex.[22]

Conservatives often bemoan that America seems to have lost its moral compass, but when it comes to sex, drugs, and rock and roll, compared to their parents' generation, the kids these days are . . . practically Victorian. (Or perhaps they're all just "straight edge," like the adherents of the punk rock movement who eschewed the standard vices like booze and drugs.) Whatever it is, while millennials have their flaws, being a bunch of rowdy heathens isn't exactly one of them, and you're more likely to find them going out and doing community service than to find them causing trouble.

Yet, at the same time that young Americans are avoiding those good old-fashioned harbingers of moral decay, you won't find them clutching their pearls in horror at those who choose a different path. Frankly, millennials may be a well-behaved bunch, but they're unlikely to care what *you're* up to or get bothered if your lifestyle is different. Living with your girlfriend before you get engaged? No problem. Smoking pot? Well, you're not hurting anyone. Gay, straight, transgender, bisexual . . . who cares? What you do in your own bedroom is your own business. Put simply, this generation doesn't view many old, traditional "taboos" as being immoral, particularly if that "taboo" has no clear victim or leads to no real harm.[23] This pops up in our national discourse as the assertion that young people are more "socially liberal," a sort of catchall term that implies young people are more tolerant and open-minded about lifestyle choices and private behavior.

In general, yes, today's young Americans are pretty comfortable with a wide array of lifestyles that would have been marginalized or frowned upon in years past. Take sex: attitudes have certainly become less conservative in recent years, and at a fairly rapid pace. Today, only three out of ten people in the U.S. view sex between unmarried adults as morally unacceptable, and only 7 percent view contraception use as morally unacceptable.[24] On the issue of homosexuality, society's views have changed dramatically in the last few decades. (To grasp the magnitude and speed with which this change has taken place, recall that in the 2008 election President Obama was opposed to same-sex marriage. Four years later, both he and Hillary Clinton were "evolving" on the issue.)

In the late 1980s the General Social Survey, one of the largest and longest-running comprehensive studies of American social and cultural trends, revealed that about three out of four American adults at the time found same-sex relationships to be wrong; by 2010 that had fallen to just 43.5 percent. Young people are a heavy driver of these changes, with only 26 percent of adults under age 30 viewing homosexual behavior as "always wrong."[25] Polling by Harvard's Institute of Politics found only 27 percent of young Americans felt homosexual relationships were morally wrong and six out of ten said that a friend's sexual orientation is not important.[26]

So then, if many activities that were once frowned upon are now accepted and embraced, what *do* young people define as wrong? Turns out that there are some things where society isn't budging, where "moral acceptability" isn't increasing—or in some cases, are even more frowned upon. The common theme with all of them? Causing harm to another.

Married and having an affair? Some 89 percent of those under fifty have said that's wrong, making it actually *more* unacceptable to younger people than for those over age 65.[27] Or take medical testing on animals, the death penalty, and abortion: society hasn't grown any more comfortable with those things in the last fifteen years, and in the case of both animal testing and the death penalty, it is the young who are more likely to find them morally objectionable.[28] And despite abortion constantly being lumped into the "social issues" bucket, and frequent discussion about how Republicans need to change their position in order to keep up with the times, the times *aren't* really changing much on abortion. About half of Americans think that abortion is "morally wrong" and there's little difference between the attitudes of those over and under age fifty.[29] This has been the case for at least the last decade, in contrast to the issue of gay rights, where public opinion is shifting rapidly and is seriously divided by generation.[30]

Young Americans still have a strong sense of right and wrong—they just define "right and wrong" in a different way than previous generations might have, with morality being tightly bound to the concept of harm. Without a victim, it seems there is no crime. Jonathan Haidt, a preeminent social psychologist and author of *The Righteous Mind: Why Good People Are Divided by Politics and Religion*, has noted that most questions of morality can be broken down into several areas, such as harm, fairness, loyalty, authority, and purity. These days, a cursory look at young voter attitudes about what is or isn't morally acceptable suggests harm and fairness are more or less where the next generation of voters thinks we ought to focus our public policy. Hand in hand with this shift away from certain older social norms—those pertaining to things like sexual purity or spiritual authority—has come a decline in religiosity in America's young.

In the Broadway musical *Guys and Dolls*, Sarah Brown and her Salvation Army compatriots try to save bad boy Sky Masterson from his drinking and gambling ways through evangelism, noting that dice games and booze can lead only to the devil himself; today, the more compelling sales pitch would point out the risks of liver damage and potential financial ruin.

While faith and spirituality still play a large role in the lives of young Americans, there's a widening gulf between having faith and showing up to church every Sunday. Millennials are less likely to affiliate formally with and regularly attend services for a religious faith—particularly Christianity—even at the same time that principles like "Do unto others" and "Love one another" remain at the core of their moral code. Significantly more young Americans call themselves "religiously unaffiliated" than do older generations, but the declines in religious affiliation are not confined to the young; both Generation Xers and the baby boom generation are slightly less religiously affiliated than they were just a few years ago. They're not getting more religious as they get older—in fact, they've become less likely to be affiliated with a particular faith.[31] And looking at adults of all ages, over time, the proportion of Americans who say they have a "great deal" of faith in "church or organized religion" has fallen from 43 percent in 1973 to only 25 percent today.[32]

As a generation, young Americans don't seem particularly distressed about the decline in religiosity, with only a third thinking that the diminishing number of religious Americans is a bad thing—and with even religious millennials less likely than their elders to view it as such.[33] Nearly half of those under age thirty say that one need not believe in God in order to be moral.[34]

The fact is that religion is not viewed as all bad or all good, but as something that calls us to love one another *and* judge one another. This leads to some conflicted feelings, to say the least. While a majority of young Americans think that religion holds answers to the problems facing us today, they are significantly less likely to hold that view than older generations. Roughly four out of ten Americans under age 30 think religion is "old-fashioned and out of date."[35] Some 63 percent of those between the ages of 18 and 24 have said that they think modern-day Christianity "consistently shows love for other people," but a similar percentage think that Christianity today is "judgmental" and "anti-gay."[36]

The reasons for the disconnect go beyond issues of sex and gay rights, however. For instance, young Americans are significantly more likely to believe in the theory of evolution, with fewer than three out of ten saying "God created humans in present form within the last 10,000 years."[37] Only 28 percent of millennials think public school libraries should ban books with "dangerous ideas" compared with 43 percent of Generation Xers and a majority of those from the Silent Generation, those born from the mid-1920s to the mid-1940s.[38]

So traditional "religiosity" is on the decline, viewed more often as old-fashioned or out of touch with how young people live. But make no mistake: the vast, vast majority of young Americans still identify with a faith of some kind, and for most, that faith is a critical element of their lives. Only about a quarter say they outright don't identify with a religion, and Harvard University's survey of young adults has found that some 79 percent of religiously affiliated young people consider their religion an important part of their lives.[39] Millennials still have faith, it just looks a lot different from what it did in decades past.

Take some lighter examples from modern Christianity and its influence in pop culture: perhaps surprisingly, one out of five adults aged 18 to 29 say they've listened to Christian rock music in the last week, according to a Pew Research Center study.[40] During September 2012, Christian artist TobyMac's album *Eye on It* debuted at the top of the Billboard 200. Not the Christian charts. The Billboard 200. I discovered my favorite band, Mute Math, from a bonus track on a Christian music compilation album I bought in 2004; two years later, after *Rolling Stone* had written about them with the moderately snarky headline "Mute Math Loves Jesus but Isn't Terrible," they were appearing at festivals like Bonnaroo, and could be spotted playing Jimmy Kimmel's late-night talk show.[41]

Or consider a comical example from the world of sports: Take the rise of Tim Tebow, the beloved Heisman Trophy–winning quarterback from the University of Florida, who was often seen kneeling down in prayer after a touchdown or with Bible verses written under his eye black, putting his religious faith in the forefront of his public life. Polling done during Tim Tebow's astonishingly successful playoff run as quarterback of the Denver Broncos in early 2012 found that young people were more likely than those over age 30 to think that Tebow's success "could be attributed to divine intervention." (Frankly, I'm stunned this data even exists.)[42] But call the Broncos' playoff run that season a miracle if you like: young people are about as likely as older people to believe in miracles, as well as angels, demons, heaven, hell, and an afterlife, all despite being significantly less religious.[43]

But Christian record sales and the number who think that God meddles in football playoff games probably aren't really useful or complete indicators of what modern faith or moral life looks like for young

Americans today. So we've got religious rock and belief in the stuff of Dan Brown novels. But what about the fact that young adults in the 2000s were slightly *more* likely to say they pray daily than did young adults in the 1980s or 1990s?[44] Or that teenagers in the 2000s were significantly more likely to be doing community service than teenagers were in previous decades?[45] Or that more than six out of ten college students said they'd done community service during the last year?[46]

Yes, only one out of five young people thinks religious values should play a more important role in our government. Religious disaffiliation is increasing, and young people are uninterested in enforcing religious norms about sex and science through policy. At the same time a majority of young people say that America is heading in the wrong moral direction.[47] There's clearly a hunger to see America go on a different path, a growing sense that, to be virtuous, we should first and foremost help those around us; that the role of religion in politics should be reimagined; that faith shouldn't be excised from our society.

For conservatives, who have typically benefited from the votes of the more religious among us, the way forward is neither to walk away from faith nor to double-down on winning the culture wars. Perhaps, instead, the way forward is to consider what a policy agenda that puts "Love one another" at its core might truly look like in modern America.

☆

Reese Witherspoon has been on a lot of magazine covers. Nearly every glossy fashion magazine has been graced by Witherspoon's presence, and during October 2014 she appeared on perhaps the most prominent and prestigious cover of them all: *Vogue*. The Academy Award–winning Witherspoon—famous for star turns in films such as *Sweet Home Alabama*, *Legally Blonde*, and *Walk The Line*—is most certainly deserving of such an honor, and I count myself among her fans.

Vogue was not the only magazine where Witherspoon would appear on the cover during that fall, however, though the other periodical is one you're probably less likely to pick up at your local bookstore or airport newsstand. Unless, of course, you picked up the November/December 2014 issue of *Relevant* magazine.

Relevant, "a magazine on faith, culture, and intentional living," describes itself as "the leading platform reaching Christian twenty- and thirtysomethings."[48] For over a decade, *Relevant* has had both an online platform and a print magazine focused on reaching young Christian readers, and they say they reach over two million every month. Most movie stars are more likely to appear on a magazine touting sex advice, Hollywood gossip, or insights on the latest trend in handbags; yet here was an undeniably A-list actress sitting down for a cover story with a magazine for young Christians.

In the interview, religion is not the main topic. Instead, the interview focuses on Witherspoon's upcoming film role, in which she plays an immigration worker helping refugees from South Sudan, and on her visit to refugee camps to see for herself the humanity of the crisis. "You don't have to be a perfect person to do something great for somebody else," she tells the interviewer. "It's not just for the saints of the world. We can all do something."[49]

Witherspoon was not the first mainstream celebrity to appear on *Relevant*'s cover: the prior issue had featured *Parks and Recreation*'s Nick Offerman, the actor who plays the role of Ron Swanson, arguably TV's greatest portrayal of a libertarian. Nor was Witherspoon's interview somehow out of place in the magazine for its lack of "preachiness" or Jesus name drops; *Relevant*'s tone is light, thoughtful, and warm. This isn't to say the magazine shies away from its Christianity—far from it. The print magazine is full of advertisements from service organizations looking to recruit readers to pursue a life of service through teaching in low-income schools or volunteering overseas. Alongside an interview with artist Shepard Fairey, notable for his famous blue and red "HOPE" portrait of Obama, *Relevant* digs into Christian perspectives on dating. A perusal of the *Relevant* online magazine uncovers "The Unexpected Things Millennials Want in Church" and "15 of Soren Kierkegaard's Most Challenging Quotes" right next to "The Best Violin Cover of 'Shake It Off' You'll Hear All Day," referring to the pop song by Taylor Swift. Article after article underscores the idea that, while living a life of faith isn't always easy, you shouldn't disconnect from the modern world in order to live it.

It also isn't afraid to get a little political. "Why Immigration Reform Is a Christian Cause" and "Pope Francis' Other Pro-Life Campaign"—a piece about the pope's push to abolish the death penalty and reform justice systems—definitely challenge what a non-Christian might think of as the political leanings of an evangelical Christian publication. Of course, this isn't just generational: faith leaders have often taken views that differ from those of the Tea Party on things like foreign aid programs and immigration reform. These are the sorts of conversations taking place in the pages of the premier young adult Christian publication, and ought to be a wake-up call to those assuming young men and women of faith are naturally going to be right-of-center voters; or that the core political questions directed at a new generation of evangelical Christians are primarily about those controversial "culture war" issues that get the most media attention.

In 2006, the Institute of Politics at Harvard University polling grouped young voters into four categories: traditional conservatives, who favor limited government and lean right on things like abortion; traditional liberals, who favor expanded government and lean left on things like abortion; "secular centrists," who fill that sort of libertarian-ish role; and, finally, "religious centrists."

"With a very large concentration of African American and Hispanic students, the Religious Centrists support solid free trade, strongly support universal healthcare and are very protective of the environment," wrote the report's authors in 2006. "When Religious Centrists watch the nightly news, they are more likely than other college students to

believe that recent immigration is good and that the government response to Hurricane Katrina is a serious question of morality."[50] While
not the largest group of voters, researchers said the "religious centrists"
were particularly notable because they were winnable by either party
and were more highly motivated to vote than their "secular centrist"
counterparts in the political middle. And while we normally view
"moral issues" in politics as being those hot buttons like abortion,
prayer in schools, and same-sex marriage, these voters viewed economic issues as fundamentally moral issues as well.

I've heard time and time again from young voters across the country that they wish politicians would leave religion out of political
rhetoric—that they'd embrace "separation of church and state" and
focus on economic problems. But at the same time, the majority of
Americans affiliate with some form of religion that calls for people to
care for their neighbor. Aren't these moral questions at the *heart* of how
our economy does—or doesn't—work? Why have we allowed "faith in
politics" to become defined primarily by the culture wars that young
voters are loath to keep fighting?

"The legacy of Christian political activism in America spans not just
the culture wars, but America's founding, the abolition of slavery, and
the advancement of civil rights. To Christian leaders, and many Christians themselves, it was incomprehensible that they came to occupy
such a small space of our political discourse," wrote Michael Wear in
the *Atlantic*, reflecting on his time working for President Obama on
faith-based initiatives.[51] Wear, when profiled by Glenn Beck's site *The
Blaze* (hardly a pro-Obama news outlet), was described thusly upon
his appointment on the 2012 Obama campaign: "The 23-year-old,
who interned during the president's 2008 campaign, is an evangelical
whose age could bring innovation and vibrancy to the campaign's religious outreach projects."[52]

Wear is right that the influence of political Christianity has at times
been instrumental in advancing the cause of freedom rather than op-

posing it. And certainly, if you attended the Values Voter Summit held in Washington in September 2014, you heard the word "freedom" uttered an awful lot, primarily in the context of preserving religious freedom, the freedom to bear arms, freedom from national education standards, or freedom from "big government." "As out-of-wedlock births increase, as marriage declines, as more children go to sleep at night in fatherless homes the demand for bigger government grows. As Judeo-Christian values decline, the heavy-hand of government fills the vacuum. If Libertarians want to achieve the goal of reducing the size and scope of government, they should join with social conservatives and support the pro-family agenda," said the description of one panel discussion on the agenda.[53] Speeches by luminaries on the right like Rick Santorum and Mike Huckabee focused on a message about fighting radical Islam, the role of the Bible in schools, protecting Israel, and traditional "religious right" issues.

Louisiana governor Bobby Jindal also spoke at the summit, discussing his opposition to the Affordable Care Act and a whole host of Obama Administration policies. Embedded in his speech, however, was a nugget I found particularly interesting. "Now don't get me wrong. I'm all for capitalism and a strong economy," said Jindal. "But capitalism and free enterprise will fail in a country where people don't respect the rule of law, they don't care for each other, they don't share a common view of the dignity of all mankind as God's creation. Put simply, culture matters."[54]

It wasn't the first time that a prominent Republican speaker at the Values Voter Summit devoted some speech time to the way that culture, doing right by your fellow man, is essential to making our economic system work. During the 2012 campaign, for instance, then vice presidential nominee Representative Paul Ryan spoke at length about how our value of caring for one another is essential to a free society: "We Americans give ourselves to every kind of good cause. We do so for the simple reason that our hearts and conscience have called us to work that needs doing, to fill a place that sometimes no one else can fill. It's like that with our families and communities, too. The whole life of this nation is carried forward every day by the endless unselfish things people do for one another, without even giving it much thought. In books, they call this civil society . . . [A] lot of good happens without government commanding it, directing it, or claiming credit for it. That's how life is supposed to work in a free country."[55]

In the summer of 2014, Ryan released an outline of a legislative plan for fixing broken federal antipoverty programs. As Reihan Salam, coauthor (with Ross Douthat) of *Grand New Party: How Republicans Can Win the Working Class and Save the American Dream*, wrote at *Slate* upon the roll-out of Ryan's plan: "Though the plan is very much a work in progress—Ryan's team calls it a 'discussion draft' to underline that it is not a final product—it includes some of the most thought-provoking ideas to have ever come from the halls of Congress, where ideas traditionally go to die."[56] Elizabeth Kneebone, a scholar focused on reforming poverty programs for the center-left think tank the Brookings Institution, wrote: "By not engaging in a budget cutting exercise as in the past, Ryan has framed his proposals as an effort to start a conversation in Washington about real policy reforms to more effectively fight poverty and promote economic opportunity."[57]

The plan would take the nearly one hundred federal welfare and assistance programs and consolidate them to reduce overlap and inefficiency, and then would offer states the ability to take federal funding for these programs as a block grant, requiring that the states give recipients multiple options for how they can receive assistance—including through community-based nonprofits.

Though she was skeptical of some elements of Ryan's plan, Kneebone noted, "Ryan's Opportunity Grant tackles a very real problem. In our work on suburban poverty, time and again we have seen communities trying to craft more scaled, integrated and outcome-driven solutions to confront growing suburban poverty, only to be stymied by a fragmented and inflexible federal anti-poverty policy framework. Not only has the system failed to respond to today's shifting geography of poverty, it has often impeded more efficient and effective strategies to address poverty in struggling communities." The remote and complicated federal antipoverty system is failing to deliver the results and is actually making it tougher for successful local support systems to function and thrive.

Predictably, there are plenty of Democrats who don't believe it's possible for someone like Ryan, primarily known for being a fiscal hawk dedicated to balancing budgets and slimming down government excess, to actually want to alleviate poverty by reforming— rather than gutting—programs that provide the social safety net to those in need. I say "predictably" because there's actually research suggesting that political liberals think it is impossible for someone who *is* conservative, like Paul Ryan, to genuinely care for helping the poor. In Jonathan Haidt's aforementioned research on moral attitudes—harm, fairness, loyalty, authority, and purity—he found that political liberals are primarily driven by those questions of harm and fairness, while conservatives are driven by a mix of many. As a result, while conservatives can understand where political liberals are coming from, even as they disagree, political liberals often see conservatives as being not just wrong but as *bad people*. (Perhaps this is why liberals are more likely than conservatives to block someone on Facebook for having opposing political views.)[58]

Ryan's plan was unlikely to convince strongly liberal people that, yes, conservatives do care about helping people emerge from poverty and build prosperous and fulfilling lives. Nonetheless, it is vital for conservatives to continue to engage in this kind of thinking, to promote ideas for improving upon our nation's terribly lackluster safety net programs not by first cutting them but by first *fixing them*. It also means making programs flexible enough to rely upon, rather than replace, the charitable work being done in communities across the country.

Politically, for conservatives to thrive and win the next generation, we have to credibly prove ourselves on the moral dimensions of "care" and "fairness," to show how our convictions don't just compel us to cut taxes for rich people but instead to apply our beliefs to improving the status of the least fortunate. But this isn't just about looking friendly and warm and like we care; it is about *actually* putting forward ideas that will better the lives of our brothers and sisters—ideas that actually mesh perfectly with many of the other values held by young Americans today: a commitment to community service and a preference for localized solutions. It's not a hard sell to tell young people that government is lousy at solving problems; the challenge for conservatives is to demonstrate what *does* solve problems and how those solutions can be supported and built upon.

One of the most vocal conservatives on this issue is Yuval Levin, a fellow at the Ethics & Public Policy Center and editor of the thoughtful, must-read center-right journal *National Affairs*. In 2014, with the release of the YG Network's *Room to Grow* policy manifesto for conservatives, Levin tackled the question of reforming the social safety net thusly: "Conservatives must instead help the public see that the agenda they offer is rooted not just in fiscal concerns but in a political, moral, and social vision much better aligned with the realities of American life and the character of Americans' aspirations."[59]

When French historian Alexis de Tocqueville visited the United States of America in its early days, hoping to study our young democracy, he noted the way in which we crazy Americans loved forming associations and clubs to tackle problems. In *Democracy in America*, his book about what he saw on his visit, he wrote: "The Americans make associations to give entertainments, to found seminaries, to build inns, to construct churches, to diffuse books, to send missionaries to the antipodes; in this manner they found hospitals, prisons, and schools. If it is proposed to inculcate some truth or to foster some feeling by the encouragement of a great example, they form a society. Wherever at the head of some new undertaking you see the government in France, or a man of rank in England, in the United States you will be sure to find an association." Even to this day we're a nation of joiners and problem solvers—it is built into our country's DNA.

When Levin speaks about the center-right approach to caring for the poor and reforming our welfare programs, he differentiates the liberal and conservative viewpoints largely on the basis of the role that such associations have to play. He notes that "the premise of conservatism has always been that what matters most about society happens in the space between the individual and the state—the space occupied by families, communities, civic and religious institutions, and the private economy—and that creating, sustaining, and protecting that space and helping all Americans take part in what happens there are among the foremost purposes of government." Rather than just sending tax dollars off to Washington and having the government hand it back to the needy in an inefficient, convoluted process with dozens of programs of varying levels of effectiveness, can we do better at alleviating poverty—at truly "loving thy neighbor"—with reforms that make space for local, community-based organizations to do what they do best?

I spoke with Levin about his thoughts on previous policy ideas in this area, and he noted that this isn't just a call for a retread of "faith-based initiative" programs that the government has had in the past. "If we don't think of it as 'checking the box,' as 'what are we doing for religious people,' but instead of what are we doing for *people in need*, it's easy to see how some of those services can be provided by religious groups, because that's what they do: they care for the poor—not *because* they're religious but because they care for the poor." People who join organizations that are doing good work because their faith calls them to care for others—organizations that are providing valuable services that the government is lousy at providing—should be supported. "It'd be crazy for government to ignore the existence of that call to care and help when it is at least parallel to what government wants to do. And because it is face-to-face and hand-to-hand, it is done better," says Levin.

Reforming outdated government programs that aren't efficient; encouraging people to give charitably or to give of their time to better those around them; emphasizing local, flexible action—these are all part of a thoroughly conservative and profoundly timely approach to caring for the poor. And it meshes with the values of the next generation of Americans—including their thoughts about faith and morality—not by being trendy or fashionable, but by affirming something that is profoundly timeless about America: our commitment to caring for one another within our own communities.

EIGHT

Showing Up and Reaching Out: How to Speak to America's Most Diverse Generation

In American politics, it is sometimes said that candidates for office have to attend a lot of "rubber chicken dinners," sharing a meal with group after group of voters, dining on the same sort of fare night after night after night. They go from event to event, putting in the time to meet with and listen to constituents, and this ritual often involves eating. Shake more hands, eat more chicken, rinse and repeat.

Jason Kenney, a member of the Canadian Parliament, often finds himself out on the campaign trail, having meals with constituents as he hears their concerns and courts their votes. But as the Conservative Party's top liaison to Canada's ethnic minority communities, Kenney's typical dinner campaign stop sounds a bit, well, tastier than "rubber chicken."

"Kenney's Twitter feed chronicles an exhausting life of dinners and receptions, a lifestyle that made his former colleague Rahim Jaffer call him the 'minister for curry in a hurry,'" wrote *MacLean's* of Kenney when he served as the government's citizenship and immigration minister.[1] Nowadays, as minister of employment, social development, and multi-culturalism in Canada's Conservative government, Kenney appears to be keeping up the pace: some four years after the *MacLean's* article's head-line declared him to be Prime Minister Stephen Harper's "secret weapon [who is] reinventing the Conservative party," Kenney's Twitter feed shows a stream of visits with refugees, new Canadian citizens, and a whole host of meetings and meals with various religious and ethnic groups.

In case you'd never heard of Jason Kenney before picking up this book today, let me clarify something right off the bat: Kenney is not, himself, a racial or ethnic minority. He's a 40-something-year-old white guy. But that hasn't stopped him from being a tireless and quite successful envoy from Canada's Conservative Party to ethnic minority communities. It's easy to find photos of him, say, donning a head cov-ering to attend a parade in the Sikh community, or wearing traditional silk dress for a Chinese tea ceremony. He's even reportedly earned the nickname "Smiling Buddha" from some groups of Chinese-Canadians.[2] One day he's speaking Chinese at a World Falun Dafa Day event in Ottawa, the next he's on Canadian TV discussing temporary foreign worker programs. Kenney may be a white guy in a suit, but he's put in the work of building ties with Canada's ethnic minority communities, listening to their concerns and championing their causes.

As a result, he's become the face of the Conservative Party's efforts to shed their image as anti-immigrant and intolerant, winning over a more diverse group of voters in the process. "For decades, the Liberals took for granted the support of Canada's immigrant communities," noted Kenney in a speech to the 2011 Conservative Policy Convention in Ottawa. "And while Conservatives have always actually been the party of diversity, we allowed our adversaries to monopolize political relationships with cultural communities."[3]

In previous elections, Conservatives were badly beaten among minority voters. Indeed, in the 2000 election, roughly 70 percent of all Canadian voters from ethnic minority communities cast their ballots for the Liberal Party—a percentage that is similar to that enjoyed by Democrats these days in the U.S.

Conservatives at the time faced image challenges similar to those of today's Republican Party. Their party was not viewed as welcoming or diverse. Yet, by the 2008 election, as a result of the work of Kenney and his Conservative Party allies, the Liberals were winning fewer than four out of ten of those minority voters, with the Conservatives right on the Liberals' heels. Since taking power, Canada's Conservatives have expanded their majority in Parliament, up from 98 seats prior to the 2006 election to over 160 seats in 2014. Much of this success came from Conservatives making inroads with ethnic minority communities. "The Liberals were able to coast to victory in 2000 with the support of two key groups: visible minorities and Catholics. By 2008, the Liberals could no longer count on their loyalty," wrote a group of political scientists led by McGill University's Elisabeth Gidengil that studied data about Canadian elections. "In fact, minority voters were almost as likely to vote Conservative in 2008 as they were to vote Liberal."[4]

And the Conservatives haven't let up in the fight. "Despite the federal Liberals' attempts, under leader Justin Trudeau, to win back ethnic voters, the Conservatives continue to raise more money from Chinese-Canadians than any other party, new fundraising data suggest," reported the *National Post* during the summer of 2014. "The data appear to indicate the Tories' continuing ethnic outreach, spearheaded by cabinet minister Jason Kenney, is connecting with the fast-growing numbers of Canadians who trace their roots to China and Taiwan."[5]

There's the old line "Eighty percent of success is showing up." When it comes to expanding the reach of the Conservative Party to Canadian voters of all races and ethnicities, Jason Kenney *shows up*. Canada's Conservatives *show up*.

Republicans need to show up too.

More white people are dying in America than are being born. In the summer of 2013, the U.S. Census Bureau announced that the nation's racial majority experienced a population decline. The drop-off was small, with around 12,400 more deaths than there were births among white non-Hispanics living in America.[6] But the next year the Census Bureau announced a continuation of the trend, and this time the decline was over twice as large, what the bureau calls a "natural decrease" of over 27,000.

Yet, even as America has fewer and fewer white people each year, the nation's population continues to grow—big-time. The aging of America's white population comes at a time when, for every Hispanic-American who passes away, over six bundles of joy are born in the Hispanic community. That six-to-one ratio is impressive. But the Latino community is not alone; for the Asian-American community, the ratio is four to one, and for African-Americans there are over twice as many births as there are deaths.

Nearly four million newborns were welcomed into the world in the United States between the summer of 2012 and 2013. Less than half of them were white non-Hispanic. (The Census Bureau does not currently count Hispanic as a distinct racial group, so people are assigned to a race such as white or black, and are then given the separate designation of Hispanic or non-Hispanic.) These demographic trends are not a product of immigration from abroad; this is homegrown change driven by new American citizens, born here, who in the decades to come will grow up, become voters, and profoundly affect the political makeup of America. The face of America is changing *fast*, and as it does, it is reshaping the nation's future in powerful ways.

Today, those four million babies are being potty trained and are learning their ABCs. In the presidential election of 2032, they will cast their first ballots. But even while they are still in diapers, the demographic shifts evident in their parents' and grandparents' generations are having a dramatic impact on the American political landscape.

The racial and ethnic diversity of America's voting public has been increasing for decades now. In the presidential election that brought Jimmy Carter into the White House, 89 percent of voters were white. Only 1 percent were Hispanic, and only 9 percent were black. Since that election, the share of voters who are white has shrunk with each passing presidential election save one.[7] Since the presidential election of 1992, Hispanics have grown enormously as a share of the electorate, increasing from 2 percent of voters to 10 percent. Black and Asian-American voters have also ticked upward in their numbers. The trend lines are consistent and point in one direction: toward growing diversity.

Diversity in the electorate, in and of itself, does not doom Republicans. Republicans actually won over Asian-American voters during the 1990s, and during the George W. Bush administration Republicans improved in their performance with Hispanic voters each time Bush was on the ballot. With few exceptions, the overall trend over the last twenty years has been unmistakable, with minority voters trending away from the GOP and toward the Democrats. At the same time that minority voters are becoming a bigger and bigger chunk of the voting public, those voters are becoming less and less Republican.

This is not a brand-new phenomenon and it did not happen overnight. The fact that this change has been under way for decades makes it all the more stunning that, in 2012, it appeared that the Romney presidential campaign banked on capturing enough of the white vote to win the election. In a 2012 article by Ron Brownstein in the *National Journal*, he quoted an unnamed Republican strategist who noted that the strategy of the Romney team was to win at least 60 percent of all white voters. The thought was that despite the expectation that Romney would not do well with other voter groups, so long as he was able to win six out of ten white voters, he would be able to win the election. The strategy, therefore, was to try to win as many white votes as possible. The strategist was quoted as saying, "This will be the last time anyone will try this."[8]

It wound up being one try too many.

Consider this: in the 2012 presidential election, Mitt Romney won the youth vote—among young white people. Despite Obama winning over young white voters by a 10-point margin against John McCain in the 2008 election, those fortunes flipped four years later, with Romney winning 51 percent of white voters under age 30, and Obama only winning 44 percent.

Mitt Romney lost the election. *Who cares if he won young white people?* But consider this: if Mitt Romney won young white voters by a reasonably healthy margin, then *how could he possibly lose the youth vote overall so badly, by 23 points?*

The answer is simple: the youth vote is awfully diverse, and young people who are *not* white broke overwhelmingly for President Obama. Some Republicans were relieved that Mitt Romney did better among young voters than John McCain had in 2008, but, digging deeper into the data, it appears that almost all of that improvement came from the changing attitudes of young white voters. Young African-Americans, Latinos, and those of other ethnicities all gave comparable levels of support to President Obama in 2012 as they had four years earlier.

Yes, the story of the future of American politics is going to be heavily influenced by the values, beliefs, and preferences of the younger generation. Millennial voters will make a major imprint on elections for decades to come. But this story is as much one about race and diversity as it is about student loans and start-ups. The average Hispanic-American is under the age of 30, while the average American overall is nearly "over the hill."[9] Political pundits and commentators often talk about "winning the youth vote" or "winning the Latino vote" as if they are separate issues, different boxes to check on a voter outreach "shopping list." The reality is that America's growing diversity is intertwined with the new attitudes of the younger generation, and this fact will only become more apparent with each passing election. For instance, it is not uncommon for Univision to beat out traditional English-language networks' top ratings among viewers under age 50. When *Amores Verdaderos* is beating out *The Bachelorette* among viewers aged 18 to 34, political advertisers on the right who want to reach young people need to wake up to the new demographic reality.[10]

If Republicans are to draw their votes primarily from the pool of white voters in America, they are simply on an unsustainable path. While some Republican campaigns have made a splash by courting minority voters, they are often the exception rather than the rule. On the airwaves, for instance, Republicans typically get outspent by Democrats by massive margins in terms of advertising on Spanish-language media. On the ground, Republicans have not traditionally put in the same effort in having field offices in Hispanic communities, organizing people on the ground, and building relationships over time rather than just showing up right before Election Day and saying, "Vote for me."

When Republicans do show up and make an effort to win voters who aren't white, it makes a difference. Take Chris Christie's reelection campaign in New Jersey; Christie actually *won* among Hispanic voters, according to the exit polls. He didn't just *do well* with them, he outright *won*—and in a blue state no less. He also did far better than most Republicans do among African-American voters, picking up 21 percent of their votes. After the election, Univision interviewed Christie campaign manager Mike DuHaime about the campaign's efforts to reach Latino voters, with DuHaime noting, "It was part of the campaign from the very beginning: we were going to be doing English-language ads and Spanish-language ads, English-language direct mail, Spanish-language direct mail." They hired field staff who spoke Spanish and made sure these efforts weren't just a side project. "It was always part of the bigger campaign. Too often, campaigns view them separately, and they shouldn't."[11] The RNC, too, said they focused on reaching Hispanic and African-American voters in New Jersey during Christie's reelection, spending a six-figure sum on the effort.[12]

Or take the 2014 election of Greg Abbott to the office of governor of Texas: despite Democratic efforts to turn Texas into a swing state on the strength of their performance with the state's large Latino population, the Abbott campaign countered with millions spent on Spanish-language media and numerous field offices in Hispanic regions of the state. The Abbott campaign made outreach a priority and it paid off at the ballot box, with Abbott outperforming his predecessor, Governor Rick Perry, among Latino voters.[13]

In the 2014 midterm elections, Republicans did quite well across the country by winning large proportions of white voters, while non-white and young voters sat home and did not turn out to vote in large numbers. That will not necessarily be the case in the presidential election in 2016 and is unlikely to be the case in the elections beyond. We live in an era when each election feels like a wave election, because the voters who show up in midterm elections look very different from the voters who show up in presidential elections. Winning only in mid-terms is not a long-term strategy for accomplishing much of anything.

If Republicans ever want to win over the millennial generation, they will have to improve their standing with young voters of all races and ethnicities. And if they want to stand a chance in that presidential election of 2032, they had better start planning how they'll get there.

☆

Most conversations about expanding the GOP's demographic appeal start in the same place: the need to pass an immigration reform plan.

In the Republican "Growth and Opportunity Report," the 2013 post-election analysis sometimes referred to darkly as an "autopsy," party leaders took a look at the myriad reasons why Republicans struggled to win in the 2012 election and assessed what needed to be done for the party to move forward. Among other things, the report rightly identified the GOP's declining appeal among nonwhite voters as a key problem that needed addressing if Republicans were to win in the future. Most of the recommendations offered throughout the report were about the party's processes: how the party chooses nominees through primary contests, expectations for good election polling, the need to hire more analytics staff.

There was, however, a notable exception where the authors of the report went as far as to recommend a particular policy position that the party should adopt: support for comprehensive immigration reform.

"We are not a policy committee, but among the steps Republicans take in the Hispanic community and beyond, we must embrace and champion comprehensive immigration reform. If we do not, our Party's appeal will continue to shrink to its core constituencies only. We also believe that comprehensive immigration reform is consistent with Republican economic policies that promote job growth and opportunity for all," said the report.[14]

Certainly, Americans of all political stripes think that the immigration system is in need of repair and reform. The Public Religion Research Institute, one of the foremost research organizations that studies public opinion on issues like immigration, found over seven out of ten Americans think the current system is broken.[15] Nonetheless, not all Republicans, including many prominent conservative commentators, were excited about the inclusion of this recommendation in the report.

Indeed, despite the Senate's passage of a comprehensive immigration reform package in 2013, driven by a bipartisan group of senators including Republican Marco Rubio of Florida, the Republican House of Representatives did not pick up the bill. Republican disagreement over immigration policy is hardly a new phenomenon: George W. Bush's own policy proposal failed in 2006 in large part due to opposition from within his own party, despite having support at the time from people like Governor Rick Perry of Texas.[16] And though the venerated Ronald Reagan declared "I believe in the idea of amnesty" during a 1984 presidential debate and granted legal status to millions during his presidency, the word "amnesty" is now radioactive within the GOP.[17] Even reforms that garner clear bipartisan support in public opinion polling, such as a path to citizenship for undocumented Americans brought to the U.S. as children, face pushback and opposition from activists and in Congress.

The reality is that the political math is very complicated for Republicans on the issue of immigration, at least in the near term. Even with young voters, the picture is unclear. Few young voters of any political persuasion are happy with the current state of the nation's immigration system, and neither party has a decisive lead on the issue among young voters. In the fall 2014 survey by Harvard's Institute of Politics, some 61 percent of young people disapproved of the president's handling of the issue of immigration. When asked which party they trusted more to handle the issue, four out of ten young voters said they were not sure, while 32 percent chose the Democrats and 26 percent chose the Republicans. Republicans hold a slight edge on the issue with young white voters; Democrats hold a significant edge with voters who aren't white. (Only 10 percent of young black voters and 14 percent of young Hispanic voters trust the GOP most on the issue.)

To be sure, Democrats have run into trouble over immigration policy too. For instance, in 2007, Hillary Clinton famously botched a response to a question about whether she'd support giving driver's licenses to undocumented workers, first sounding supportive of the policy and later recanting.[18] Ahead of the 2014 midterm elections, there were a number of news reports of frustration and anger within the Democratic coalition, particularly among immigration reform advocates, who had publicly deemed President Obama the "deporter-in-chief."

Nonetheless, there is no doubt that Republicans have the tougher needle to thread on the issue and that, even when it comes to the attitudes of young voters, the path forward politically is far from clear-cut.

Republicans are not the only right-of-center party in a difficult political position when it comes to immigration. One need only look across the Atlantic Ocean to see the trouble that center-right parties in Europe are facing these days on the issue of immigration, balancing increasingly diverse national populations with increasingly anxious racial and ethnic majorities. In the 2014 European Parliament elections, extreme right-wing anti-immigrant parties did exceptionally well, riding on a tide of anxiety and anger fueled in part by the economic struggles of the eurozone.[19] The rise of these far-right nationalist parties has come at a cost to the existing center-right parties in many countries. Take, for instance, the 2014 national elections in Sweden, where the Moderate Party—Sweden's right-of-center, pro-market political party—was knocked out of power, not because their major opposition on the political left made substantial gains, but because nearly thirty of their parliamentary seats fell into the hands of the far-right Sweden Democrats, an anti-immigrant party that had surged in popularity and with whom no other party was eager to enter into a coalition.[20] Or look to France, where Marine Le Pen's National Front Party, fueled by a potent blend of economic populism and anti-immigrant sentiment, has eaten into the center-right party's voting base even as President François Hollande, a Socialist, has become extremely unpopular.

The American political system is quite different from that of countries in Europe. Though there is no National Front to pull voters away from the GOP, there is great concern about how embracing immigration reform might affect Republican fortunes in the *short term*. Will "base" voters stay home and not turn out to vote or, worse, abandon the party? Are young voters, particularly young voters who are Hispanic, likely to be won over to the GOP? Would support for immigration reform, including a pathway to citizenship for the undocumented, lead to a net addition or subtraction of voters for the Republican Party? The answer, at least for the moment, is unclear.

The immigration system needs fixing, and over the long term, Republicans have a serious political interest in being a part of the solution. For young voters who might be open to a Republican economic message but feel the party is hungry for deportations, rhetoric that sounds hostile and anti-immigrant all but shuts down the opportunity for conversation. But it is important to note that comprehensive immigration reform is not a cure-all for Republican woes with young or minority voters. Only a handful of young voters name immigration as their top issue; most are focused on economic issues and government debt.[21] For instance, black voters hold views similar to white voters' on the need for immigration reform, with fewer than half telling the Pew Research Center that they think passing immigration reform is extremely or very important.[22] Fewer than half of Asian-Americans say that the nation's immigration system needs major changes or an overhaul.[23] And among Hispanic adults, even during the summer of 2014, in the midst of the border crisis, the proportion of Hispanics who named immigration as their top issue was only one out of four, while 40 percent said the economy was most important.[24]

It is clear that young nonwhite voters don't trust the Republican Party to handle the issue of immigration. This is a serious problem and may prevent a growing segment of the voting public from being willing to listen to anything else the GOP has to say. However, even assuming Republicans make progress on this front, a Republican-backed comprehensive immigration plan is *not* a magic spell for winning over young Hispanic voters.

It is absolutely the case that there needs to be a public policy answer to the question of what to do about the millions of immigrants living in the United States without legal status. It is absolutely the case that we need to reform how we deal with legal and illegal immigration. This issue is not going *anywhere*, and smart Republicans will play an active role in shaping the solutions rather than standing on the sidelines in opposition. However, comprehensive immigration reform is *not* the sole driver of the GOP's woes with nonwhite voters, and it will not be the sole salvation of the party's hopes for the political future. The story is much more complicated.

During one of my focus groups in 2013, immediately following the presidential election, I asked a roomful of young Latino voters what they thought about the Republican Party, and the responses were not particularly focused on immigration. Instead, this quote from a participant seems to best sum up the challenge for Republicans:

"[They have] that mentality that you're born like royalty and the peasants stay peasants. I don't think that is the view that America was founded on.

"This is supposed to be a land of opportunity."

☆

Late in the evening, on a night just before Thanksgiving in 2014, a grand jury in St. Louis declined to indict police officer Darren Wilson for shooting and killing Michael Brown, a young unarmed black man, on the streets of Ferguson, Missouri. Wilson's testimony indicated that Brown had attempted to take his gun from him, escalating the encounter and requiring the use of deadly force, resulting in Brown's tragic death. Media reports portrayed Brown as having put his hands up in the air to surrender before being shot. In the summer days following Brown's death, the streets of Ferguson resembled a war zone, with journalists arrested, tear gas, looting, curfews, and armored vehicles being used against protesters by police. The grand jury's subsequent decision not to bring charges against Wilson led to more protests, outrage, and frustration across the country. The evidence released in the case muddied the waters about what did and did not happen on that street in Ferguson, and the debate over what to do about the tragedy in Ferguson raged on. Polls showed public opinion on the case was sharply divided by race.

Yet, if there was a divide over the grand jury's decision in the Ferguson case, there was very little debate over a similar grand jury decision that would come down a week later. Eric Garner, an African-American man and father of six, had been accused of selling untaxed cigarettes; his encounter with NYPD officers on Staten Island turned fatal when he was placed in what appeared to be a chokehold and repeatedly cried out that he could not breathe. Unlike the Ferguson case, there was clear, unambiguous, horrific video evidence demonstrating that Garner did not pose a threat to the officers. While most of America could only speculate on what had happened in Ferguson, they could watch the tragedy of Eric Garner play out on YouTube. When the grand jury declined to indict the police officer who killed Garner, the outrage was nearly universal. Rare is the day when Al Sharpton and Bill O'Reilly agree, and yet, the death of Eric Garner and lack of indictment in the case brought the two together.

Garner's death was also not the last tragedy of its kind. In South Carolina during the spring of 2015, an African-American man named Walter Scott was shot in the back while unarmed and running away from a white police officer during a traffic stop. The killing was caught on video, and officer Michael Slager was charged with murder.

Many Americans will hear the rallying cry of the protesters in the aftermath of the Brown and Garner and Scott cases—"Black lives matter"—and think it is obvious, self-evident. *Of course* black lives matter. We may truly want to think that racism is a thing of the past in America. We may want to say that we don't see color anymore, that we have made enormous progress as a nation, that we are a "post-racial" America. But although racism may not look the way it did in decades past, with segregated water fountains and restrooms, a look at the data paints a disappointing picture, demonstrating that we have plainly not achieved racial equality in America. One need only look at our schools and prisons to see that, tragically, we are not yet equal.

Particularly disturbing are the ways in which African-Americans are disproportionately affected by our nation's criminal justice system.

Of the 1.5 million people held in state or federal prison, among the male inmates, less than a third were white in 2013.[25] We incarcerate so many of our fellow citizens that one out of every twenty-eight kids in our country has a parent in jail. (In order to reach out to those kids, the beloved children's television program *Sesame Street* has actually created a character, Alex, a blue-haired puppet who also has an incarcerated parent.)[26] One in twelve working-age African-American men is in jail, and our nation's incarceration rate significantly surpasses that of other industrialized nations.[27]

Many of those who are in jail for nonviolent offenses might not be there if their skin was a different color. Take, for instance, the crime of marijuana possession: the ACLU claims that despite roughly equal rates of pot use by whites and blacks, black Americans are almost four times as likely to be arrested for marijuana offenses and that black Americans are significantly more likely to be charged with a drug crime in America than are white Americans.[28] In Arkansas, the outgoing Democratic governor Mike Beebe pardoned his own son, found guilty of felony marijuana possession in 2003, before he left office; most young men aren't lucky enough to have a father in the governor's mansion and don't get a penalty of just probation and fines when they're caught with pot.[29] The cost to our society of locking up so many, *particularly* those who have not committed a violent offense, is extraordinary, both in terms of the fiscal costs to government and in the human toll it takes in the disproportionately affected African-American community.

Both racial and generational divides exist in public opinion about race, justice, and law enforcement. Overall, according to the Public Religion Research Institute study, a majority of Americans disagree that "blacks and other minorities receive equal treatment as whites in the criminal justice system." Four out of ten African-Americans have "very little" confidence that police officers in their community will not use excessive force on suspects, significantly less confidence than among white adults.[30] According to the Pew Research Center, while younger African-Americans are actually *less* likely than their elders to think that racial discrimination is the main reason why black Americans "can't get ahead these days," younger African-Americans are *more* skeptical of the police and the justice system than their parents and grandparents are. Younger adults, both white and black, are significantly more likely than older adults of their own race to say that police should not be able to stop someone just because that person looks "suspicious."[31]

Younger voters are more likely than older voters to think something needs to change in how we police our streets and enforce our laws. These issues don't necessarily have a partisan angle: both limited-government Republicans and social-justice Democrats can find reasons why we should rethink how we make arrests and whom we incarcerate. In California, for instance, voters passed Proposition 47, which downgraded a number of nonviolent felonies to misdemeanors and provided an opportunity for thousands of those in state prisons for nonviolent offenses a chance to rebuild their lives when released. The measure was supported by both Newt Gingrich and Jay-Z, hardly a traditional set of allies.[32]

It might be hard to imagine many issues where Tea Party movement senators would find themselves standing side by side with liberal stars like Senators Dick Durbin of Illinois and Cory Booker of New Jersey, yet folks like Rand Paul (R-KY) and Mike Lee (R-UT) have emerged as champions of criminal justice reform. For instance, Senators Booker and Paul cosponsored the REDEEM Act, which included things like reducing harsh penalties faced by juvenile offenders—penalties that often ruin those teens' chances at a productive adult life. Senators Lee, Durbin, and Pat Leahy (D-VT) have cosponsored a bill that would reduce some drug-related mandatory minimums and reduce overcrowding in federal prisons.

Senator Lee, the conservative from Utah, has also spoken out on the need for reform, noting: "Prevailing law-enforcement strategies have helped make communities safer around the country. And yet, the current system, for all its merits, nonetheless leaves too many Americans behind—some of them reformed offenders languishing in prison . . . some of them innocent men, women, and children on the outside, trapped in fraying communities with too little security and too few fathers, uncles, and older brothers. A generation of tougher-on-crime policies has created new challenges that it's up to our generation now to meet."[33]

Republicans are too often afraid to wade into these waters. Being a "law-and-order" Republican is rarely a risky move, and being "tough on crime" is the stuff of a thousand successful campaign ads. Calling for reform opens one up to criticism for being soft on crime or making it harder for police to do the noble work of keeping people safe. Even given high-profile cases where nonthreatening encounters with police have turned fatal, most young voters do trust the police to treat them and their friends fairly.[34] However, calling for a reduction in the penalties faced over something like possession of marijuana makes sense for young voters, the vast majority of whom think marijuana should be legal under at least some circumstances.[35]

Furthermore, acknowledging that there are disparities in how our justice system sometimes treats people of different races can seem, wrongly, like a concession to the left. Journalist Wesley Lowery, writing for the *Washington Post*, spoke with a variety of Republican operatives about outreach to black voters ahead of the 2014 midterms, noting: "To compete, they acknowledge, they have to be willing to discuss issues of race, prejudice and discrimination that often make members of their party uncomfortable."[36]

We can acknowledge that police have an incredibly difficult job, putting their lives on the line to protect us, and also say we need to find ways to prevent the next Eric Garner tragedy before it happens. We can argue that all of the time and money spent fighting nonviolent crime, locking up kids for possessing small amounts of pot and closing the door of opportunity for those accused of petty violations of the law, would be better spent fighting *violent* crime and keeping *those criminals* behind bars. We know that the vast majority of law enforcement officers are doing brave, essential work protecting their fellow citizens, while at the same time we know that the justice system is too often levying harsh, life-destroying penalties on those who have committed only minor offenses, and is doing so disproportionately to those who aren't white.

The conservative case for justice reform makes complete sense. In addition to saving on the enormous expense to taxpayers that comes with incarcerating so many criminals, standing for limited government should include standing against overcriminalization. In fact, in 2011, the conservative Heritage Foundation decried the massive increase in the number of federal criminal offenses on the books in recent decades, noting: "Congress seems to have forgotten that it can repeal bad laws. It can and should. The worst, most unjust criminal offenses should be thrown into the legislative dumpster."[37] But there's more than just the fiscal or size-of-government argument to be made by conservatives. Justice reform is profoundly pro-family. It creates opportunity where it had previously been lost.

Senator Mike Lee put it thusly: "If you brought together all the children in the United States with a parent in prison, they would make up a city roughly the size of Chicago. These children and their families and neighborhoods too often find themselves locked in a different kind of prison: of poverty, instability, immobility, and isolation . . . [T]he real benefits of criminal justice reform won't be found in government budgets, or even in courtrooms and prisons, but in homes and classrooms and churches and sidewalks in neighborhoods where hope can start to make a comeback."[38]

If Republicans are to improve their standing with voters who are not white, they must commit to removing barriers to opportunity that exist for people who are not white. There are economic barriers, there are educational barriers, and there are legal barriers. All must be addressed; denying their existence does nothing to solve the problem or to create harmony. No one political party has cornered the market on being the party to best advance the cause of "race relations" in America. Harvard's Institute of Politics survey asked young voters in fall 2014 which party they trusted more to handle the issue of race relations, and the top answer was—as with immigration—"Not sure." Yet these overall results, too, mask significant differences between black and white young people, including the fact that young African-Americans are much more distrustful of the Republican Party. To champion equality and harmony, Republicans must credibly show how they want to create more opportunity for young people of all races. That starts very fundamentally by proving we agree: black lives matter. And we have the policy reform ideas to prove our commitment.

Our nation is experiencing a moral crisis and a devastating loss of potential. To be a political party that champions freedom, family, and opportunity, it is essential to acknowledge where the government has thrown up roadblocks—roadblocks that particularly affect Americans from communities of color. It has become common on the right to say that we should not and cannot guarantee people equal outcomes, but we ought to strive for equal opportunity. That starts with the law.

☆

When Jason Kenney sits down with voters in Canada's ethnic minority and immigrant communities, he isn't just dining, shaking hands, and putting in face time. He's not just showing up. He's got a message: *Conservatives share your values.*

"Most new Canadians are natural, small-c conservatives: in their values, in the way they live their lives, in their aspirations," says Kenney. "By making a sustained effort to reach out on the basis of our shared values, we could turn those small-c conservatives into big-C

Conservatives."[39] Family, enterprise, equality of opportunity, hard work, and personal responsibility are all values that Kenney argues are at the core of his Conservative Party as well as the immigrant communities into which he goes to listen. "Canadians of all backgrounds, particularly new Canadians, are drawn to our party not in spite of our values, like the media thinks, but *because* of our conservative values."

Kenney's strategy for broadening the Conservative Party base in Canada was about putting in the effort to show voters of all ethnicities that they matter and are welcome in his party. But showing voters that the door to your party is open is not enough. You have to give them a reason to come in. And so the second piece of his strategy, focusing on shared values, is perhaps the most important.

The values Kenney mentions—family, faith, entrepreneurship, personal responsibility, opportunity—all sound like they come straight out of the Republican playbook as well. There is a vast overlap between those values and the values of young Americans, including and particularly young voters of racial and ethnic minorities.

Take entrepreneurship, careers, and hard work: young African-American and Hispanic voters are even more likely than their white counterparts to say they want to start their own business one day.[40] Nearly nine out of ten young Latinos—more than for the general population of young adults—say that being successful in a career is "very important" to them, and although traditional priorities like having children and being religious are less of a priority to second- and third-generation Hispanic young adults, career success is very important to nearly 90 percent of young Hispanics of each generation. They're also much more likely than other young adults to say that hard work is how one gets ahead in the U.S. today.[41]

Or take opportunity: young Americans—particularly those from minority communities—are troubled by what they perceive as a lack of a chance to succeed. There is a huge generational divide on this issue. Put simply, young Americans are much more likely than their

parents or grandparents to think lack of opportunity is a major problem and that not everyone has a chance to reach the top. Race and eth-
nicity also play a big role: today, while half of white Americans believe
that "one of the biggest problems in the country is that not everyone
is given an equal chance to succeed in life," that view is held by three-
quarters of African-Americans and roughly 60 percent of Hispanics.[42]

Some Republicans have been focused on the issue of opportunity.
The RNC's postelection report was named the "Growth and Opportunity Project," underscoring their view that economic growth and opportunity have to be the core of the GOP agenda and message. Some
major Republican lawmakers, such as Senator Marco Rubio, have also
struck this chord. In 2014, Senator Rubio gave a speech in honor of the
fiftieth anniversary of the "war on poverty" in which he noted:

"We are still a country where hard work and perseverance can earn
you a better life. The vast majority of Americans today live lives much
better than their parents. Yet we are rightfully troubled that many of
our people are still caught in what seems to be a pervasive, unending
financial struggle. It bothers us because we are a people united by the
belief that every American deserves an equal opportunity to achieve
success."[43]

The trouble with Republicans on this issue is that, while we value
opportunity, we don't all see where opportunity is lacking in America.
In a poll done by the nonpartisan Public Religion Research Institute,
only about a third of Republicans said, "One of the big problems in
the country is that we don't give everyone an equal chance in life,"
while a majority of Republicans agreed with the statement "It is not
really that big of a problem that some people have more of a chance in
life than others." While Senator Rubio and others have made the case
that Republicans ought to focus on opportunity, not all Republican
voters think that a lack of opportunity is the biggest problem—or is
even a problem at all.

The core of the Republican Party's problem with young voters from racial and ethnic minorities is not exclusively about immigration, or justice reform, or a particular policy area. It is about opportunity. This is linked, of course, to opportunity for those who were brought illegally here as children or those whose lives will be ruined by a conviction over a minor nonviolent criminal offense. Taking steps to increase opportunity with policy changes in these arenas is something Republicans ought to pursue.

But, more broadly, for Republicans to win with young voters from racial and ethnic minority communities, we have to talk about shared values, most important the shared value of equal opportunity. *And we have to genuinely share that value.* This means acknowledging areas where equal opportunity does not exist today and seeking to create it in those areas. We may reject the Democratic view that equality of outcomes is an important goal: some will work harder than others, some will have better ideas than others, and people should reap the benefits of their work. The goal should not be that we all end up in the same place but rather that we all have a chance to make it across the finish line.

The future of politics in America will be shaped by the sea change in the country's demographic makeup. Republicans will absolutely have to improve their standing outside the core group of white voters who have sustained GOP victories in recent midterm elections. The issues Republicans face in winning over young voters and winning over nonwhite voters are inextricably linked, and overcoming the party's struggles with both groups will involve a similar prescription.

Republicans have to be in the opportunity business. They have to show up and talk to voters they have previously neglected. They have to listen to the concerns of voters with whom they have not always agreed. And, most important, they have to have something to say about the ways in which Republican ideas can create opportunity for *all* Americans, regardless of the color of their skin or the date of their birth.

NINE

Vote by Numbers:
What Campaigns Are Learning
from Silicon Valley

Jesse Kamzol meets me in the newly redone Data and Digital Department at the Republican National Committee headquarters in DC. I have been in this part of the RNC building before, years earlier when it housed the RNC's Research Department, and it did not look anything like this the last time I was here. "This used to be a cube farm," says Jesse. "It was a dumping ground for old equipment." What was once a relatively dark cave full of cubicles is now bright and open, with long rows of white desks filling the space. On one wall, a cluster of large TV screens display digital metrics, and the remaining walls are covered in posters that declare "Always Challenge the Old Ways" or "Innovate and Die." It feels like a war room mixed with a Silicon Valley start-up, which is exactly the point.

"He's the guy behind the new GOP.com site that just launched today. He probably hasn't slept in ten days," Jesse says, gesturing to a desk down one of the rows, where a young man with headphones in is typing away, looking surprisingly alert. I'm visiting the RNC just a few weeks before the 2014 midterm elections, and things are in high gear and dozens of staffers are at work trying to maximize Republican chances of victory. At another desk, a staffer is looking at a detailed map on his screen with a multitude of different boundaries and lines defining where various voting precincts begin and end, as well as other important points of political geography. Jesse remarks, "He's doing our GIS work." (GIS means Geographic Information Systems, dealing with data about where things are located.) The staffer is wearing bulky over-ear Beats headphones. He seems "in the zone"; I don't dare interrupt to ask him for more detail on what he's up to.

Jesse and I go into a small conference room where the poster on the wall declares: "The best way to predict the future is to create it."

That is what Jesse and his team are trying to do.

After the 2012 election, the Republican Party went through a very public airing of grievances. Everyone had an opinion on why Republicans were lost in the wilderness and seemed unable to win elections at the national level. The 2013 "Growth and Opportunity Project" report released by the RNC assessing the party's challenges put it succinctly: "Voter data and analytics are where Republicans most clearly trail Democrats according to an internet survey of 227 GOP campaign managers, field staff, and other political professionals, consultants, and vendors."[1] Democrats had systems that did an effective job of keeping track of each voter or potential voter, systems that were repeatedly and frequently updated with new information about each person's probable political preferences and likelihood to vote. By constantly collecting more and more information about voters, the Obama team was able to make accurate predictions about how many voters would show up and whether or not those were Romney voters or Obama voters. Most important, that information drove strategy decisions and let the Obama campaign target exactly the voters they wanted to reach, persuade, or encourage to vote. Republicans had lagged behind in this area and were publicly shamed for it after the 2012 election; the team at the RNC was determined to write a new story for the 2014 election and beyond.

"We were putting together 'big data' national voter files two decades ago," Kamzol says, dismissing the notion that Democrats are the pioneers of the voter data world. "You had to store the data on tapes. They were this big," he says, gesturing to indicate the size of a large textbook. "It took eighteen of these just to store the Florida voter file." The "voter file," generally built from a publicly available list of all voters in a certain geographic area, is the backbone of a campaign. It starts with everyone who is a registered voter and ultimately includes all of the other information a campaign can get its hands on about an individual (like whether or not you are registered Republican or voted in the last election or might have a dog). It's that information that tells a campaign who their voters might be and lets the campaign know how to reach them.

"Us and the Democrats, we start with the same dirty data," Jesse reminds me. In the world of data science, "dirty data" means data that is potentially inaccurate or badly organized. Dealing with that dirty data through "data cleaning"—making the data as accurate, uniform, and usable as possible—is one of the most important and most labor-intensive tasks.

Here's the best way to think about data cleaning: Let's say you're organizing an end-of-season party for a softball league. You want to send all of the players an invitation, but you only have the roster for your own team, and there are seven other teams in the league. You want to send people an invitation in the mail and then also send them an e-mail. The captain of your team sends you the contact list of all of your teammates as a spreadsheet. She's good with computers and very organized, so she has a column for first names and another column for last names. There's a column for phone numbers, and one for e-mail addresses. The column for addresses has separate columns for street, city, state, and zip, which will make it much easier for you to print out mailing labels.

Unfortunately, most of the other coaches didn't collect the exact same type of information. One captain has stored his teammates' entire addresses in just one column of the spreadsheet instead of separating out city and zip. First and last names are also stored in just one column instead of being separated into two columns. There seem to be a lot of typos in a few of the other team contact lists. Some of the people who joined the league midseason aren't included, and at least a few people have changed addresses. One list has a bunch of duplicates. One captain doesn't have the information as a spreadsheet, just a list he's copied and pasted into an e-mail to you. What a mess. How are you going to put all of this information into one consistent list that you can use to make mailing labels and keep track of RSVPs?

Now imagine doing that task with lists compiled by thousands of different county entities across all fifty states, for *hundreds of millions of people*. Instead of a softball team roster being a bit sloppy, it's *a whole county*. This is the challenge of political data. "There are probably only ten people alive who have actually built a national voter file completely from scratch. It isn't as easy as it looks," says Jesse.

No kidding. The task of building a national voter file is uniquely challenging. In the state of Florida, for instance, voters register as being affiliated with a particular political party. When I lived in Florida, you could look me up in the voter file and see that next to my name I was listed as "Republican." In the state of Virginia, however, they don't ask voters to choose a party on their registration forms. The way that one state stores a voter's address or voting history may be completely different from the way another state stores the same information. Someone might move from one county to another, and there will be a discrepancy that needs to be fixed. Or someone might move to a new state entirely, making it hard to link their new voter profile with their old voter history.

There will also be lots of human error involved. "County clerks are hard to work with sometimes," Jesse points out. "And if the nice old lady who types the data into the county file enters someone's address wrong, too bad. So we have to go through and clean the country's worth of data every few months."

Add to this the roughly 260 million consumers nationwide that the RNC has purchased data about—some of whom are not currently listed as registered voters—and you can see how the challenge of creating a simple, clean data set might be an enormous undertaking requiring a lot of manpower and a lot of brainpower. "Have you ever seen the movie *Wall-E?*" Jesse asks. "That's how we've been repurposed. Our job is to take whatever kind of data we get, to compound it, and to store it efficiently."

Jesse did not begin his career in politics as a data guy. In 2006 he worked on his first race, a congressional campaign in Florida, then worked in the world of government affairs before landing at the RNC, working in the Strategy Department, which has since been renamed Data and Digital to more accurately reflect the work they do these days. One of the major challenges in the campaign data world is finding the right talent for the job, and it has required more than a little cross-training, pulling political operatives and teaching them how to work with data, while at the same time recruiting data science pros and schooling them on the wild world of politics. Jesse's colleague, Azarias Reda, a twenty-something PhD in computer science, is heading up the RNC's efforts to build better tools to use data to engage and activate voters. "We've been pairing tech people with political people so they learn from each other. I now know just enough about data to be dangerous. Azarias now knows enough about politics to be dangerous. We're a good team."

☆

Azarias Reda has been tasked with helping Republicans build tools to make the most of the big data revolution.

Recruited from the world of tech start-ups and boasting a résumé that includes stints at LinkedIn and at Microsoft Research in India, Reda is not the usual political operative. He did not come up through the ranks of, say, the College Republicans or an internship on Capitol Hill. At the time I sat down with Reda, he'd been at the RNC less than a year. Of course, in the start-up world, where a year is a lifetime, new ideas are always being hatched, and then developed or abandoned, at lightning speed. "You want to fail fast or have an inflection point where you really take off," Reda tells me when discussing his life in the start-up world before his time in Washington. Bringing that breakneck pace of change to the sometimes stubbornly slow world of politics was one of many challenges Reda encountered upon his arrival in the political world, a world which is now adapting to the rapidly expanding possibilities offered by the explosion of available data.

The things that can be done today with data are extraordinary compared with just a decade or two ago. A major retailer like Target, for instance, doesn't just know what type of food you like or what type of pet you might have. Target can tell if you're pregnant.

In a 2012 *New York Times Magazine* article on how corporate marketers have been using consumer data to predict and influence behavior, it was revealed that statisticians at the retail behemoth were trying to find ways to identify loyal customers who were about to embark on a new (and expensive) chapter of their lives. Written by Charles Duhigg, author of *The Power of Habit: Why We Do What We Do in Life and Business*, the article chronicles how Target discovered that major life events make customers more likely to change where they shop. By grabbing these consumers early, a retailer like Target can better work to ensure their loyalty before the big-ticket baby-purchasing decisions

have to be made. Target studied the purchasing habits of customers to examine what products people tend to buy a few months *before*
they start buying diapers and cribs, creating an index of roughly two
dozen products that signal someone might be pregnant. If a customer
switches to buying a non-scented lotion or unusually large bags of
cotton balls, researchers found that these items signaled it might be
time to send the customer ads about maternity wear and strollers.
(In the story, a father actually complained to Target that his teenage
daughter was receiving baby-themed ads, only to very shortly thereafter apologize upon learning that Target's prediction had been all too
correct: she *was* pregnant.)[2]

While a retailer like Target has the advantage of being able to track
your individual purchases at their store, breathe easy: campaigns do
not have *that* level of specificity. Alex Lundry is quick to note that
while the data is interesting and valuable, it is not overly specific
and far less creepy than it may seem at first glance. "There's another
misperception that we are Big Brother, that we know all these things;
but if people could see the data, they'd be disappointed. It's done in
a way that is helpful to marketers like us but isn't nakedly revelatory.
There's no transaction level data, there's not as much detail as you
might expect. Say there's a flag on the file that says 'technology interest': that may be on your record because you subscribe to *Wired*; it may
be because you have a frequent buyer card at Best Buy; it may be there
because you filled out a warranty for your computer. There are likely
lots of ways to get flagged, so we don't know how you got marked as
'technology interest.'"

Mitt Romney and Barack Obama did not know that you picked up
a jumbo size bag of cotton balls. (And they probably wouldn't have
cared anyhow.) They don't know what kind of dog food or what color
sweater you bought. But while they won't see your transactions, they
can get information about notable patterns and lifestyle habits. They
may not know what type of yarn you buy or if you prefer Michaels to

Jo-Ann Fabric, but they do know if you're likely to have a knitting habit. "Sometimes 'knitting' pops in a model. It's an indicator that someone's older and angry about Obamacare," says Kamzol in our conversation about how campaigns use this consumer data to learn more about voters. In fact, every person I spoke with who works with this kind of data noted that for each individual, there are thousands of possible flags or indicators about lifestyle habits or preferences. There are limits to how valuable these thousands and thousands of data points can be; for every time something like knitting or having a dog winds up being truly meaningful, there are countless other times where it doesn't mean much. "It's nice to have information about magazine subscriptions and such," says Azarias, but the big variables, like age and gender, tend to matter more. Not to mention, as sexy as this consumer data stuff is, it is just one piece of the political data puzzle, and publicly available things like voting history and political contributions are the most essential.

Nonetheless, the data can still shed light on how attached someone might be to their candidate or political party and if they're willing to change. In the same way that Target was on the hunt for customers who might be on the brink of changing their purchasing habits, campaigns can go on the hunt for voters who might be on the brink of changing their *voting* habits. It's not enough to know how likely someone is to vote or which way they lean politically; perhaps even more valuable is the ability to know who might be open to changing their mind, regardless of where they fall on the political spectrum.

Kamzol gave as an example the idea of finding what he calls "conflicted voters." "Let's say we know someone grew up in Michigan, drives a hybrid car, listens to Willie Nelson, and registered Republican," Kamzol says. In that case, the "hybrid car" flag might indicate someone leans Democratic, but being registered Republican is a pretty sure sign that the person is a Republican. Hence: "conflicted voter." Republicans used this kind of information to great effect in the 2014 election to pinpoint voters who didn't vote very often but were probably Republican or at least would be open to voting for Republicans with the right pitch.

The hunt for conflicted voters is just one of a huge variety of ways that campaigns use data to target and mobilize voters. To illustrate how an entity like the RNC uses all of the data that is out there, Reda walks me through the life of political data for a hypothetical voter named Chris.

"Let's say Chris just moved to Research Triangle Park," he says, referring to an area in North Carolina with a number of major research institutions and universities. "Our first interaction with him, before he even registers to vote there, is to see if we have history from where he used to live. We work with the 'change-of-address' data to see who is moving."

If Reda's team discovers that Chris used to be registered as a Republican in his old state, they can let the North Carolina Republican Party know that perhaps they should reach out to him and remind him to register to vote at his new address. Once Chris registers, then he will be added to the North Carolina "voter file" and his voter registration info will be updated in the RNC's database as well.

Political geography is one absolutely essential element, particularly for an entity like the RNC, which, unlike a single national presidential campaign, needs to be able to serve campaigns of all sorts. Those campaigns' voters might reside in a whole host of different boundaries. Think about the last time you went to vote. You didn't just vote for offices like president or governor: you probably also voted for state legislators and county commissioners and town councils and such. You live inside a particular political precinct, a state legislative district, maybe a certain town boundary or a congressional district that slices through your county. While your friend who lives on the other side of town may have had the same options for president or governor, perhaps they have a different state representative and are in a different school district. An organization like the RNC needs to know which voters can vote in which races, up and down the ballot. The task of figuring out which voters fall into which set of boundaries at *every* level is one of the most critical tasks, and that's the next thing the RNC will do with our hypothetical voter, Chris, once he re-registers in North Carolina: they'll figure out what districts and such he lives in.

It is at this point that the RNC, if it hasn't already, will also try to match Chris up with all of the consumer data it has and begin trying to make assumptions about his political preferences. Remember how campaigns build models that try to predict things like someone's political party or issue priorities? How they try to figure out the recipe for which ingredients make someone likely to be, say, a conservative Republican or someone who is really interested in gun control? It is also important to remember that those "ingredients" aren't frozen in time and that your predictive model might change. (Recall the example with Romney and the dog: prior to the Seamus story coming out, there may have been no relationship between owning a dog and supporting Mitt Romney. As events change, so might your model.)

Groups like the RNC will constantly refresh those models, doing large-scale surveys and experiments to update what they know. Maybe the RNC never actually surveys our hypothetical voter, but they do survey a bunch of other people in Research Triangle Park because they want to talk about how Republicans make it easier for people to launch successful start-ups. Let's say they find that people with similar characteristics to Chris tend to be interested in hearing more about regulations on small businesses and seem very enthusiastic about voting.

This is where Reda says things get especially fun: handing the insights over to the campaigns on the ground.

"The real power comes when other people can access this," says Reda. "The thing that will change most as we move forward is shifting this out there to the campaigns themselves. We want to make data easier to work with so other applications can be built upon it." For instance, people can build a "walk app," an app that can run on a volunteer's mobile device like a phone or tablet and tell them the voters they should go talk to and what they should say to each particular voter when they come to the door.

If a campaign is going to send volunteers out door-to-door in Chris's neighborhood, they can know that he's a Republican and they can know that he's probably interested in hearing what Republicans want to do to help people starting up small companies, and a walk app can tell them this. The idea of sending voters out with a detailed list of targets isn't new. The difference is that nowadays any campaign that is reasonably up-to-date shouldn't be sending people out with clipboards and paper surveys. They should be plugged directly into one of these data sources like the RNC's and should be able to both access and feed data about our hypothetical voter, Chris, right back into the system.

But according to Reda, "This is just scratching the surface." And of course we aren't done with Chris after he gets that visit from the volunteers. Maybe during that interaction he mentioned that he's definitely planning on voting early. Great! That information can go right into the data file. The volunteers can ask Chris for his e-mail address so they can contact him with information on early voting.

Now that the campaign has Chris's e-mail address, they can do even more. "The tie right now between on- and off-line lives is via an e-mail address," Reda explains, noting that once they can match you up with things like your Twitter account, they can analyze anything you might put out there, publicly, online. "What you say about Obamacare on Twitter can then go back and inform the voter file."

Finally, the data can tell you when you can *stop* reminding Chris to go vote. If the RNC's data suggests that Chris is definitely going to vote and vote Republican, or already has voted, they can shift resources away from contacting him and instead focus on people who are definitely Republican but are less likely to show up at the polls. In 2014, the RNC political director, Chris McNulty, told the *Washing-*

ton Examiner that some volunteers were confused that their walk app wasn't telling them to knock on certain doors of known Republican voters; it was intentional and all part of the GOP's effort to focus their volunteers on turning out the more than one million unlikely voters (called "low-propensity voters" in the campaign world) who, based on the statistical models, were expected to be Republicans.[3]

It is through this multistep process that a campaign can gain a multidimensional portrait of you, make all kinds of reasonably informed assumptions about your political attitudes, and try to push all the right buttons to ensure that on Election Day you'll cast a vote for the GOP. As creepy as this all may sound to you as a voter, for Reda, building tools that better engage and motivate people to participate in the electoral process is a noble thing.

"I'm a first-generation immigrant, born in Ethiopia," Reda informs me. "Politics is not my passion. But in Ethiopia people just don't get involved." After years in the start-up and academic worlds pursuing a career in computer science, he came to the RNC job so that he could use his skills to get more people engaged and involved in their democracy. "Whatever shade of ideology you have, at the end of the day, this country has democracy right. Candidates here win because they have better ideas, not because they have better tech," he says.

"What we are doing is enabling democracy."

☆

It's the Sunday before Election Day 2014 and, unsurprisingly, most of the ads on television are political. I'm in Massachusetts for a fellowship at Harvard University, which puts me in the Boston media market, given that I can walk a few blocks from my apartment and see the Boston skyline across the Charles River. There's a lot going on in state politics this year, and a lot of the ads are for Massachusetts politicians or ballot campaigns: ads for and against Richard Tisei, an openly gay candidate running as a Republican for a Massachusetts seat in the

House of Representatives; ads by Martha Coakley and Charlie Baker, the candidates for governor of Massachusetts; ads encouraging voters to oppose a ballot initiative about bottle recycling. If I was registered to vote here, I'd probably be a good target for these campaigns, because I'm a frequent voter and possibly a "cross-pressured" one.

But these Massachusetts ads aren't all I'm seeing on the air. I also keep seeing ads about Jeanne Shaheen and Scott Brown, the two candidates who are facing off in the race for New Hampshire's Senate seat. Every so often I see an ad about someone running for Congress . . . in New Hampshire. I've seen ads for and against Marilinda Garcia, a young Republican woman running for Congress . . . in New Hampshire.

People who live here in Boston cannot vote for New Hampshire candidates like Jeanne Shaheen or Scott Brown or Marilinda Garcia. But money—*lots* of money—is being spent serving up TV ads to people like me who can't vote in those races. Likewise, every time one of these Charlie Baker TV ads runs, there are people who live in New Hampshire who are seeing it even though they can't participate in Massachusetts state elections.

This is *terribly* inefficient.

It's not that the borders of the Boston media market *themselves* are wrong or a bad idea. If I hopped in a car and drove from Cambridge up to Nashua, I'd be there in less than an hour. There are tons of Patriots and Red Sox fans in New Hampshire, and advertisers for fast-food chains or retailers or consumer brands don't really care what state or county you live in. It's perfectly sensible that people who live in Manchester would get the Boston local news channels and see Boston ads.

No, the problem is that media market boundaries don't care about political geography whatsoever. They have nothing to do with what your oddly shaped congressional district looks like on a map, and they don't even match up with state borders in many cases. The vast majority of people in New Hampshire live in the Boston media market, but the vast majority of people in the Boston media market do not live in New Hampshire.

This leads to a lot of wasted money. When a New Hampshire campaign pays money to air their ad during the Patriots-Broncos game on the local CBS station, a Boston-based station, they aren't just paying to show that ad to New Hampshire voters, they're paying to show that ad to *every single person in the Boston area* who tunes in to watch the Tom Brady–Peyton Manning showdown, even if most of those viewers are not even eligible to vote in that race.

And that's *eligible* to vote, to say nothing of being an actual *target*. "Much of this 'data revolution' in politics has only touched 'addressable communication,' like mail, phones, e-mail," said Alex Lundry. "Addressable" means just what it sounds like: some kind of communication that can be addressed directly to you as a person. Remember, now that campaigns know huge amounts of information about every voter, they can specifically pinpoint the *exact* voters they want to persuade to turn out. Campaigns know which doors to knock on and which doors to skip. The broadcast airwaves do not make such distinctions. "With TV and radio," notes Lundry, "it is broadcast, it goes out to everyone watching or listening."[4]

The campaign may know that they should send me something in the mail about how great their candidate is, but they also know they can save postage and skip sending anything to my next-door neighbor because, well, she doesn't have many characteristics that suggest she'll show up at the polls this year anyhow or be open to voting Republican. But when it comes to that ad airing during the Patriots game, even though I might be a target voter and my neighbor has never voted in her life, we both count in the TV ratings, we're both being shown the ad, and we're both costing the campaign money.

That may not be the case for long.

Millions of people watching TV these days *do* have an address of sorts: the set-top box that brings TV into their home.[5] And nowadays, those cable boxes make it possible for you to personally, specifically be targeted with ads.

"Call it direct mail for TV: First used by the Obama campaign in 2012, these 'addressable' ads allow campaigns to target a list of voters and match them with Dish and DirecTV's 20 million subscribers," wrote *USA Today* of a newly announced plan by Dish/DirecTV to let campaigns buy targeted individually focused ads.[6] DirecTV's senior vice president of ad sales noted: "Campaigns can focus their message to a precise set of potential voters and eliminate the spending waste."[7]

Let's go back to our hypothetical voter, Chris. We know he lives in the Research Triangle area of North Carolina, and so he lives in the Raleigh-Durham media market. We know he's a registered Republican, and we know he's someone who our campaign would like to turn out to vote. We want to make sure he gets our message about small businesses. Sure, we can send him mail and knock on his door, but the reality is that most of a campaign's money is spent on TV.

So what can we do?

We can go to our voter file and find all of the voters who we have reason to believe are Republicans interested in small business, like Chris. We've got our TV ad about what we want to do to make it easier for people to be entrepreneurs. We can create a list of the people we'd like to show that ad to, and ship that list to the TV provider. From there, the voters we want to reach are the voters who will see our ad. Instead of blanketing the airwaves with an ad and paying to show it to tons of people who aren't our target, we show up right in Chris's living room with a message tailored just for voters like him. For now, this addressable TV is just a small piece of the puzzle in a political campaign, but it is quite likely to grow in importance in the coming years, and smart campaigns would be foolish not to explore the way they can send TV ads to exactly the voters they want.

On top of addressable TV, however, campaigns have tools *now* at their disposal to find target voters and show them ads on TV more effectively using big data. Consider this: your set-top-box data is a two-way street. You aren't just consuming TV shows and ads; you're also sending back information about what you watch. When you settle in on the couch with a pint of Ben & Jerry's and turn on an episode of *Say Yes to the Dress* on a Friday night, your cable box knows.

And that data is for sale.

Typically the way we know "what people watch" is through Nielsen's TV ratings that look at broad demographic groups. If you want to reach, say, men aged 25 to 54, putting an ad on during that Patriots football game isn't a terrible idea. But "men aged 25 to 54" isn't very specific, is it? Not all "men aged 25 to 54" are the same, and not all men aged 25 to 54 are your target voters. Maybe there are certain shows that your target voters watch in greater numbers than the Pats game? What if you knew that you could reach many of those target voters by putting an ad on during, say, *Jimmy Kimmel Live* the next night, and could do it for much, much less money?

"Our political targets are not wholesale chunks, like 'women 35-plus' anymore. They're much more precise and nuanced, so there's this disconnect between the info we have about our targets and the information we have to buy TV and radio," says Lundry. It used to be that campaigns would target voters in these larger chunks. You still hear political pundits talk about campaigns this way: "The campaign needs to do better with young women"; "This candidate is really trying to reach senior citizens." But campaigns nowadays don't have to think solely about these large chunks of voters; they can know who their "swing voters" are individually rather than as a big, monolithic block. The traditional ratings can tell you how many women over the age of 35 watch a show, but they can't tell you how many "swing voters" watch a show.

This, too, is starting to change. In 2012, the Oregon-based firm Rentrak worked with the Obama campaign's media team to help guide their decisions about where to place their TV ads by going beyond the usual age and gender demographics. The Obama people could hand over a list, saying, "These are the people we think are swing voters," and then Rentrak could match that list up with the actual viewing behavior of those voters. Instead of the usual TV ratings, the Obama campaign could get back information about what shows their target voters tended to watch.

"Using Rentrak's quarter-hour ratings, the OFA team began airing television ads in local markets in crucial swing states. OFA tended to buy 60 networks deep and broader schedules than normal across stations. The Romney campaign stuck to 18 networks deep and tighter schedules within stations," says Rentrak of the role they played in Obama's victory.[8] While the Romney campaign mostly focused on airing ads on broadcast channels such as ABC and CBS, the Obama campaign was able to find pockets of target voters who tended to watch more obscure channels at unusual times of day, and got those ads in front of the target for much less money.

Republicans are catching up. "This comes out of a frustration with seeing how TV was done on the presidential level in 2012," Lundry says. "TV continues to be the biggest line item in a campaign's budget, and it's the least data-driven, the least targeted. We're increasing the efficiency of 70 to 80 percent of the budget by 15 to 25 percent." In a presidential campaign, that can mean millions and millions of dollars.

For decades TV advertising has been the main way that political candidates have entered the living rooms of Americans, long before the world of "big data." But in the future, when you hear those familiar words, "I'm So-and-so, and I approved this message," you can feel comforted—or unsettled—to know that the candidate may as well be saying: . . . *and I approved this message just for you* . . .

☆

"I came in expecting the challenges to be technical. This is not rocket science. This is straightforward stuff," Azarias Reda says during our chat at RNC Headquarters.

"I found instead the challenge is really that we are changing culture."

This is something I have heard over and over again. Reda's colleague Jesse Kamzol also notes that persuading campaigns to see value in making data-driven decisions and relying on data to improve their campaign efforts is key. Too often, the story of the Democrats' data advantage over Republicans seems to boil down to the idea that Democrats have more data or bigger computers or fancier technology. That misses what's really going on. The problem isn't that the sides have different tools. The problem is that one side is more focused on *using* those tools well and letting data drive decision making. Republicans have had a habit of running campaigns on a mix of gut decisions and assumptions about "what worked last time," while Democrats in recent years have gotten better at letting data guide decisions about which voters to target and how best to target them.

"It's worth emphasizing that [the Romney campaign] had 95 to 98 percent of the same data and tools as the Obama campaign had access to," Alex Lundry notes when I pose this question to him. Where, then, were they behind? "Having and trusting a culture of data-driven decision making. Having a system set up that allowed analytics to drive a lot of the key decisions. It's not to say the people on the campaign didn't want to be data-driven or that they specifically ignored data; it's just that it's a very tough thing to do to ask people to go against decades of conventional wisdom and what many felt in their gut was right to do."

Reda has found the same thing. "You have a campaign system where the outcome is binary, where it is difficult to tell what worked or what didn't, so the system isn't 'free market' at all. It's based on history or relationships, so new technology has a high bar of entry, and there are interests that want to keep the old system," Reda maintains. "Campaigns don't always want to take advantage of what's available to them."

What *is* available today is extraordinary. It used to be that campaigns had a limited picture of who you are. They knew the basics: your name, your voting history, and your zip code. Nowadays, almost everything we do—swiping our credit card, changing the channel, posting a tweet—is knowable, and usable, by campaigns eager to court votes.

How campaigns identify and interact with voters these days can be enhanced and made more efficient through the smart analysis of data. Used properly, data can tell a campaign which voters are likely to be supporters and which voters can be persuaded to join your side. It can tell a campaign who is likely to vote and who might need a stronger nudge. It can tell a campaign who should be contacted with a message about immigration reform and who should be contacted with a message about education reform. It can help a campaign get better bang for its buck.

But all the data in the world is useless if there aren't talented consultants and staff on campaigns who know how to use it wisely. Where Republicans have lagged behind the left is in having the pool of people who can actually do data analysis well. The RNC or other groups can build amazing databases and can run experiments to figure out what buttons to push to move voters, but if campaigns themselves aren't making use of the tools or don't have people on their teams who understand data, who know how to use data, who are willing to *trust* what we can learn from data, then Republicans will just have a very nice, very large database and won't do any better in elections.

To be sure, sophisticated data systems won't *win* anyone an election outright. An uninspiring candidate can't be saved just because his campaign can pinpoint likely voters who eat sushi or who have a knitting habit. A campaign might efficiently target TV ads to swing voters, but if the ads are lousy and poorly done, nobody will be persuaded. In a close race of evenly matched opponents, better data and targeting can help give one side an edge over the other, but it isn't a substitute for substance.

The real benefit of data is that it can allow campaigns to be much smarter about nearly everything they do. It can help campaigns be more intelligent about who they talk to and to be more effective with what they say. It can give a campaign an awareness of what the battlefield looks like at any given moment so that they aren't caught off guard by shifts in public opinion or left unprepared on Election Day.

Republicans have made real strides in catching up to the Democrats in terms of data and analytics; after all, it was Democrats much more than Republicans who were taken by surprise on Election Day in 2014 by the massive margins of victory for GOP candidates across the country. It was Republicans more than Democrats who were able to target their voters and get them to go to the polls in that midterm. But that's just one election. The battlefield is constantly changing. Technology is constantly evolving. Running last election's playbook is a surefire recipe for failure.

Reaching and appealing to voters today and in the future requires smart, data-driven campaigning that fully takes advantage of the vast amount of information that is out there and constantly adapts to a changing political landscape. Campaigns that win in the future won't just make decisions based on the gut instinct of one or two election gurus or clump voters into over-broad groups based on a few factors like gender or age. People are multidimensional: they have complex tastes and preferences and habits that are all connected to the same sorts of values that drive their political decision making. The more we learn about that complexity and the more we can analyze it, the better we can get at knowing what the future of elections will look like.

CONCLUSION

Win the Future by Fighting the Past

"I feel like a monk."

I looked down at my phone and saw the text come in from Dad, featuring a picture of two boxes full of beer bottles sitting in a bathtub. I had given him a home brewing kit for Christmas, much to my mother's consternation, and finally, the end product—a brown ale I had lovingly named "Johnnybräu"—was nigh.

For all that globalization and mass production was once viewed as a threat to crafting and craftsmanship, the do-it-yourself, local, personal economy is alive and well. The online homemade goods site Etsy connects over a million crafty individuals with willing buyers, making at-home handiwork a profitable venture or hobby with ease.[1] Farmers' markets have grown more prevalent and popular as shoppers want to support people in their own communities and eat fresher food. Mass-produced and corporate is the wave of the past; small-batch and personal is the taste of the moment.

Nowhere has the rise of the local, unique, independently made craft products movement hit it bigger than in beer. While beer sales overall slightly declined in 2013, sales of *craft beer* were up over 17 percent in that same year.[2] This isn't just some urban hipster phenomenon, either. Even in my suburban neighborhood back home in Orlando, there's now a great little bar named House of Beer nestled into a strip mall and offering hundreds of different types of craft and international beer. People want choices, they want something unique, and they want something that tastes good.

While it is unlikely that my dad will turn Johnnybräu into a commercial enterprise, more and more craft breweries are popping up and offering an incredible array of choices for beer drinkers. Young consumers in particular have gravitated away from big brands and toward craft beers, and companies like Anheuser-Busch are trying hard to turn around the decline in sales of old standbys like Budweiser because of the public's growing preference for the taste and uniqueness of the beers.[3]

And yet, in my home state of Florida in 2014, legislators passed a bill that would make it harder for craft breweries to sell their wares. "After Prohibition, you had a three-tiered model develop where there's a manufacturer, a distributor, and a vendor. There are slight variations, like Pennsylvania where liquor stores are run by the state. But in Florida it is mandatory that alcohol must go to a distributor before it can go to a vendor and be sold to customers," says Josh Aubuchon, the advocate and lobbyist who fought on behalf of the craft brewers during the legislative battle. Each state chooses to regulate beer sales differently, and in Florida a bill was proposed—backed by the major brewers and beer distributors—that would prevent craft brewers from selling their own beer in taprooms without first selling it to a distributor and then buying it back.[4] Aubuchon described the bill to me this way: "These brewers would have had to cut a check to the distributor even if the distributor didn't take the case out of the brewer's fridge."

The debate pitted independent brewers against the established big names in a legislative battle that in the end wasn't about party or ideology—it was about protecting established businesses from competition and threats to their business model. "Since about 2006 or 2007, these craft breweries have started to grow," Aubuchon says. "But then there's the old guard distributors, who I love to refer to as a government mandated regional monopoly." He notes the enormous power that distributors wield in politics because of their money and long-term ties to communities, but also points out that craft brewers and their customers were a force to be reckoned with. "We'd blast something out on social media, and our breweries would all send the message to their fans and followers. Senator Jack Latvala, our champion on this, he's been around politics for a long time and he said he'd never seen anything like the coverage, interest, and comments on the issue."

Florida's legislature is dominated by Republicans in both chambers; the debate wasn't particularly partisan. Aubuchon noted that it was many of what he called "old-guard" Republicans who were in support of the distributors, while younger Republican legislators took the other view. "The old-guard Republicans were supporting it but the younger legislators see this and say, 'This isn't Republican principles; we're not doing this.'"

Beer isn't the only thing in the U.S. that you have to buy through a middleman. States typically require that sales of cars be done through dealers, which winds up keeping companies like Tesla from being able to sell directly to consumers.[5] Want to avoid relying on the power company and get your energy *directly from the sun*? Nope—in many states, legislative battles rage about whether or not people should have to pay extra fees to the existing utilities if they choose to pay to install solar panels on their own homes.

These regulations are always sold on the grounds of fairness or as a way of protecting consumers, of course. Dealers provide good local service, so of course we need regulations that require they be the only place you can buy a car. It's only fair that people who put solar panels on their roof pay their fair share to keep the utilities going. We need to keep ride-sharing companies shut down because they are unfair to cab companies and are risky. The craft beer industry should have to sell their products through a middleman because that's what is best for consumers.

In all of these cases, producers and consumers are forced to pay a little bit more or jump through an extra set of hoops because government regulations say so, and keeping these regulations in place is often a bipartisan affair. Too often these days, regulations are being proposed because innovation that threatens the incumbents must be slowed down or stopped. If Republicans want to win over the young voters of today and tomorrow, they can't afford to be the ones who are pressing the brake pedal.

This isn't just about beer, of course. That millennials prefer craft beer over big brands may seem like a minor point but does shed light on the underlying values and preferences that ultimately drive more than just their drinking habits. Young people have a desire to be unique, to try something new and adventurous, to express their individuality. They pride themselves on independent thinking and they care about supporting the little guy. Some express this through the choice of beer they drink and buy. Caring about supporting local small businesses might lead me to pick an IPA brewed down the road, or it might cause me to vote for a candidate who has made local small-business tax cuts a priority. The reason why campaigns today can draw conclusions about voters based, in part, on their consumer habits is that all of these choices are coming from the same value set. My beer doesn't drive my vote or vice versa, but both choices are a reflection, in some small way, of the same set of values and preferences that make me a unique individual.

And at the same time, my ability to express my preferences and live the way I want is threatened by government regulation or big entities that protect an old model of doing business. Whether it's getting a growler of craft beer or a ride across town or an affordable college education, there are numerous ways that the status quo makes it hard for me as a young person to live how I want. Whether it is how we care for the poor, how we deal with drug crime, how we educate our children, how we get our health insurance, or how we balance work and family, we have a set of policies in place today that are not quite aligned with how young people think we can best create opportunity and prosperity in the future.

Throughout this book, I've tried to highlight areas in politics and policy that are ready for change, where the old ways of doing things just don't work for young people. This applies to the old methods of campaigning, which increasingly fail to reach young people and neglect the power of data and analytics. But this also applies to our message and our policies. We have a public sector, an education system, a welfare system, and a regulatory framework that is suited to a different era, and neither party has taken up the cause of modernity and reform.

There are massive political challenges awaiting Republicans in the future. As a party, we have relied on older voters, white voters, religious voters, married voters, voters in rural or less-dense suburbs. All of these groups are shrinking. This is happening gradually, of course, but trends that have been in motion for years are slowly going to make it harder and harder for Republicans to continue to have the same coalition. They will need to win a new group of voters: today's young voters.

"Prediction" is a dangerous word in my line of work. Many people who have tried to "predict" elections in recent years have wound up publicly embarrassed, as polls have failed to accurately portray how voters might vote. People who "predicted" Republican dominance in the mid–2000s look pretty foolish today. People who "predicted" Republicans would never win an election again after Obama reshaped the electorate looked pretty foolish when Republicans took back Congress. A year is a lifetime in politics, and today's confidently made pronouncement about the future is tomorrow's punch line.

When Patrick Ruffini and I launched Echelon Insights in 2014, we hoped to bring the incredible power of data, analytics, and research to bear on campaigns of all types. However, we tried hard in our pitch to strike the appropriate balance between telling the world how exciting the brave new world of political data could be and being humble about precisely what data can tell us. Data does not mean we know the future; it just means we can quantify our uncertainty. It makes us smarter, in part, because it lets us know how much we *don't* know. We can assign a probability to how we think someone might vote, but even if we give someone a 95 percent chance of acting one way, it means we think there's still a 5 percent chance they won't. Nothing is certain, and especially not in politics.

This book makes a lot of predictions. I look at polls and trends and try to project what issues and values will be instrumental in selecting our nation's political leaders over the coming decades. I do so knowing that, a few years from now, the political environment will probably be very different. We are on the edge of a presidential election that may redefine what it means to be Republican or Democrat. We live in a world that is unstable and often scary, where every day could mean an escalation of tensions or a terrorist attack that profoundly alters the landscape. (I intentionally avoid, for instance, commenting on international relations and issues of national security in this book precisely for that reason.)

I've presented data that suggests Republicans are at risk of losing my generation, and have tried to predict what the political future could look like. Even knowing that it is risky to say you know what the future holds, I still think that the data tells a story of huge pending risk and enormous potential rewards for Republicans. Stealing a metaphor from Wayne Gretzky, my goal in this book is to show people "where the puck is going" in hopes that Republicans will skate there. I try, wherever possible, to provide data that backs up why I think the puck is heading in a particular direction.

Anyone can say that they think the way forward for the Republican Party is to "be more like me" or "do more things I agree with." I have tried to be very aware of my own biases and preferences, and even where I may disagree with my own generation, I try to present a clear picture of where I think smart political folks will look if they want to win in the future. I think that the opportunities for Republicans to reach my generation are many, and hope I've made the case for Republicans to focus on reforming out-of-date, broken institutions and systems while becoming more inclusive and connected.

I remain optimistic about the prospects for center-right politics in the U.S. and abroad. As a Republican, despite the enormous amount of evidence suggesting that the road ahead of the GOP is a rough one, I see great opportunity. I've encountered scores of bright rising stars who are poised to change the way their parties connect with young people. Over and over, I hear from the rightward-leaning young people I meet that while they don't feel invested in the Republican Party and politics of *today*, they're hopeful that someday soon they will feel truly represented by the leaders of their party—that eventually the political leaders of today will begin to propose policies that really understand the reality of young lives.

The good news for Republicans is that this moment offers a wide array of challenges that can be best solved by applying conservative principles to modern problems. There are countless arenas—education, welfare, transportation, and more—where the status quo is being defended by the left and where it is Republicans who are best positioned to disrupt the old ways of doing things that have failed so many young people.

The other piece of good news for Republicans is that the gap in how positively young voters view the Republican and Democratic Parties has narrowed. No longer are young people enamored of Obama or of Democrats. The grand promises of "Hope and Change" from 2008 have failed to materialize, and although the president has been given some credit for trying, it hasn't been enough. Headlines like "Obama Losing the Confidence of Key Parts of the Coalition That Elected Him," are becoming less and less surprising.[6] Young voters are now beginning to tune out *both* parties. It does not warm my heart that the way Republicans will get a second shot at my generation is because *both* parties are failing to reach them, but nonetheless, here we are. The door for the GOP has reopened. Now we must choose to walk through it.

Change won't happen overnight, and it won't happen with a cute slogan, a change of a policy position, or a single charismatic candidate. It must, however, happen quickly. Each election that passes where Republicans stick to the usual playbook is another two to four years where attitudes will be cemented. Once the image of what it means to be Republican is locked in, it is terribly hard to change, and the image young people have of Republicans today is not one we want to stick.

Ever since I've begun researching the values and attitudes of millennials, I've focused on how the Republican Party can adapt in order to win over this new generation and remain competitive. I'm often asked if the Republican Party needs to change its policies and its principles in order to do so, or if it can get by with a fresh tone and a new message. There are certainly areas, like same-sex marriage, where the established Republican platform position is out of sync with where young voters are at and where the country is heading, and where a change in approach will have to happen in order for the Republican Party to compete for millennial voters in the future. And there are tactical things about how we communicate with voters that certainly require an update and a willingness to embrace new technology. However, there are huge areas of overlap between where Republicans and young voters stand. The Republican Party does not need to become the Democratic Party to win young voters, nor should it.

Message changes alone will not be enough. Product metaphors are frequently invoked when people talk about the plight of the GOP and the need to win young voters, and I've often referred to the party "brand" throughout the course of the book. Some will say that Republicans need to mostly change the packaging and marketing of their product if they want to reach young people. I challenge that notion, because I am not confident Republicans have tried to think through the product they have to offer in the first place.

Young voters are not strongly ideological. They don't view government as inherently great or inherently evil. They're tuning out *both* parties. They just want to see problems solved. They want someone to propose some kind of governing agenda that makes sense given the realities of modern living. They want policy makers to make reforms that indicate they have an idea of what it is like to be young in America today. They want to know someone cares about creating opportunity. They want to know someone is thinking about where America is heading and how we can make that future look a little brighter.

This should be the core of the Republican agenda and message—the "product"—in the coming years.

I'm a firm believer that we can get the right medium to reach young people and that we can craft a message that tries to speak to young people's values. However, if we don't have the substance and the ideas to back it up, it will be for naught. Sometimes, people running for office love to get the cute, snappy phrase or single message that they think will win them a debate and earn them the hearts and minds of voters. I believe that our leaders will need to work a little harder than that in order to win over young voters.

This book is not a call for policy makers to chase what is trendy. It is a wake-up call that the world has changed and our politics have failed to keep up. At the core, the values that young people espouse and that guide their thinking about politics are far from passing fads: opportunity, individuality, compassion, hard work, community, and responsibility are timeless.

From these years of study about what young people want, I've assembled a collection of ideas that policy makers can use to find common ground with young people—ideas that align with rather than run contrary to established conservative principles. I've gone through the major polling "crosstabs" that strategists use to segment voters—what your family looks like, what your race or heritage is, how you were educated, how you make a living, where you live, and what your faith looks like—and have tried to find areas of opportunity for Republicans in each. The media coverage of Republican struggles with young voters often focuses heavily on the obvious points of generational disagreement, but I believe there is a far wider array of areas where young voters and conservative ideas overlap. These aren't just rooted in ephemeral tastes and the attitudes of the day; these are linked to core parts of peoples' identity, and reflect the values that I believe are central to my generation and how we will look at politics throughout our lifetimes. My hope is that the reforms and messages provide a framework for smart Republicans who want to get set on a course to win, not just in 2016, but in 2046 and 2076.

By running campaigns that make it a priority to reach voters with whom Republicans have struggled in the past, we have an opportunity to expand the reach of our ideas and earn more chances to put them into action. This means going outside of the usual comfort zone, with new audiences and new channels that Republicans have not reached as effectively in recent years. It means building smart, data-driven campaigns that are ahead of the curve.

It also means coming in with a new message, one that is optimistic, reform oriented, inclusive, and forward-looking. We have the ability to take our existing message about the size of government, fiscal responsibility, the plight of overregulation, and the scourge of ineffective bureaucracy, and focus on how our principles lead to opportunity and prosperity for people, particularly young people. We have the ability to take what we know about individuals and to identify which of our ideas is the most relevant to improving their lives, and we also have the technology to get that message to people in ever-changing ways.

Perhaps most important, more than finding the right message and the right channel, to really get Republicans on the right track and win over the next generation means actually putting our principles to work.

Republicans didn't get the brand of being the "old" party by accident. We've bumbled our way through recent elections, failing to describe a coherent agenda that speaks to the values of young people, and failing to reach them on their terms, where they turn to listen to their leaders. We've too often decided that young voters don't matter because they don't vote or they're going to wind up Republican one day anyhow. What we've missed is that, not only are we losing them for the long haul, but we're also ignoring how young Americans influence the *entire* electorate and political discussion.

Conservatism often means a respect for tradition, a reverence for the way things have been in the past, a belief that some but not all change is good, a healthy skepticism of how much we can engineer a bright future. I'm not suggesting that, in order to win young voters, conservatives should forget our heritage and blindly forge ahead, destroying the past in our wake. But too often we can get caught in the trap of looking back longingly at the way things were. When young voters complain that the Republican Party wants things to go back to being like they were in the 1950s, I want to believe that they're wrong, but there's undoubtedly a fair bit of nostalgia that some older conservatives feel for a prior era.

In trying to hold on to the past too tightly, we can miss the ways that our worldview is actually new and fresh and ideally suited to where the country is going. Republicans should not fear the changes I've described in this book; they should embrace them.

When I look at "where the puck is heading" in American politics and culture, I'm excited about where we're going. I'm nothing if not optimistic. I've combed through volumes of data and have come away hopeful. I see the way that we're eager as a generation to try new things, not because we think something new is always inherently going to be better, but because it has the potential to be. I see the amazing things that technology allows us to achieve today, the countless ways we can connect with one another and genuinely improve the quality of life of millions of people. I see the way that we care deeply for our families and those in their communities and feel a sense of responsibility for them. I see the way that we set high expectations and are then hungry for the opportunity to meet them.

America does not look the way it used to. Generational shifts are gradually reshaping our nation in powerful and profound ways. The technological, demographic, and cultural changes we are witnessing today did not begin yesterday and will not evaporate tomorrow.

And it is young Americans who are leading the way.

ACKNOWLEDGMENTS

Writing a book is no easy task, and writing your first book is an even bigger challenge. Meeting that big challenge required the love, wisdom, and encouragement of an enormous group of people. From friends and family to the folks at the La Colombe coffee shop down the street from my home who kept me caffeinated and focused, it took a great support system to make this book happen.

I first need to thank Zach Schisgal, who told me he thought the world might actually be interested in reading what I had to say. He encouraged me to take this leap, and I'm grateful for his friendship and patience as I put together the concept for this book. It has also been an honor to work with Adam Bellow of Broadside Books, who helped shepherd this book idea from outline to reality. As a novice author, Zach, Adam, and his team at HarperCollins have all given me wonderful guidance, and I am grateful that they are on my team.

To the friends and colleagues who helped with the research for this book, reviewed chapters, or offered advice on the writing process, I am lucky to have you in my orbit: Margaret Hoover, Mindy Finn, Dave Feinberg, Matt Moon, Sarah Isgur Flores, Karin Agness, Mike Shields,

Robert Draper, Doug Heye, Alex Smith, Alex Schriver, John O'Hara, Alex Lundry, Rob Kubasko, J. P. Freire, Matt Baker, Michelle Rempel, Danny Banks, Blake Patterson, Jessica Reese, Gwen Thomas, Matthew Browne, Johnny Tang, Victor Kamenker, Victor Mezacapa, Tyler Sinclair, Stephanie Slade, Sasha Issenberg, Josh Barro, Noah Kristula-Green, Sean Trende, Ryan Enos, Elise Stefanik, and Eva Guidarini all deserve great thanks. In particular, I have to single out Reihan Salam, who not only provided me with advice and encouragement about the project, but also is indirectly responsible for setting all of this—and, frankly, most of the positive things in my career—in motion.

To everyone at the Institute of Politics at Harvard University, you were my family while I was in the thick of the writing process, and I am thankful that I got to test out many of my ideas on all of you. More important, I will never forget your friendship and kindness.

I am forever indebted to Patrick Ruffini, who I have undoubtedly tormented during this process and who has borne that burden admirably. He decided to launch a company with me, Echelon Insights, right at the moment that I was focused on both this book project and the Harvard fellowship. He led Echelon to an incredible first few months during my absence. His patience and support have been extraordinary.

Writing this book has given me a deep appreciation for the teachers and mentors I have had in my life. David Winston and Myra Miller brought me into their company when I was just a kid and gave me an incredible eight-year education in politics, polling, and center-right policy. I feel lucky to have learned from the best. Teachers I have had, including Jason Wysong, David Bilka, Dan Smith, and Dorothea Wolfson, have always supported me, even if some of them disagreed with my political views. I hope that in writing this book I have made them proud.

To my family, there is no way to properly express how much you have meant to me in this process. My parents, John and Linda, are responsible for every bit of success in my life and have encouraged me even when I have doubted myself. To thank them properly would take a whole other book. My parents-in-law, Mike and Diane, I can never thank you enough for your love and incredible faith in me. I am honored to be able to call them "Mom and Dad."

Finally, and most important, I need to thank my husband, Chris. When we first began dating, his Facebook profile actually listed *Elements of Style* as one of his favorite books. After years of knowing that I'd married an English major who genuinely enjoyed editing, I finally abused my privileges. He gave me his thoughts whenever I asked, and always pushed me in the right direction. His most critical contribution, however, was his love and support. He gave me time and space to write but also gave me comfort and confidence when I needed it most. I couldn't have asked for a better husband.

NOTES

Introduction: A Front-Facing Picture of a Generation

1. Alexandra Sifferlin, "Why Selfies Matter," *Time*, September 6, 2013, http://healthland.time.com/2013/09/06/why-selfies-matter/ (accessed February 28, 2015).

2. Sarah Graham, "Take a Lot of Selfies? Then You May Be MENTALLY ILL: Two Thirds of Patients with Body Image Disorders Obsessively Take Photos of Themselves," *Daily Mail*, April 10, 2014, http://www.dailymail.co.uk/sciencetech/article–2601606/Take-lot-selfies-Then-MENTALLY-ILL-Two-thirds-patients-body-image-disorders-obsessively-photos-themselves.html (accessed February 28, 2014).

3. Dr. Gwendolyn Seidman, "Are Selfies a Sign of Narcissism and Psychopathy?," *Psychology Today*, January 8, 2015, https://www.psychologytoday.com/blog/close-encounters/201501/are-selfies-sign-narcissism-and-psychopathy (accessed February 28, 2015).

4. Roberto Schmidt, "The Story Behind 'That Selfie,'" Agence France-Presse, December 11, 2013, http://blogs.afp.com/correspondent/?post/Selfie#.VQtzH0JnJ1J (accessed March 18, 2015).

5. Joshua Miller, "Charlie Baker Snaps Selfies in Upbeat Closing TV Ad," *Boston Globe*, October 29, 2014, http://www.bostonglobe.com/metro/2014/10/29/republican-charlie-baker-launches-final-during-campaign-for-governor/Bdd4ri8bnrhf4cEY0JHuAK/story.html (accessed February 28, 2015).

6. Yair Rosenberg, post on Twitter, March 17, 2015, https://twitter.com/Yair_Rosenberg/status/577829146048380928.

7. Ross Douthat, "The Age of Individualism," *New York Times*, February 28, 2014, http://www.nytimes.com/2014/03/16/opinion/sunday/douthat-

the-age-of-individualism.html?partner=rssnyt&emc=rss (accessed February 28, 2015).

8. Charles Blow, "The Self(ie) Generation," *New York Times*, March 7, 2014, http://www.nytimes.com/2014/03/08/opinion/blow-the-self-ie-generation.html?ref=charlesmblow (accessed February 28, 2015).

9. Nick Gillespie, "There's Nothing Wrong with Being Your Best Selfie," *Daily Beast*, March 18, 2014, http://www.thedailybeast.com/articles /2014/03/18/there-s-nothing-wrong-with-being-your-best-selfie.html (accessed February 28, 2014).

10. Sara Kehaulani Goo, "At Google, Hours Are Long, but the Consomme Is Free," *Washington Post*, January 24, 2007, http://www.washingtonpost. com/wp-dyn/content/article/2007/01/23/AR2007012300334.html (accessed December 13, 2014).

11. "More on Americans' Attitudes Toward Food," Public Policy Polling, February 27, 2013, http://www.publicpolicypolling.com/pdf/2011/PPP_ Release_Food_227.pdf (accessed December 13, 2014).

12. Dave Gilson, "Chart: Generational Attitudes About Sushi and Gay Marriage Correlate Almost Perfectly," *Mother Jones*, February 27, 2013, http://www.motherjones.com/mojo/2013/02/chart-generational-attitudes-sushi-gay-marriage (accessed December 13, 2014).

13. Yoel Inbar, David Pizarro, Ravi Iyer, and Jonathan Haidt, "Disgust Sensitivity, Political Conservatism, and Voting," *Social Psychological and Personality Science* 3, no. 5 (September 2012), p. 537.

14. Telephone interview with Alex Lundry, September 19, 2014.

15. Neil Swidley and Stephanie Ebbert, "Journeys of a Shared life," *Boston Globe*, June 27, 2007, http://www.boston.com/news/nation/articles /2007/06/27/raising_sons_rising_expectations/?page=full.

16. http://www.gallup.com/poll/171740/americans-confidence-news-media-remains-low.aspx.

17. Margaret Scammell, "Political Brands and Consumer Citizens: The Rebranding of Tony Blair," *Annals of the American Academy of Political and Social Science* 611, no. 1 (May, 2007): 176–192.

18. http://www.resurgentrepublic.com/research/obamas-likeability-is-not-enough-to-win-back-and-hold-independents.

One: The Election of 2076

1. John Colapinto, "The Young Hipublicans," *New York Times Magazine*, May 25, 2003, http://www.nytimes.com/2003/05/25/magazine /25REPUBLICANS.html (accessed December 13, 2014).

2. Robert Draper, "Can the Republicans Be Saved from Obsolescence?," *New York Times Magazine*, February 14, 2013, http://www.nytimes. com/2013/02/17/magazine/can-the-republicans-be-saved-from-obsolescence.html?pagewanted=all&_r=0 (accessed December 13, 2014).

3. Ibid.

4. "How Groups Voted in 1980," Roper Center for Public Opinion at the University of Connecticut, http://www.ropercenter.uconn.edu/elections/ how_groups_voted/voted_80.html (accessed December 13, 2014).

5. "How Groups Voted in 1984," Roper Center for Public Opinion at the University of Connecticut, http://www.ropercenter.uconn.edu/elections/ how_groups_voted/voted_84.html (accessed December 13, 2014).

6. "How Groups Voted in 1988," Roper Center for Public Opinion at the University of Connecticut, http://www.ropercenter.uconn.edu/elections/ how_groups_voted/voted_88.html (accessed December 13, 2014).

7. "How Groups Voted in 1996," Roper Center for Public Opinion at the University of Connecticut, http://www.ropercenter.uconn.edu/elections/ how_groups_voted/voted_96.html (accessed December 13, 2014).

8. Matthew Continetti, "Not the One They Were Hoping For," *Weekly Standard*, March 8, 2010, http://www.weeklystandard.com/articles/not-one-they-were-hoping (accessed December 13, 2014).

9. Michael Hais and Morley Winograd, "It's Official: Millennials Re-aligned American Politics in 2008," *Huffington Post*, December 18, 2008, http://www.huffingtonpost.com/michael-hais-and-morley-winograd/its-official-millennials_b_144357.html (accessed December 13, 2014).

10. http://www.gallup.com/poll/163133/americans-view-gop-less-favorably-democratic-party.aspx.

11. http://www.nytimes.com/interactive/2010/11/07/ weekinreview/20101107-detailed-exitpolls.html.

12. Meet the Press Transcript, NBC News, November 7, 2004, http://www. nbcnews.com/id/6430019/#.VBSR10tFEpE (accessed December 13, 2014).

13. John Judis and Ruy Teixeira, *The Emerging Democratic Majority* (New York: Scribner, reprint edition, 2004).

14. James Carville, *40 More Years: How the Democrats Will Rule the Next Generation* (New York: Simon & Schuster, 2009).

15. Frank Newport, "Party Identification Varies Widely Across Age Spectrum," Gallup, July 10, 2014, http://www.gallup.com/poll/172439/party-identification-varies-widely-across-age-spectrum.aspx (accessed December 13, 2014).

16. Keith R. Billingsley and Clyde Tucker, "Generations, Status and Party Identification: A Theory of Operant Conditioning," *Political Behavior* 9, no. 4 (1987): 305–322.

17. Amanda Cox, "How Birth Year Influences Political Views," in "The Upshot" *New York Times*, July 8, 2014, http://www.nytimes.com/interactive/2014/07/08/upshot/how-the-year-you-were-born-influences-your-politics.html (accessed December 13, 2014).

18. Stephen Nohlgren, "Appetite Big for Teenie Beanie Babies," *St. Petersburg Times*, May 26, 1998, http://www.sptimes.com/TampaBay/52698/Appetite_big_for_Teen.html (accessed December 13, 2014).

19. Kayla Webley, "A Brief History of the Happy Meal," *Time*, April 30, 2010, http://content.time.com/time/nation/article/0,8599,1986073,00.html (accessed December 13, 2014).

20. Emily Bryson York, "McDonald's Sued for Marketing Happy Meals to Children," *Los Angeles Times*, December 15, 2010, http://articles.latimes.com/2010/dec/15/business/la-fi-mcdonalds-lawsuit–20101215 (accessed December 13, 2014).

21. Joe Eskenazi, "Happy Meal Ban: McDonald's Outsmarts San Francisco," *SF Weekly*, November 29, 2011, http://www.sfweekly.com/thesnitch/2011/11/29/happy-meal-ban-mcdonalds-outsmarts-san-francisco (accessed December 13, 2014).

22. Eric Schlosser, *Fast Food Nation: The Dark Side of the All-American Meal* (New York: First Mariner Books, 2001), 43.

23. College Republican National Committee, "Grand Old Party for a Brand New Generation," June 2014, http://images.skem1.com/client_id_32089/Grand_Old_Party_for_a_Brand_New_Generation.pdf (accessed December 13, 2014).

24. Mike Viqueria, "GOPer Compares Brand to Bad Dog Food," NBC News, May 14, 2008, http://firstread.nbcnews.com/_

news/2008/05/14/4436302-goper-compares-brand-to-bad-dog-food (accessed December 13, 2014).

25. Aaron Blake, "Republican Brand: Still 'Dog Food,'" *Washington Post*, October 3, 2012, http://www.washingtonpost.com/blogs/the-fix/wp/2012/10/03/republican-brand-still-dog-food/ (accessed December 13, 2014).

26. Republican National Committee, "Growth and Opportunity Project Report," 2013, https://goproject.gop.com/RNC_Growth_Opportunity_Book_2013.pdf (accessed December 13, 2014).

27. Alexander Bolton, "Rand Paul: GOP Brand 'Sucks,'" *The Hill*, October 29, 2014, http://thehill.com/homenews/222250-rand-paul-gop-brand-sucks (accessed December 13, 2014).

Two: Snapchats from Hillary

1. Cornelia Grumman, "Dole Error Hurts Web Site Plug," *Chicago Tribune*, October 8, 1996, http://articles.chicagotribune.com/1996-10-08/news/9610080226_1_bob-dole-dole-spokeswoman-dole-fruit (accessed December 7, 2014).

2. Eric C. Newburger, "Computer Use in the United States," U.S. Census Bureau, September 1999, http://www.census.gov/prod/99pubs/p20-522.pdf (accessed December 7, 2014).

3. Eric C. Newburger, "Home Computers and Internet Use in the United States: August 2000," U.S. Census Bureau, September 2001, http://www.census.gov/prod/2001pubs/p23-207.pdf (accessed December 7, 2014).

4. U.S. Census Bureau, "Computer & Internet Trends in America," February 3, 2014, http://www.census.gov/hhes/computer/files/2012/Computer_Use_Infographic_FINAL.pdf (accessed December 7, 2014).

5. Stephen J. Blumberg and Julian V. Luke, "Wireless Substitution: Early Release of Estimates from the National Health Interview Survey, July–December 2013," National Center for Health Statistics, July 2014, http://www.cdc.gov/nchs/data/nhis/earlyrelease/wireless201407.pdf (accessed December 7, 2014).

6. Nancy Darling, "Is It Okay to Let Your Toddler Play with the iPad?," *Psychology Today*, October 19, 2011, http://www.psychologytoday.com/blog/thinking-about-kids/201110/is-it-okay-let-your-toddler-play-the-ipad (accessed December 7, 2014).

7. Pippa Norris, *A Virtuous Circle: Political Communications in Post-Industrial Societies* (New York: Cambridge University Press, 2000).

8. Lee Rainie and Scott Keeter, "Pew Internet Project Data Memo," Pew Internet and American Life Project, April 2006, http://www.pewinternet.org/files/old-media//Files/Reports/2006/PIP_Cell_phone_study.pdf.pdf (accessed December 7, 2014).

9. Aaron Smith, "Smartphone Ownership—2013 Update," Pew Research Center, June 5, 2013, http://www.pewinternet.org/files/old-media//Files/Reports/2013/PIP_Smartphone_adoption_2013_PDF.pdf (accessed December 7, 2014).

10. Ryan Lizza, "The YouTube Election," *New York Times*, August 20, 2006, http://www.nytimes.com/2006/08/20/weekinreview/20lizza.html?pagewanted=all&_r=0.

11. Thomas J. Johnson and David D. Perlmutter, eds. *New Media, Campaigning and the 2008 Facebook Election* (New York: Routledge, 2011).

12. Laura Matthews, "GOP, Tea Party Tweeted More Than Democrats in 2010 Election," *International Business Tribune*, July 22, 2011, http://www.ibtimes.com/gop-tea-party-tweeted-more-democrats–2010-election–300841 (accessed December 7, 2014).

13. Sasha Issenberg, "How President Obama's Campaign Used Big Data to Rally Individual Voters, Part 1," MIT Technology Review, December 16, 2012, http://www.technologyreview.com/featuredstory/508836/how-obama-used-big-data-to-rally-voters-part–1/ (accessed December 7, 2014).

14. Janna Anderson and Lee Rainie, "The Internet of Things Will Thrive by 2025," Pew Research Center, May 2014, http://www.pewinternet.org/files/2014/05/PIP_Internet-of-things_0514142.pdf.

15. Z. Byron Wolf, "Who Are Ron Paul's Donors?," ABC News, November 6, 2007, http://abcnews.go.com/Politics/Vote2008/Story?id=3822989&page=1 (accessed December 7, 2014).

16. Engage Research, "Inside the Cave," 2013, http://enga.ge/download/Inside%20the%20Cave.pdf (accessed December 14, 2014).

17. Darren Samuelsohn, "The GOP's 2016 Tech Deficit," *POLITICO*, October 22, 2014, http://www.politico.com/story/2014/10/the-gops–2016-tech-deficit–112121.html (accessed December 7, 2014).

18. Seamus Byrne, "A Massive Success: 10 years of World of Warcraft (Q&A)," CNET, October 29, 2014, http://www.cnet.com/news/world-of-warcraft-ten-year-anniversary-interview-ion-hazzikostas/ (accessed December 7, 2014).

19. Mark Mazzetti and Justin Elliot, "Spies Infiltrate a Fantasy Realm of Online Games," *New York Times*, December 9, 2013, http://www.nytimes.com/2013/12/10/world/spies-dragnet-reaches-a-playing-field-of-elves-and-trolls.html?_r=0 (accessed December 7, 2014).

20. Wei Wang, David Rothschild, Sharad Goel, and Andrew Gelman, "Forecasting Elections with Non-representative Polls," *International Journal of Forecasting* (September 10, 2014), http://dx.doi.org/10.1016/j.ijforecast.2014.06.001 (accessed December 7, 2014).

21. Bonnie Nardi, *My Life as a Night Elf Priest: An Anthropological Account of* World of Warcraft (Ann Arbor, MI: University of Michigan Press, 2010).

22. Peter Suderman, "The Infinite World of Bioshock," *Reason*, April 13, 2013, http://reason.com/archives/2013/04/13/the-infinite-world-of-bioshock (accessed December 7, 2014).

23. Stephen Totillo, *"Grand Theft Auto V* Mocks Republicans, Skewers Democrats," *Kotaku*, August 14, 2013, http://kotaku.com/grand-theft-auto-v-mocks-republicans-skewers-democrats–1134219480 (accessed December 7, 2014).

24. Steve Gorman, "Obama Buys First Video Game Campaign Ads," Reuters, October 16, 2008, http://www.reuters.com/article/2008/10/16/us-media-obama-idUSTRE49F1PY20081016 (accessed December 7, 2014).

25. Owen Good, "President Obama Returns to *Madden* Through In-Game Advertising," *Kotaku*, September 14, 2012, http://kotaku.com/5943462/president-obama-returns-to-madden—through-in-game-advertising (accessed December 7, 2014).

26. Sami Yenigun, "Presidential Campaigns Rock the Gamer Vote," NPR, October 1, 2012, http://www.npr.org/2012/10/01/162103528/presidential-campaigns-rock-the-gamer-vote (accessed December 7, 2014).

27. Chris Kohler, "John Edwards' Second Life Vandalized," *Wired*, March 1, 2007, http://www.wired.com/2007/03/john_edwards_se/ (accessed December 7, 2014).

28. Ben Lewis and Lance Porter, "In-Game Advertising Effects: Examining Player Perceptions of Advertising Schema Congruity in a Massively Multiplayer Online Role Playing Game," *Journal of Interactive Advertising* 10, no. 2 (Spring 2010): 46–60.

29. Tricia Duryee, "Four Types of Advertising Are Emerging in Social

Games, EA Says," *All Things D*, April 4, 2012, http://allthingsd. com/20120404/theres-four-types-of-advertising-emerging-in-social-games-ea-says/ (accessed December 7, 2014).

30. Matt Petronzio, "The Rise of Mobile in Election 2012," *Mashable*, October 2, 2012, http://mashable.com/2012/10/02/mobile-election–2012/ (accessed December 7, 2014).

31. Kyle Stock, "Highlights from the Candy Crush IPO Filing: 500 Million Downloads and Counting," *Bloomberg Businessweek*, February 18, 2014, http://www.businessweek.com/articles/2014–02–18/king-digitals-ipo-filing-shows–500-million-candy-crush-downloads (accessed December 7, 2014).

32. Entertainment Software Association, *2014 Essential Facts About the Computer and Video Game Industry*, October 2014, http://www.theesa.com/wp-content/uploads/2014/10/ESA_EF_2014.pdf.

33. Nellie Andreeva, "Sony Pictures TV to Produce Comic Book Drama Series 'Powers' for PlayStation," *Deadline Hollywood*, March 19, 2014, http://deadline.com/2014/03/sony-pictures-tv-to-produce-drama-series-powers-for-playstation–701727/ (accessed December 7, 2014).

34. Brian Fung, "Microsoft Is Using Your Data to Target Political Ads on Xbox Live," *Washington Post*, March 7, 2014, http://www.washington post.com/blogs/the-switch/wp/2014/03/07/microsoft-is-using-your-data-to-target-political-ads-on-xbox-live/ (accessed December 7, 2014).

35. Alexis Madrigal, "AMA: How a Weird Internet Thing Became a Mainstream Delight," *Atlantic*, January 7, 2014, http://www.theatlantic.com/technology/archive/2014/01/ama-how-a-weird-internet-thing-became-a-mainstream-delight/282860/?single_page=true (accessed December 7, 2014).

36. Abby Phillip, "Martin O'Malley Did a Reddit AMA. It Didn't Go Very Well," *Washington Post*, May 5, 2014, http://www.washingtonpost.com/blogs/the-fix/wp/2014/05/05/martin-omalley-did-a-reddit-ama-it-didnt-go-very-well/ (accessed December 7, 2014).

37. Erin La Rosa, "21 Cats Who Are Totally Empowered by Their Halloween Costume," *BuzzFeed*, October 30, 2014, http://www.buzzfeed.com/erinlarosa/cats-who-are-totally-empowered-by-their-halloween-costume (accessed December 7, 2014).

38. National Republican Congressional Committee, "13 Animals That Are

Really Bummed About ObamaCare," March 22, 2013, http://www.nrcc. org/2013/03/22/13-animals-that-are-really-bummed-about-obamacare/ (accessed December 7, 2014).

39. Nick Bilton, "Disruptions: Indiscreet Photos, Glimpsed Then Gone," *New York Times*, May 6, 2012, http://bits.blogs.nytimes.com/2012/05/06/ disruptions-indiscreet-photos-glimpsed-then-gone/ (accessed December 7, 2014).

40. Henry Blodget, "EXCLUSIVE: How Snapchat Plans to Make Money," *Business Insider*, November 20, 2013, http://www.businessinsider.com/ how-snapchat-will-make-money–2013–11 (accessed December 7, 2014).

41. Evelyn M. Rusli and Douglas MacMillan, "Snapchat Fetches $10 Billion Valuation," *Wall Street Journal*, August 26, 2014, http://online.wsj. com/articles/snapchat-fetches–10-billion-valuation–1409088794?tesla=y (accessed December 7, 2014).

42. Billy Gallagher, "Taco Bell Asks Twitter Followers to Add Them on Snapchat, Users May Soon See Snaps From Brands," *TechCrunch*, May 1, 2013, http://techcrunch.com/2013/05/01/taco-bell-joins-snapchat/ (accessed December 7, 2014).

43. Cotton Delo, "McDonald's Joins Throng of Marketers Experimenting with Snapchat," *Advertising Age*, February 26, 2014, http://adage. com/article/digital/mcdonald-s-joins-marketers-experimenting-snapchat/291875/ (accessed December 7, 2014).

44. Marc Graser, "Marriott Signs Content Deals with YouTube, Snapchat Stars, 'Ghost Whisperer' Producers Through New Studio (EXCLUSIVE)," *Variety*, October 31, 2014, http://variety.com/2014/digital/ news/marriott-signs-content-deals-with-youtube-snapchat-stars-ghost-whisperer-producers-through-new-studio–1201344180/ (accessed December 7, 2014).

45. Jose Delreal, "Generation Opportunity to Campaign on Snapchat," *POLITICO*, December 9, 2013, http://www.politico.com/story/2013/12/ snapchat-obamacare-generation-opportunity–100890.html (accessed December 7, 2014).

46. Mike Allen, "Sen. Rand Paul joins Snapchat," *POLITICO*, January 15, 2014, http://www.politico.com/story/2014/01/rand-paul-snapchat–102199.html (accessed December 7, 2014).

47. Harvard Institute of Politics, "Survey of Young Americans' Attitudes

Toward Politics and Public Service, 26th Edition: September 26–October 9, 2014," October 29, 2014, http://www.iop.harvard.edu/sites/default/files_new/fall%20poll%2014%20-%20topline.pdf.

48. John Dick, "Snapchat, Facebook, and the Generation Divide of Social Media," CivicScience, December 6, 2013, http://civicscience.com/snapchat-facebook-and-the-generational-divide-of-social-media/ (accessed December 7, 2014).

Three: Saying No to the Dress (but Yes to the Diapers)

1. Chuck Bennett, "Obama Wedding Registry Fundraising Strategy Not a Hit with Brides," *New York Post*, July 16, 2012, http://nypost.com/2012/07/16/obama-wedding-registry-fund-raising-strategy-not-a-hit-with-brides/.

2. Sue Shellenbarger, "The Gifts on Every Wedding List," *Wall Street Journal*, June 8, 2011, http://online.wsj.com/article/SB10001424052702304906004576371352048939270.html.

3. Maeve Reston, "Voter Data Crucial to Romney's Victory," *Los Angeles Times*, January 10, 2012, http://articles.latimes.com/2012/jan/10/nation/la-na-romney-analysis–20120111.

4. Pew Research Center, "The Decline of Marriage and Rise of New Families," November 18, 2010, http://www.pewsocialtrends.org/files/2010/11/pew-social-trends–2010-families.pdf.

5. Rick Klein, "Obama: 'I Think Same-Sex Couples Should Be Able to Get Married," ABC News, May 9, 2012, http://abcnews.go.com/blogs/politics/2012/05/obama-comes-out-i-think-same-sex-couples-should-be-able-to-get-married/.

6. Eytan Bakshy, "Showing Support for Marriage Equality on Facebook," Facebook, March 29, 2013, https://www.facebook.com/notes/facebook-data-science/showing-support-for-marriage-equality-on-facebook/10151430548593859 (accessed December 11, 2014).

7. "Survey of Young Americans' Attitudes Toward Politics and Public Service, 23rd Edition: March 20–April 8, 2013," Harvard Institute of Politics, http://www.iop.harvard.edu/sites/default/files_new/spring_poll_13_Topline.pdf.

8. Tim Townsend, "Conservatives Continue to Oppose Same-Sex Marriage but by Smaller Margins," Pew Research Center, October 11,

2013, http://www.pewresearch.org/fact-tank/2013/10/11/conservatives-continue-to-oppose-same-sex-marriage-but-by-smaller-margins/.

9. Pew Research Center, "Gay Marriage: Key Data Points from Pew Research," June 10, 2013, http://www.pewresearch.org/key-data-points/gay-marriage-key-data-points-from-pew-research/.

10. Kay Hymowitz, Jason S. Carroll, W. Bradford Wilcox, and Kelleen Kaye, *Knot Yet: The Benefits and Costs of Delayed Marriage in America*, National Marriage Project at the University of Virginia, March 2013, http://nationalmarriageproject.org/wp-content/uploads/2013/03/KnotYet-FinalForWeb.pdf (accessed December 11, 2014).

11. W. Bradford Wilcox, "Tie the Knot," *Slate*, March 25, 2013, http://www.slate.com/articles/double_x/doublex/2013/03/marry_in_your_twenties.html.

12. Pew Research Center, "The Decline of Marriage and Rise of New Families," November 18, 2010.

13. Melanie Hicken, "Average Wedding Bill in 2013: $28,400," CNN Money, March 10, 2013, http://money.cnn.com/2013/03/10/pf/wedding-cost/index.html (accessed December 11, 2014).

14. National Exit Polls 2012, accessed via CNN.com, http://www.cnn.com/election/2012/results/race/president (accessed December 11, 2014).

15. Ronald Brownstein, "The Hidden History of the American Electorate," *National Journal*, August 23, 2012, http://www.nationaljournal.com/2012-conventions/the-hidden-history-of-the-american-electorate–20120823.

16. "Some Employers Helping Couples with Daycare," *Palm Beach Post*, December 17, 1980, B2, http://news.google.com/newspapers?nid=1964&dat=19801217&id=_8cyAAAAIBAJ&sjid=rs0FAAAAIBAJ&pg=1212,147507 (accessed December 11, 2014).

17. David Bauder, "Fox News' Megyn Kelly Lands in Prime Time with New Show, " Associated Press, October 9, 2013, http://bigstory.ap.org/article/fox-news-megyn-kelly-heading-prime-time.

18. Jacob Weisberg, "Yahoo's Marissa Mayer: Hail to the Chief," *Vogue*, August 16, 2013, http://www.vogue.com/magazine/article/hail-to-the-chief-yahoos-marissa-mayer/#1.

19. Pew Research Center, "Breadwinner Moms," May 29, 2013, http://www.pewsocialtrends.org/files/2013/05/Breadwinner_moms_final.pdf.

20. Pew Research Center, "Modern Parenthood," March 14, 2013, http://

www.pewsocialtrends.org/files/2013/03/FINAL_modern_parenthood
_03–2013.pdf.

21. Pew Research Center, "Modern Parenthood."

22. Lauren Weber, "Why Dads Don't Take Paternity Leave," *Wall Street Journal*, June 12, 2013, http://online.wsj.com/news/articles/SB100014241 27887324049504578541633708283670.

23. Maureen Dowd, "Plowshares into Pacifiers," *New York Times*, August 15, 1996, http://www.nytimes.com/1996/08/15/opinion/plowshares-into-pacifiers.html.

24. Rich Morin, "The Public Renders a Split Verdict on Changes in Family Structure," Pew Research Center, February 16, 2011, http://www.pewsocialtrends.org/2011/02/16/the-public-renders-a-split-verdict-on-changes-in-family-structure/.

25. Pew Research Center, "The Public Renders Split Verdict on Changes in Family Structure," February 16, 2001, http://www.pewsocialtrends.org/files/2011/02/Pew-Social-Trends-Changes-In-Family-Structure.pdf.

26. Daniel A. Smith, Matthew DeSantis, and Jason Kassel, "Same-Sex Marriage Ballot Measures and the 2004 Presidential Election," *State and Local Government Review* 38, no. 2 (2006): 78–91, http://www.clas.ufl.edu/users/dasmith/SLGR2006.pdf.

27. College Republican National Committee, "Grand Old Party for a Brand New Generation," June 2013, http://images.skem1.com/client_id_32089/Grand_Old_Party_for_a_Brand_New_Generation.pdf (accessed December 11, 2014).

28. American Association of University Women, "The Simple Truth about the Gender Pay Gap," Fall 2014, http://www.aauw.org/files/2014/09/The-Simple-Truth_Fall.pdf (accessed December 11, 2014).

29. Senator Deb Fischer, "What Women Want," *POLITICO*, April 9, 2014, http://www.politico.com/magazine/story/2014/04/what-women-want–105520.html#ixzz3JC7HVml8 (accessed December 11, 2014).

30. Kay Hymowitz, "Longer Maternity Leave Not So Great for Women After All," *Time*, September 30, 2013, http://ideas.time.com/2013/09/30/longer-maternity-leave-not-so-great-for-women-after-all/ (accessed December 11, 2014).

31. "Why Swedish Men Take So Much Paternity Leave," *Economist*, July 22, 2014, http://www.economist.com/blogs/economist-explains/2014/07/economist-explains–15 (accessed December 11, 2014).

32. Patrick Brennan, "Mike Lee Inroduces Pro-Growth, Pro-Middle Class Tax Reform," *National Review Online*, September 17, 2013, http://www.nationalreview.com/corner/358728/mike-lee-introduces-pro-growth-pro-middle-class-tax-reform-patrick-brennan (accessed December 11, 2014).

33. W. Bradford Wilcox and Andrew J. Chernin, "The Marginalization of Marriage in Middle America," Brookings Institution, August 2011, http://www.brookings.edu/~/media/research/files/papers/2011/8/10%20strengthen%20marriage%20wilcox%20cherlin/0810_strengthen_marriage_wilcox_cherlin.pdf.

34. Child Care Aware of America, "Parents and the High Cost of Child Care," August 2012, http://www.naccrra.org/sites/default/files/default_site_pages/2012/cost_report_2012_final_081012_0.pdf (accessed December 11, 2014).

35. Internal Revenue Service, "Ten Things to Know About the Child and Dependent Care Credit," March 7, 2011, http://www.irs.gov/uac/Ten-Things-to-Know-About-the-Child-and-Dependent-Care-Credit (accessed December 11, 2014).

36. Melissa Langsam Braunstein, "The Nanny Tax," *National Review*, April 13, 2012, http://www.nationalreview.com/articles/295891/nanny-tax-melissa-langsam-braunstein (accessed December 11, 2014).

Four: Taking Uber to Whole Foods

1. Daniella Medina, "The Road Less Traveled: Fewer Teens Getting Driver's Licenses and Hitting the Road," *Miami Herald*, June 7, 2014, http://www.miamiherald.com/news/local/community/miami-dade/article1965650.html.

2. Nin-Hai Tseng, "Why Car Companies Can't Win Young Adults," *Fortune*, August 16, 2013, http://fortune.com/2013/08/16/why-car-companies-cant-win-young-adults/.

3. U.S. Census Bureau, "Quarterly Homeownership Rates by Age of Householder, 1994 to Present," http://www.census.gov/housing/hvs/data/histtab19.xls (accessed December 11, 2014).

4. Kevin Cirilli, "Fewer Young People Buying Homes," *The Hill*, November 3, 2014, http://thehill.com/policy/finance/222679-fewer-young-people-buying-homes.

5. Martin Gervais and Jonas Fisher, "Why Has Homeownership Fallen

Among the Young?," Federal Reserve Bank of Chicago, March 6, 2009, http://eprints.soton.ac.uk/71045/1/0907.pdf (accessed December 11, 2014).

6. David Dayen, "Yes, Millennials Actually Are Living in Their Parents' Basements," *New Republic*, July 9, 2014, http://www.newrepublic.com/article/118619/millennials-living-parents-numbers-behind-trend (accessed December 11, 2014).

7. "Fusion Millennial Political Poll 2014."

8. Hart Research Associates, "How Housing Matters: The Housing Crisis Continues to Loom Large in the Experiences and Attitudes of the American Public," MacArthur Foundation, April 2014, http://www.macfound.org/media/files/How_Housing_Matters_2014_FINAL_REPORT.pdf (accessed December 11, 2014).

9. Derek Thompson, "The End Of Ownership: Why Aren't Young People Buying More Houses," *Atlantic*, February 29, 2012, http://www.theatlantic.com/business/archive/2012/02/the-end-of-ownership-why-arent-young-people-buying-more-houses/253750/?single_page=true.

10. Christopher B. Leinberger and Mariela Alfonzo, "Walk This Way: The Economic Promise of Walkable Places in Washington, D.C.," Brookings Institution, May 2012, http://www.brookings.edu/~/media/Research/Files/Papers/2012/5/25%20walkable%20places%20leinberger/25%20walkable%20places%20leinberger.pdf (accessed December 11, 2014).

11. Claire Cain Miller, "Where Young College Graduates Are Choosing to Live," in "The Upshot," *New York Times*, October 20, 2014, http://www.nytimes.com/2014/10/20/upshot/where-young-college-graduates-are-choosing-to-live.html?abt=0002&abg=0.

12. Tom Vanderbilt, "What's Your Walk Score?," *Slate*, April 12, 2012, http://www.slate.com/articles/life/walking/2012/04/walking_in_america_how_walk_score_puts_a_number_on_walkability_.html.

13. Cracker Barrel Old Country Store, "Investor Presentation," September 2014, http://files.shareholder.com/downloads/CBRL/3718206258x0x783794/75792c78–659c–4775–89f9–127ad33fd849/September%202014%20Investor%20Presentation.pdf (accessed December 11, 2014).

14. David Wasserman, "Will the 2012 Election Be a Contest of Whole Foods vs. Cracker Barrel Shoppers?," *Washington Post*, December 9, 2011, http://www.washingtonpost.com/opinions/will-the–2012-election-be-a-contest-of-whole-foods-vs-cracker-barrel-shoppers/2011/09/28/gIQAMuXDiO_story.html.

15. David Wasserman, "Senate Control Could Come Down To Whole Foods vs. Cracker Barrel," *FiveThirtyEight*, October 8, 2014, http://fivethirtyeight.com/features/senate-control-could-come-down-to-whole-foods-vs-cracker-barrel/.

16. Seth C. McKee, "Rural Voters and the Polarization of American Presidential Elections," *PS: Political Science and Politics* 41, no. 1, 101–108.

17. James G. Gimpel and Kimberly A. Karnes, "The Rural Side of the Urban-Rural Gap," *PS: Political Science and Politics* 39, no. 3, 467–472.

18. National Exit Polls 2004, accessed via http://www.cnn.com/ELECTION/2004/pages/results/states/US/P/00/epolls.0.html (accessed December 11, 2014).

19. National Exit Polls 2014, accessed via http://elections.nbcnews.com/ns/politics/2012/all/president/#exitPoll (accessed December 11, 2014).

20. Elizabeth Williamson and Dante Chinni, "Shifting Demographics Tilt Presidential Races in American Suburbs," *Wall Street Journal*, April 30, 2014, http://www.wsj.com/articles/SB10001424052702304672404579182214229099376.

21. Josh Kron, "Red State, Blue City: How the Urban-Rural Divide Is Splitting America," *Atlantic*, November 30, 2012, http://www.theatlantic.com/politics/archive/2012/11/red-state-blue-city-how-the-urban-rural-divide-is-splitting-america/265686/?single_page=true.

22. Drew Desilver, "How the Most Ideologically Polarized Americans Live Different Lives," Pew Research Center, June 13, 2014, http://www.pewresearch.org/fact-tank/2014/06/13/big-houses-art-museums-and-in-laws-how-the-most-ideologically-polarized-americans-live-different-lives/.

23. Pew Research Center, "Table 3.2: Ideal Community Type," June 12, 2014, http://www.people-press.org/2014/06/12/ideal-community-type/ (accessed December 11, 2014).

24. Matt Yglesias, "When Is a Taxi Not a Taxi?," *Slate*, December 15, 2011, http://www.slate.com/articles/technology/technocracy/2011/12/uber_car_service_exposing_the_idiocy_of_american_city_taxi_regulations_.html.

25. Evelyn M. Rusli and Douglas MacMillan, "Uber Gets an Uber-Valuation," *Wall Street Journal*, June 6, 2014, http://www.wsj.com/articles/uber-gets-uber-valuation-of–18–2-billion–1402073876.

26. Serena Saitto, "At $40 Billion, Uber Would Eclipse Twitter and Hertz,"

Bloomberg.com, November 26, 2014, http://www.bloomberg.com/news/2014–11–26/uber-said-close-to-raising-funding-at-up-to–40b-value.html.

27. Dustin Volz, "Can Marco Rubio Uber His Way to the Youth Vote?," *National Journal*, March 24, 2014, http://www.nationaljournal.com/tech/can-marco-rubio-google-and-uber-his-way-to-the-youth-vote–20140324.

28. Byron Tau and Kevin Robillard, "GOP Chases Youth Vote with Uber," *POLITICO*, August 6, 2014, http://www.politico.com/story/2014/08/uber-republicans-youth-vote–109785.html#ixzz3LcK411Xt.

29. Julian Hattem, "RNC Circulates Petition, Raises Funds off of Uber," *The Hill*, August 6, 2014, http://thehill.com/policy/technology/214488-rnc-circulating-petition-fundraising-off-uber.

30. Fernanda Santos, "Licensed and Illegal Vans Fight It Out," *New York Times*, June 9, 2010, http://www.nytimes.com/2010/06/10/nyregion/10vans.html?pagewanted=all&_r=0.

31. Lauren Drell, "Your City Needs These 7 Open Data Apps," *Mashable*, November 7, 2012, http://mashable.com/2012/11/07/open-data-city-apps/.

32. Laura Drees and Daniel Castro, "State Open Data Policies and Portals," Center for Data Innovation, August 18, 2014, http://www2.datainnovation.org/2014-open-data.pdf.

33. Code for America, "2015 Partners," http://www.codeforamerica.org/governments/2015-cities/ (accessed December 11, 2014).

34. Joel Gurin, "How Open Data Is Transforming City Life," *Forbes*, September 12, 2014, http://www.forbes.com/sites/techonomy/2014/09/12/how-open-data-is-transforming-city-life/.

35. Tarryn Mento, "New San Diego Data Chief Wants to Get Government Records in Public's Hands," KPBS News, December 10, 2014, http://www.kpbs.org/news/2014/dec/10/san-diego-making-progress-open-data-new-hire/.

36. Jaime Fuller, "The Most Interesting Mayor You've Never Heard Of," *Washington Post*, March 10, 2014, http://www.washingtonpost.com/blogs/the-fix/wp/2014/03/10/the-most-interesting-mayor-youve-never-heard-of/.

Five: Start-Ups and Stock Markets

1. James Montgomery, "Barack Obama and 'Boxers or Briefs': MTV's History Of Politics," MTV News, October 25, 2012, http://www.mtv.com/news/1696244/ask-obama-live-mtv-politics-history/ (accessed December 14, 2014).

2. Michael Scherer, "Inside the Secret World of the Data Crunchers Who Helped Obama Win," *Time*, November 7, 2012, http://swampland.time.com/2012/11/07/inside-the-secret-world-of-quants-and-data-crunchers-who-helped-obama-win/ (accessed December 14, 2014).

3. "Barack Obama Addresses Unemployment Among Young People," MTV, October 26, 2012, http://www.mtv.com/videos/news/850462/president-barack-obama-addresses-unemployment-among-young-people.jhtml#id=1696102 (accessed December 14, 2014).

4. Library of Congress, "Bill Summary & Status, 112th Congress (2011–2012), H.R.3606, Major Congressional Actions," http://thomas.loc.gov/cgi-bin/bdquery/z?d112:HR03606:@@@R (accessed December 14, 2014).

5. United States Senate, "U.S. Senate Roll Call Votes 112th Congress–2nd Session: H.R.3606," http://www.senate.gov/legislative/LIS/roll_call_lists/roll_call_vote_cfm.cfm?congress=112&session=2&vote=00055 (accessed December 14, 2014).

6. Kristen Soltis Anderson, "Conservative Ideas Are Our Biggest Strength with Young Americans," *National Review Online*, August 24, 2012, http://www.nationalreview.com/corner/314916/conservative-ideas-are-our-biggest-strength-young-americans-kristen-soltis-anderson (accessed December 14, 2014).

7. Bureau of Labor Statistics, "Number of Jobs Held, Labor Market Activity, and Earnings Growth Among the Youngest Baby Boomers: Results from a Longitudinal Survey," news release, July 25, 2012, "http://www.bls.gov/news.release/pdf/nlsoy.pdf (accessed December 14, 2014).

8. Robert E. Hall, "The Importance of Lifetime Jobs in the U.S. Economy," *American Economic Review* 72, no. 4, 716 (available at http://web.stanford.edu/~rehall/Importance-AER-Sep–1982.pdf; accessed December 14, 2014).

9. Henry S. Farber, "Is the Company Man an Anachronism? Trends in Long Term Employment in the U.S., 1973–2006," prepared for con-

ference on the Transition to Adulthood, MDRC, New York, January 27–28, 2006, http://dataspace.princeton.edu/jspui/bitstream/88435/dsp 01ft848q61h/1/518.pdf (accessed December 14, 2014).

10. PricewaterhouseCoopers, "Millennials at Work: Reshaping the Workplace," 2012, http://www.pwc.com/en_M1/m1/services/consulting/documents/millennials-at-work.pdf (accessed December 14, 2014).

11. Harvard Kennedy School of Government, "Class of 2013 Employment Overview," 2013, http://www.hks.harvard.edu/var/ezp_site/storage/fckeditor/file/pdfs/degree-programs/oca/employment_overview.pdf (accessed December 14, 2014).

12. Bureau of Labor Statistics, "Employer Costs for Employee Compensation—September 2014," December 10, 2014, http://www.bls.gov/news.release/ecec.nr0.htm (accessed December 14, 2014).

13. The Pew Charitable Trusts and the Laura and John Arnold Foundation, "Recruiting and Retaining Public Sector Workers," September 2014, http://www.pewtrusts.org/~/media/Assets/2014/09/Recruitingand RetainingPublicSectorWorkersIssueBrief.pdf (accessed December 14, 2014).

14. Achievers, "Class of 2014: Your Next Generation of Top Talent," 2014 http://go.achievers.com/rs/iloverewards/images/Achievers_WP _Classof2014_v2.pdf (accessed December 14, 2014).

15. LinkedIn Talent Solutions, "Students and Recent Grads Talent Pool Reports," May 2013, https://business.linkedin.com/content/talent-solutions/global/en_us/index/site-forms/asset?resPath=/content/talent-solutions/global/en_us/site-resources/tips-and-insights/global-student-and-recent-grads-talent-pool-reports/jcr:content/tipsAndInsight&cqRetPath=/content/dam/business/talent-solutions/global/en_US/site/pdf/datasheets/linkedin-talent-pool-report-students-and-recent-grads.pdf (accessed December 14, 2014).

16. PricewaterhouseCoopers, "Millennials at Work: Reshaping the Workplace," 2012, http://www.pwc.com/en_M1/m1/services/consulting/documents/millennials-at-work.pdf (accessed December 14, 2014).

17. U.S. Office of Personnel Management, "Millennials: Finding Opportunities in Federal Service," 2014, http://www.fedview.opm.gov/2014FILES/FEVS_MillennialsReport.pdf (accessed December 14, 2014).

18. U.S. Office of Personnel Management, "Federal Employee Viewpoint Survey Results," 2014, http://www.fedview.opm.gov/2014FILES/2014_

Governmentwide_Management_Report.PDF (accessed December 14, 2014).

19. American Federation of Teachers, "Opposition to Pay for Performance for Public Employees," 2000, http://www.aft.org/resolution/opposition-pay-performance-public-employees#sthash.z7tnGxMr.dpuf (accessed December 14, 2014).

20. Bureau of Labor Statistics, "Labor Force Statistics from the Current Population Survey: Union Affiliation of Employed Wage and Salary Workers by Occupation and Industry," http://www.bls.gov/cps/cpsaat42.htm (accessed December 14, 2014).

21. Gerald Mayer, "Selected Characteristics of Public and Private Sector Workers," Congressional Research Service, March 21, 2014, http://fas.org/sgp/crs/misc/R41897.pdf (accessed December 14, 2014).

22. Pew Research Center, "Favorable Views of Business, Labor Rebound," June 27, 2013, http://www.people-press.org/files/legacy-pdf/6–27–13%20Business%20and%20Labor%20Release.pdf.

23. Carl Campanile, "Voters: Ax the Worst," *New York Post*, February 3, 2011, http://nypost.com/2011/02/03/voters-ax-the-worst/ (accessed December 14, 2014).

24. Stephen Barr, "Unions Oppose Senate's Pay-for-Performance Bill," *Washington Post*, June 30, 2006, http://www.washingtonpost.com/wp-dyn/content/article/2006/06/29/AR2006062902029.html (accessed December 14, 2014).

25. Stephen Barr, "A Closer Inspection of Airport Screeners' Pay," *Washington Post*, July 31, 2007, http://www.washingtonpost.com/wp-dyn/content/article/2007/07/30/AR2007073001471.html (accessed December 14, 2014).

26. "Recruiting and Retaining Public Sector Workers."

27. Robert L. Clark, Lee A. Craig, and Jack W. Wilson, *A History of Public Sector Pensions in the United States* (Philadelphia: University of Pennsylvania Press, 2003), http://www.pensionresearchcouncil.org/publications/pdf/0–8122–3714–5–1.pdf (accessed December 14, 2014).

28. Patrick Seburn, "Evolution of Employer-Provided Defined Benefit Pensions," *Monthly Labor Review*, Bureau of Labor Statistics, September 1991, http://www.bls.gov/mlr/1991/12/art3full.pdf (accessed December 14, 2014).

29. William Wiatrowski, "The Last Private Industry Pension Plans: A

Visual Essay," *Monthly Labor Review*, Bureau of Labor Statistics, December 2012, http://www.bls.gov/opub/mlr/2012/12/art1full.pdf (accessed December 14, 2014).

30. Mark Miller, "The Vanishing Defined Benefit Pension and Its Discontents," Reuters, May 6, 2014, http://www.reuters.com/article /2014/05/06/us-column-miller-pensions-idUSBREA450PP20140506 (accessed December 14, 2014).

31. Alicia H. Munnell, Kelly Haverstick, and Mauricio Soto, "Why Have Defined Benefit Pensions Survived in the Public Sector?," Trustees of Boston College, Center for Retirement Research, December 2007, http://crr.bc.edu/wp-content/uploads/2007/12/slp_2.pdf (accessed December 14, 2014).

32. Josh Barro, "How Congress Can Help State Pension Reform," *National Affairs*, Summer 2012, 92, http://www.nationalaffairs.com/ doclib/20120619_Barro_Indiv.pdf (accessed December 14, 2014).

33. Ray Long and Monique Garcia, "Illinois Approves Major Pension Overhaul," *Chicago Tribune*, December 4, 2013, http://www.chicagotribune. com/news/ct-illinois-governors-race-pensions-met–1203–20131204- story.html#page=1 (accessed December 4, 2013).

34. Jennifer Levitz, "Rhode Island's Deal on Pensions Overhaul Falls Apart," *Wall Street Journal,* April 11, 2014, http://online.wsj.com/articles/ SB10001424052702303873604579495991860073278 (accessed December 14, 2014).

35. Mike Rosenberg, "New San Jose Firefighters to See Pensions Cut After Long Union Battle with City," *San Jose Mercury News*, September 24, 2014, http://www.mercurynews.com/pensions/ci_26591446/new- san-jose-firefighters-see-pensions-cut-after (accessed December 14, 2014).

36. Pew Research Center, "The Big Generation Gap at the Polls Is Echoed in Attitudes on Budget Tradeoffs," December 20, 2012, http://www. pewsocialtrends.org/files/2012/12/FINAL_policies_report.pdf (accessed December 14, 2014).

37. Pew Research Center, "The Generation Gap and the 2012 Election," November 3, 2011, http://www.people-press.org/files/legacy- pdf/11–3–11%20Generations%20Release.pdf (accessed December 14, 2014).

38. Pew Research Center, "Attitudes About Aging," January 30, 2014,

http://www.pewglobal.org/files/2014/01/Pew-Research-Center-Global-Aging-Report-FINAL-January–30–20141.pdf (accessed December 14, 2014).

39. Reason/Rupe Foundation, "Millennials: The Politically Unclaimed Generation," July 10, 2014, http://reason.com/assets/db/2014-millennials-report.pdf (accessed December 14, 2014).

40. UBS, "Think You Know the Next Gen Investor? Think Again," *UBS Investor Watch*, 2014, http://www.ubs.com/content/dam/Wealth ManagementAmericas/documents/investor-watch–1Q2014-report.pdf (accessed December 14, 2014).

41. Ted Johnson, "How Funny or Die Got Barack Obama on Zach Galifi-anakis' 'Between Two Ferns,'" March 11, 2014, http://variety.com/2014/digital/news/president-obama-on-zach-galifianakis-between-two-ferns-watch–1201129329/ (accessed December 15, 2014).

42. Jeffrey Gottfried and Monica Anderson, "For Some, the Satiric 'Colbert Report' Is a Trusted Source of Political News," Pew Research Center, December 12, 2014, http://www.pewresearch.org/fact-tank/2014/12/12/for-some-the-satiric-colbert-report-is-a-trusted-source-of-political-news/ (accessed December 15, 2014).

43. Larry Levitt, Gary Claxton, and Anthony Damico, "The Numbers Behind 'Young Invincibles' and the Affordable Care Act," Kaiser Family Foundation, December 17, 2013, http://kff.org/health-reform/perspective/the-numbers-behind-young-invincibles-and-the-affordable-care-act/ (accessed December 15, 2014).

44. Judy Kurtz, "Katy Perry Tweets Obamacare Support," *The Hill*, August 2, 2013, http://thehill.com/blogs/in-the-know/in-the-know/318721-katy-perry-tweets-support-for-obamacare-at-vmas (accessed December 15, 2014).

45. Rich Lowry, "Pajama Boy, an Insufferable Man-Child," *POLITICO*, December 18, 2013, http://www.politico.com/magazine/story/2013/12/opinion-rich-lowry-obamacare-affordable-care-act-pajama-boy-an-insufferable-man-child–101304.html#.VI7liMYZJ1I (accessed December 15, 2014).

46. Harvard Institute of Politics, "Survey of Young Americans' Attitudes Toward Politics and Public Service," 26th Edition," October 2014, http://www.iop.harvard.edu/sites/default/files_new/fall%20poll%2014%20-%20topline.pdf (accessed December 15, 2014).

47. Ibid.

48. Robert E. Moffit and Nina Owcharenko, "The McCain Health Care Plan: More Power to Families," Heritage Foundation, October 15, 2008, http://www.heritage.org/research/reports/2008/10/the-mccain-health-care-plan-more-power-to-families (accessed December 15, 2014).

49. Jason Millman, "Why Uber Loves Obamacare," *Washington Post*, November 17, 2014, http://www.washingtonpost.com/blogs/wonkblog/wp/2014/11/17/why-uber-loves-obamacare/ (accessed December 15, 2014).

Six: Coding Our Way out of Student Debt

1. Bureau of Labor Statistics, "Occupational Outlook Handbook: Computer and Information Research Scientists," U.S. Department of Labor, http://www.bls.gov/ooh/computer-and-information-technology/computer-and-information-research-scientists.htm (accessed December 14, 2014).

2. Jonathan Rothwell, "Still Searching: Job Vacancies and STEM Skills," Brookings Institution, July 2014, http://www.brookings.edu/~/media/research/files/reports/2014/07/stem/job%20vacancies%20and%20stem%20skills.pdf (accessed December 15, 2014).

3. Bureau of Labor Statistics, "Labor Force Statistics from the Current Population Survey," U.S. Department of Labor, http://www.bls.gov/web/empsit/cpseea10.htm (accessed December 15, 2014).

4. Jaison R. Abel, Richard Deitz, and Yaqin Su, "Are Recent College Graduates Finding Good Jobs?," *Federal Reserve Bank of New York Current Issues in Economics in Finance* 20, no. 1 (2014), http://www.newyorkfed.org/research/current_issues/ci20–1.pdf (accessed December 15, 2014).

5. Meg P. Bernhard, "Yale Considers Proposal to Offer CS50 Next Fall," *Harvard Crimson*, October 8, 2014, http://www.thecrimson.com/article/2014/10/8/cs50-yale-harvard-proposal/ (accessed December 15, 2014).

6. Emily F. Cataldi, Caitlin Green, Robin Henke, et al., *2008–09 Baccalaureate and Beyond Longitudinal Study (B&B:08/09): First Look*, U.S. Department of Education (Washington, DC: National Center for Education Statistics), July 2011, http://nces.ed.gov/pubs2011/2011236.pdf (accessed December 12, 2014).

7. Harvard Institute of Politics, "Survey of Young Americans' Attitudes Toward Politics and Public Service: 25th Edition," April 2014, http://www.iop.harvard.edu/sites/default/files_new/Harvard_ExecSummary Spring2014.pdf (accessed December 14, 2014).

8. Cynthia Prince and others, "Building Teacher and Community Support for New Compensation Systems," Center for Educator Compensation Reform, http://www.cecr.ed.gov/researchSyntheses/Research%20Synthesis _Q%20F21.pdf (accessed December 14, 2014).

9. Jens Manuel Krogstad, "Top Issue for Hispanics? Hint: It's Not Immigration," Pew Research Center, June 2, 2014, http://www .pewresearch.org/fact-tank/2014/06/02/top-issue-for-hispanics-hint-its-not-immigration/ (accessed December 15, 2014).

10. Paul DiPerna, "2014 Schooling in America Survey," Friedman Foundation, June 2014, http://www.edchoice.org/CMSModules/EdChoice/FileLibrary/1057/2014-Schooling-in-America-Survey.pdf (accessed December 15, 2014).

11. College Republican National Committee, "Grand Old Party for a Brand New Generation," June 2013, http://images.skem1.com/client_id_32089/Grand_Old_Party_for_a_Brand_New_Generation.pdf (accessed December 11, 2014).

12. National Center for Education Statistics, *Digest of Education Statistics*, US Department of Education, 2013, http://nces.ed.gov/fastfacts/display.asp?id=76 (accessed December 12, 2014).

13. Emily F. Cataldi, Caitlin Green, Robin Henke, et al., *2008–09 Baccalaureate and Beyond Longitudinal Study (B&B:08/09): First Look.*

14. Pew Research Center, "Young Adults, Student Debt, and Economic Well-being," May 14, 2014, http://www.pewsocialtrends.org/files/2014/05/ST_2014.05.14_student-debt_complete-report.pdf (accessed December 12, 2014).

15. Selena Simmons-Duffin, "For Millions of Millennials: Some College, No Degree, Lots of Debt," NPR, November 19, 2014, http://www.npr.org/2014/11/19/362802610/for-millions-of-millennials-some-college-no-degree-lots-of-debt (accessed December 12, 2014).

16. Daniel Greenstein, "Addressing Students' Concerns in Higher Ed," Bill and Melinda Gates Foundation, December 11, 2014, http://www.impatientoptimists.org/Posts/2014/12/Addressing-Students-Concerns-in-Higher-Ed (accessed December 12, 2014).

17.   Andrew Martin and Andrew W. Lehren, "A Generation Hobbled by the Soaring Cost of College," *New York Times*, May 12, 2012, http://www.nytimes.com/2012/05/13/business/student-loans-weighing-down-a-generation-with-heavy-debt.html?pagewanted=all&_r=0 (accessed December 12, 2014).

18.   Ibid.

19.   Jordan Weissman, "Forget Elizabeth Warren," *Slate*, June 10, 2014, http://www.slate.com/articles/business/moneybox/2014/06/elizabeth_warren_student_debt_crisis_it_s_actually_tom_petri_who_has_the.html (accessed December 12, 2014).

20.   Jordan Marie Smith and Hunter Harris, "Senate Plan Could Help Grads Pay Off Student Loans," *POLITICO*, August 6, 2014, http://www.politico.com/story/2014/08/senate-plan-help-graduates-pay-off-student-loans–109789.html (accessed December 12, 2014).

21.   Center for Law and Social Policy, "Yesterday's Nontraditional Student Is Today's Traditional Student," 2011, http://www.clasp.org/resources-and-publications/publications–1/nontraditional-students-facts–2011.pdf (accessed December 15, 2014).

22.   Western Governors University, "WGU Timeline," http://www.wgu.edu/about_WGU/timeline (accessed December 12, 2014).

23.   Christopher Connell, "At No-frills Western Governors University, the Path to a College Degree Is Only as Long as Students Make It," Hechinger Institute on Education and the Media Teachers College, Columbia University, November 2011, http://hechinger.tc.columbia.edu/case_studies/wgu_case_study.pdf (accessed December 12, 2014).

24.   PR Newswire, "WGU Washington Offers Master's Degree for Aspiring English Teachers," (press release), December 8, 2014, http://www.prnewswire.com/news-releases/wgu-washington-offers-masters-degree-for-aspiring-english-teachers–300006304.html (accessed December 12, 2014).

25.   Brandon Busteed, "The Real Disruptive Innovation in Education," *Gallup Business Journal*, December 1, 2014, http://www.gallup.com/businessjournal/179564/real-disruptive-innovation-education.aspx (accessed December 12, 2014).

26.   Andrew P. Kelly, "Why Massive Open Online Courses Are More Like Health Clubs Than Hospitals," *Forbes*, May 15, 2014, http://www.aei.org/

publication/why-massive-open-online-courses-are-more-like-health-clubs-than-hospitals/ (accessed December 15, 2014).

27. Frederick M. Hess, Andrew P. Kelly, Olivia Meeks, "The Case for Being Bold," U.S. Chamber of Commerce, April 2011, http://www.aei.org/wp-content/uploads/2011/04/TheCaseforBeingBold2011.pdf (accessed December 15, 2014).

Seven: Pot and the Pope

1. Rachel Donadio, "Cardinals Pick Bergolglio, Who Will Be Pope Francis," *New York Times*, March 13, 2013, http://www.nytimes.com/2013/03/14/world/europe/cardinals-elect-new-pope.html?pagewanted=all&_r=0 (accessed December 13, 2014).

2. Pew Research Center, "The Global Catholic Population," February 13, 2014, http://www.pewforum.org/2013/02/13/the-global-catholic-population/ (accessed December 13, 2014).

3. John Guthrie, "Current Trends in Vocations & USCCB Initiatives," United States Conference of Catholic Bishops, August 19, 2014, http://www.usccb.org/beliefs-and-teachings/vocations/upload/JSPaluch-Presentation–2014.pdf (accessed December 13, 2014).

4. Pew Research Center, " 'Strong' Catholic Identity at a Four-Decade Low in U.S.," March 13, 2013, http://www.pewforum.org/files/2013/03/Strong-Catholic-Identity-version–3–13–13-for-web.pdf (accessed December 13, 2014).

5. Amy Sullivan, "Pope Benedict and the Decline of American Catholicism," *National Journal*, http://www.nationaljournal.com/politics/pope-benedict-and-the-decline-of-american-catholicism–20130211.

6. Antonio Sparado, "A Big Heart Open to God," *America*, September 30, 2013, http://www.americamagazine.org/pope-interview (accessed December 13, 2014).

7. "Pope Francis: Who Am I to Judge Gay People?," BBC News, July 29, 2013, http://www.bbc.com/news/world-europe–23489702 (accessed December, 13, 2014).

8. Nick Squires, "Rio's Copacabana Beach Transformed as Three Million Catholics Pack Sands for Sunday Mass," *Telegraph*, July 28, 2013, http://www.telegraph.co.uk/news/worldnews/southamerica/brazil/10207773/

Rios-Copacabana-beach-transformed-as-three-million-Catholics-pack-sands-for-Sunday-Mass.html (accessed December 13, 2014).

9. Mark Binelli, "Pope Francis: The Times, They Are A-Changin'," *Rolling Stone*, January 28, 2014, http://www.rollingstone.com/culture/news/pope-francis-the-times-they-are-a-changin–20140128 (accessed December 13, 2014).

10. Marco della Cava, "Pope Francis Again Demotes Hard-line U.S. Cardinal," *USA Today*, November 9, 2014, http://www.usatoday.com/story/news/world/2014/11/08/pope-francis-demotes-conservative-us-cardinal-raymond-burke/18710769/ (accessed December 13, 2014).

11. Elisabetta Povoledo and Laurie Goodstein, "At the Vatican, a Shift in Tone Toward Gays and Divorce," *New York Times*, October 13, 2014, http://www.nytimes.com/2014/10/14/world/europe/vatican-signals-more-tolerance-toward-gays-and-remarriage.html?_r=0 (accessed December 13, 2014).

12. Pew Research Center, "U.S. Catholics View Pope Francis as a Change for the Better," March 6, 2014, http://www.pewforum.org/files/2014/03/Pope-Francis-change-for-the-better-full-report.pdf (accessed December 13, 2014).

13. Samuel J. Best and Brian S. Krueger, *Exit Polls: Surveying the American Electorate, 1972–2010* (Los Angeles: Sage/CQPress, 2012), 60–61.

14. Ron Fournier, "What the Republican Party Can Learn from Pope Francis," *Atlantic*, November 13, 2014, http://www.theatlantic.com/politics/archive/2013/11/what-the-republican-party-can-learn-from-pope-francis/281478/ (accessed December 13, 2014).

15. Stephanie J. Ventura, Brady E. Hamilton, and T. J. Mathews, "National and State Patterns of Teen Births in the United States, 1940–2013," *National Vital Statistics Reports* 63, no. 4 (August 20, 2014), http://www.cdc.gov/nchs/data/nvsr/nvsr63/nvsr63_04.pdf (accessed December 13, 2014).

16. Lawrence Finer and Jessie Philbin, "Trends in Ages at Key Reproductive Transitions in the United States, 1951–2010," *Women's Health Issues* 24, no. 3, http://www.whijournal.com/article/S1049–3867(14)00008–5/pdf (accessed December 13, 2014).

17. "OJJDP Statistical Briefing Book: Juvenile Arrest Rate Trends," U.S. Department of Justice, February 25, 2014, http://www.ojjdp.gov/ojstatbb/crime/JAR_Display.asp?ID=qa05200 (accessed December 13, 2014).

18. Lloyd D. Johnston, Patrick M. O'Malley, Richard A. Miech et al., *Monitoring the Future National Survey Results on Drug Use, 1975–2013: Volume I, Secondary School Students* (Ann Arbor: Institute for Social Research, University of Michigan, 2014), http://www.monitoringthefuture.org/pubs/monographs/mtf-vol1_2013.pdf (accessed December 13, 2014).

19. Ibid.

20. Lloyd D. Johnston, Patrick M. O'Malley, Jerald G. Bachman et al., *Monitoring the Future National Survey Results on Drug Use, 1975–2013: Volume II, College Students and Adults Ages 19–55* (Ann Arbor: Institute for Social Research, University of Michigan, 2014), http://www.monitoringthefuture.org/pubs/monographs/mtf-vol2_2013.pdf (accessed December 13, 2014).

21. CBS News, "When Gambling Isn't a Sure Bet for Las Vegas," November 4, 2014, http://www.cbsnews.com/news/las-vegas-casinos-reinventing-the-strip-to-attract-new-generation/ (accessed December 13, 2014).

22. "Oh! You pretty things," *Economist*, July 12, 2014, http://www.economist.com/news/briefing/21606795-todays-young-people-are-held-be-alienated-unhappy-violent-failures-they-are-proving (accessed December 13, 2014).

23. Pew Research Center, "Sex, Drugs and the 1040," March 28, 2006, http://pewsocialtrends.org/files/2010/10/Morality.pdf (accessed December, 13, 2014).

24. Rebecca Riffkin, "Premarital Sex, Embryonic Stem Cell Research, Euthanasia Growing in Acceptance," Gallup, May 30, 2014, http://www.gallup.com/poll/170789/new-record-highs-moral-acceptability.aspx (accessed December 13, 2014).

25. Tom W. Smith, "Public Attitudes Toward Homosexuality," NORC/University of Chicago, September 2011, http://www.norc.org/PDFs/2011%20GSS%20Reports/GSS_Public%20Attitudes%20Toward%20Homosexuality_Sept2011.pdf (accessed December 13, 2014).

26. Harvard Institute of Politics, "Survey of Young Americans' Attitudes toward Politics and Public Service, 25th Edition: March 22–April 4, 2014," April 2014, http://www.iop.harvard.edu/sites/default/files_new/Harvard_ToplineSpring2014.pdf (accessed December 13, 2014).

27. Pew Research Center, "Sex, Drugs and the 1040."

28. Rebecca Riffkin, "Premarital Sex, Embryonic Stem Cell Research, Euthanasia Growing in Acceptance."

29. Pew Research Center, "Abortion Viewed in Moral Terms," August 15, 2013, http://www.pewforum.org/2013/08/15/abortion-viewed-in-moral-terms/ (accessed December 13, 2014).

30. Pew Research Center, "Sex, Drugs and the 1040."

31. Pew Research Center, "Nones on the Rise," October 9, 2012, http://www.pewforum.org/files/2012/10/NonesOnTheRise-full.pdf (accessed December 13, 2014).

32. Gallup data on religion, http://www.gallup.com/poll/1690/religion.aspx (accessed December 13, 2014).

33. Pew Research Center, "Growth of the Nonreligious," July 2, 2013, http://www.pewforum.org/2013/07/02/growth-of-the-nonreligious-many-say-trend-is-bad-for-american-society/ (accessed December 13, 2014).

34. Pew Research Center, "The American-Western European Values Gap," November 17, 2011, http://www.pewglobal.org/2011/11/17/the-american-western-european-values-gap/ (accessed December 13, 2014).

35. Frank Newport, "Majority Still Says Religion Can Answer Today's Problems," Gallup, June 27, 2014, http://www.gallup.com/poll/171998/majority-says-religion-answer-today-problems.aspx (accessed December 13, 2014).

36. Robert P. Jones, Daniel Cox, and Thomas Banchoff, "A Generation in Transition," Public Religion Research Institute, April 19, 2012, http://publicreligion.org/site/wp-content/uploads/2012/04/Millennials-Survey-Report.pdf (accessed December 13, 2014).

37. Frank Newport, "In U.S., 42% Believe Creationist View of Human Origins," Gallup, June 2, 2014, http://www.gallup.com/poll/170822/believe-creationist-view-human-origins.aspx (accessed December 13, 2014).

38. Pew Research Center, "Trends in American Values: 1987–2012," June 4, 2012, http://www.people-press.org/2012/06/04/section–6-religion-and-social-values/ (accessed December 13, 2014).

39. Harvard Institute of Politics, "Survey of Young Americans' Attitudes Toward Politics and Public Service, 25th Edition: March 22–April 4, 2014."

40. Pew Research Center, "Religion and Electronic Media: One-in-Five Americans Share Their Faith Online," November 6, 2014, http://www.

pewforum.org/files/2014/11/Religion-and-Electronic-media–11–06-full. pdf (accessed December 13, 2014).

41. Kevin O'Donnell, "CMJ Madness: Mute Math Loves Jesus but Isn't Terrible," *Rolling Stone*, November 2, 2006, http://www.rollingstone. com/music/news/cmj-madness-mute-math-loves-jesus-but-isnt-terrible–20061102 (accessed December 13, 2014).

42. Poll Position, "National Survey of 1,076 Registered Voters," January 10, 2012, http://media.pollposition.com.s3.amazonaws.com/wp-content/up-loads/Poll-Position-crosstabs-divine-intervention.pdf (accessed December 13, 2014).

43. Pew Research Center, "Religion Among the Millennials," February 2010, http://www.pewforum.org/files/2010/02/millennials-report.pdf (accessed December 13, 2014).

44. Ibid.

45. Corporation for National and Community Service, "Volunteer Growth in America," December 2006, http://www.nationalservice.gov/ pdf/06_1203_volunteer_growth.pdf (accessed December 13, 2014).

46. Kent E. Portney, Lisa O'Leary, Elyse S. Arezzini et al., "National Survey of Civic and Political Engagement of Young People," Tufts University, February 2007, http://activecitizen.tufts.edu/wp-content/uploads/Final-Report1.pdf (accessed December 13, 2014).

47. Harvard Institute of Politics, "Survey of Young Americans' Attitudes Toward Politics and Public Service, 25th Edition: March 22–April 4, 2014."

48. "The RELEVANT Story," *Relevant*, http://www.relevantmagazine.com/ relevant-story (accessed December 13, 2014).

49. Tyler Huckabee, "Reese Witherspoon," *Relevant*, November/December 2014, http://www.relevantmagazine.com/culture/film/reese-witherspoon (accessed December 13, 2014).

50. Harvard Institute of Politics, "Spring 2006 Survey: Executive Summary," April 11, 2006, http://www.iop.harvard.edu/spring–2006-survey-executive-summary (accessed December 13, 2014).

51. Michael Wear, "The Changing Face of Christian Politics," *Atlantic*, February 17, 2014, http://www.theatlantic.com/politics/archive/2014/02/ the-changing-face-of-christian-politics/283859/ (accessed December 13, 2014).

52. Billy Hallowell, "Meet the 23-Year-Old Obama Hired to Head His

Religious Campaign Outreach," *Blaze*, May 15, 2012, http://www.theblaze.com/stories/2012/05/15/meet-the–23-year-old-who-obama-hired-to-head-his-religious-campaign-outreach/ (accessed December 13, 2014).

53. Values Voter Summit agenda, http://www.valuesvotersummit.org/schedule (accessed December 13, 2014).

54. Family Research Council, "Remarks by Louisiana Governor Bobby Jindal," September 26, 2014, http://downloads.frcaction.org/EF/EF14184.doc (accessed December 13, 2014).

55. "Paul Ryan Values Voter Summit speech (full text, video)," *POLITICO*, September 14, 2012, http://www.politico.com/news/stories/0912/81222_Page3.html#ixzz3JBbBtgE3 (accessed December 13, 2014).

56. Reihan Salam, "Paul Ryan's Anti-Poverty Plan Is Paternalistic," *Slate*, July 24, 2014, http://www.slate.com/articles/news_and_politics/politics/2014/07/paul_ryan_s_anti_poverty_plan_is_paternalistic_it_s_also_a_thoughtful_compassionate.html (accessed December 13, 2014).

57. Elizabeth Kneebone, "Place and the Paul Ryan Poverty Plan," Brookings Institution, July 29, 2014, http://www.brookings.edu/blogs/the-avenue/posts/2014/07/29-paul-ryan-poverty-plan-kneebone (accessed December 13, 2014).

58. Pew Research Center, "Political Polarization and Media Habits: From Fox News to Facebook," October 21, 2014, http://www.journalism.org/files/2014/10/Political-Polarization-and-Media-Habits-FINAL-REPORT–10–21–2014.pdf (accessed December 13, 2014).

59. Yuval Levin, "The Solution: A Conservative Governing Vision," *Room to Grow*, YG Network, 2014, http://ygnetwork.org/wp-content/uploads/2014/05/Room-To-Grow.pdf (accessed December 13, 2014).

Eight: Showing Up and Reaching Out

1. Paul Wells, "Jason Kenney: Harper's Secret Weapon," *MacLean's*, November 29, 2010, http://www.macleans.ca/authors/paul-wells/harpers-secret-weapon/ (accessed December 13, 2014).

2. Joe Friesen, "Jason Kenney: The 'Smiling Buddha' and His Multicultural Charms," *Globe and Mail*, January 29, 2010, http://www.theglobeandmail.com/news/politics/the-smiling-buddha-and-his-multicultural-charms/article4388303/ (accessed December 13, 2014).

3.   "Jason Kenney Speech to CPC Convention," Ottawa, Canada, June 14, 2011, https://www.youtube.com/watch?v=rz-zoqHuayg (accessed December 14, 2014).

4.   Elisabeth Gidengil et al., "The Anatomy of a Liberal Defeat" (paper presented at the annual meeting of the Canadian Political Science Association, May 2009).

5.   Glen McGregor, "Conservative Support Grows Among Chinese-Canadians, Despite Liberal Push to Regain Ethnic Voters," *National Post*, July 31, 2014, http://news.nationalpost.com/2014/07/31/conservative-support-grows-among-chinese-despite-liberal-push-to-regain-ethnic-voters/ (accessed December 13, 2014).

6.   Carol Morello and Ted Mellnik, "White Deaths Outnumber Births for First Time," *Washington Post*, June 13, 2013, http://www.washingtonpost.com/local/white-deaths-outnumber-births-for-first-time/2013/06/13/3bb1017c-d388–11e2-a73e–826d299ff459_story.html.

7.   National exit polls. The one exception is 1992, where a dip in the African-American vote led to an uptick in the share of white voters.

8.   Ronald Brownstein, "Obama Needs 80% of Minority Vote to Win Presidential Election," *National Journal*, August 24, 2012, http://www.nationaljournal.com/thenextamerica/politics/obama-needs–80-of-minority-vote-to-win–2012-presidential-election–20120824 (accessed December 13, 2014).

9.   Pew Research Center, "Median Age for Hispanics Is Lower Than Median Age for U.S. Population," July 2, 2012, http://www.pewresearch.org/daily-number/median-age-for-hispanics-is-lower-than-median-age-for-total-u-s-population/ (accessed December 13, 2014).

10.   Anna Marie de la Fuente, "Univision to Big Four: We're No. 1 and Rising," *Variety*, July 30, 2013, http://variety.com/2013/tv/news/univision-to-big-four-were-no–1-and-rising–1200569566/ (accessed December 13, 2014).

11.   Univision Insights Team, "Christie's Hispanic Outreach Part of Overall Campaign Strategy," June 18, 2014, http://corporate.univision.com/hispanic-vote/christies-hispanic-outreach-part-of-overall-campaign-strategy/ (accessed December 13, 2014).

12.   Jenna Portnoy, "Republican National Committee Spends Big to Persuade Jersey Minorities to Vote GOP," *New Jersey Star-Ledger*, October

26, 2013, http://www.nj.com/politics/index.ssf/2013/10/rnc_hispanic_
outreach.html (accessed December 13, 2014).

13. Rosalind S. Helderman and Peyton Craighill, "GOP Gains Trac-
tion Among Hispanic Voters with Aggressive Outreach," *Washington
Post*, November 5, 2014, http://www.washingtonpost.com/politics/
gop-gains-traction-among-hispanic-voters-with-aggressive-outreach-
campaigns/2014/11/05/dcbe20ec–6520–11e4–9fdc-d43b053ecb4d_
story.html (accessed December 13, 2014).

14. Republican National Committee, "Growth and Opportunity Project
Report," 2013, http://goproject.gop.com/RNC_Growth_Opportunity_
Book_2013.pdf (accessed December 13, 2014).

15. Public Religion Research Institute, "PRRI Religion & Politics Tracking
Survey," December 4, 2014, http://publicreligion.org/site/wp-content/
uploads/2014/12/PRRI-Religion-Politics-Tracking-Survey-Dec.–2014-
Topline.pdf (accessed December 13, 2014).

16. All Things Considered, "A Reagan Legacy: Amnesty for Immigrants,"
National Public Radio, July 4, 2010, http://www.npr.org/templates/
story/story.php?storyId=128303672 (accessed December 13, 2014).

17. All Things Considered, "A Reagan Legacy: Amnesty for Illegal Immigrants," National Public Radio, July 4, 2010, http://www.npr.org/templates/
story/story.php?storyId=128303672 (accessed December 13, 2014).

18. Carolyn Lochhead, "Obama Takes a Big Risk on Drivers' License Issue,"
San Francisco Chronicle, January 28, 2008, http://www.sfgate.com/politics
/article/Obama-takes-big-risk-on-driver-s-license-issue–3296561.php
(accessed December 13, 2014).

19. Richard Wike, "In Europe, Sentiment Against Immigrants, Minorities Runs High," Pew Research Center, May 14, 2014, http://www.
pewresearch.org/fact-tank/2014/05/14/in-europe-sentiment-against-
immigrants-minorities-runs-high/ (accessed December 13, 2014).

20. Dylan Matthews, "The Left Won Sweden's Election—Thanks to
Surging Support for the Far-Right," *Vox*, September 15, 2014, http://
www.vox.com/2014/9/15/6151901/sweden-democrats-social-democrats-
election-results-far-right (accessed December 13, 2014).

21. Fusion, "Fusion Millennial Political Poll 2014," November 17, 2014,
http://fusion.net/story/20274/fusions-massive-millennial-poll-the-
complete-results/ (accessed December 14, 2014).

22. Pew Research Center, "Public Divided over Increased Deportation of

Unauthorized Immigrants," February 27, 2014, http://www.people-press.org/files/legacy-pdf/02–27–14%20Immigration%20Release.pdf (accessed December 13, 2014).

23. Ana Gonzalez-Barrera and Mark Hugo Lopez, "Asian-Americans Split on Whether U.S. Immigration System Works or Needs a Major Overhaul," Pew Research Center, January 30, 2014, http://www.pewresearch.org/fact-tank/2014/01/30/asian-americans-split-on-whether-u-s-immigration-system-works-or-needs-a-major-overhaul/ (accessed December 13, 2014).

24. Andrew Dugan, "In U.S., More Hispanics Name Immigration as a Top Problem," Gallup, September 19, 2014, http://www.gallup.com/poll/176180/hispanics-name-immigration-top-problem.aspx (accessed December 13, 2014).

25. E. Ann Carson, "Prisoners in 2013," U.S. Department of Justice Bureau of Justice Statistics, September 30, 2014, http://www.bjs.gov/content/pub/pdf/p13.pdf (accessed December 13, 2014).

26. Elizabeth Flock, "'Sesame Street' Tackles Incarceration Through Muppet with Father in Jail," *U.S. News & World Report,* July 17, 2013, http://www.usnews.com/news/articles/2013/07/17/sesame-street-tackles-incarceration-through-muppet-with-father-in-jail (accessed December 13, 2014).

27. Economic Mobility Project and the Public Safety Performance Project of the Pew Charitable Trusts, *Collateral Costs: Incarceration's Effect on Economic Mobility,* 2010, http://www.pewtrusts.org/~/media/legacy/uploadedfiles/pcs_assets/2010/CollateralCosts1pdf.pdf (accessed December 13, 2014).

28. American Civil Liberties Union, "The War on Marijuana in Black and White," June 2013, https://www.aclu.org/files/assets/aclu-thewaronmarijuana-rel2.pdf (accessed December 13, 2014).

29. Andrew DeMillo, "Beebe Formally Announces Plan to Pardon Son," December 5, 2014, http://bigstory.ap.org/article/0852ac4b09a1434eaf9d2faf4fb9197d/beebe-formally-announces-intent-pardon-son (accessed December 13, 2014).

30. Bruce Drake, "Ferguson Highlights Deep Divisions Between Blacks and Whites in America," Pew Research Center, November 26, 2014, http://www.pewresearch.org/fact-tank/2014/11/26/ferguson-highlights-deep-divisions-between-blacks-and-whites-in-america/ (accessed December 13, 2014).

31. Kim Parker, "Within the Black Community, Young and Old Differ on Police Searches, Discrimination," Pew Research Center, August 27, 2014, http://www.pewresearch.org/fact-tank/2014/08/27/within-the-black-community-young-and-old-differ-on-police-searches-discrimination/ (accessed December 13, 2014).

32. Matt Sledge, "California Voters Deal Blow to Prisons, Drug War," *Huffington Post*, November 5, 2014, http://www.huffingtonpost.com/2014/11/05/california-prisons_n_6070654.html?&ncid=tweetlnkushpmg00000067 (accessed December 14, 2014).

33. Senator Mike Lee, "Speeches: A Conversation on Criminal Justice," February 11, 2014, http://www.lee.senate.gov/public/index.cfm/speeches?ID=4708f70b-e254–4009–9092–2ff03c58045e (accessed December 13, 2014).

34. Fusion, "Fusion Millennial Political Poll 2014."

35. Ibid.

36. Wesley Lowery, "Republicans Ramp Up Minority Outreach Nationwide Ahead of 2016," *Washington Post*, October 24, 2014, http://www.washingtonpost.com/politics/republicans-ramp-up-minority-outreach-nationwide-ahead-of-2016/2014/10/24/2e6c3ab8–5870–11e4-bd61–346aee66ba29_story.html (accessed December 13, 2014).

37. Heritage Foundation, "Overcriminalization: An Explosion of Federal Criminal Law," April 27, 2011, http://www.heritage.org/research/factsheets/2011/04/overcriminalization-an-explosion-of-federal-criminal-law (accessed December 13, 2014).

38. "Speeches: A Conversation on Criminal Justice," Office of Senator Mike Lee, February 11, 2014, http://www.lee.senate.gov/public/index.cfm/speeches?ID=4708f70b-e254–4009–9092–2ff03c58045e.

39. "Jason Kenney Speech to CPC Convention."

40. Kristen Soltis Anderson, "Conservative Ideas Are Our Biggest Strength with Young Americans," *National Review Online*, August 24, 2012, http://www.nationalreview.com/corner/314916/conservative-ideas-are-our-biggest-strength-young-americans-kristen-soltis-anderson (accessed December 14, 2014).

41. Pew Research Center, "Between Two Worlds: How Young Latinos Come of Age in America: VII. Life Satisfaction, Priorities, and Values," December 11, 2009, http://www.pewhispanic.org/2009/12/11/vii-life-satisfaction-priorities-and-values/ (accessed December 14, 2014).

42. Robert P. Jones, Daniel Cox, and Juhem Navarro-Rivera, "Economic Insecurity, Rising Inequality, and Doubts About the Future," Public Religion Research Institute, September 23, 2014, http://publicreligion. org/site/wp-content/uploads/2014/09/AVS-web.pdf (accessed December 14, 2014).

43. U.S. Senator Marco Rubio, "Reclaiming the Land of Opportunity: Conservative Reforms for Combatting Poverty," January 8, 2014, http://www.rubio.senate.gov/public/index.cfm/pressreleases?ID=958d06fe–16a3–4e8e-b178–664fc10745bf (accessed December 14, 2014).

Nine: Vote by Numbers

1. Republican National Committee, *Growth and Opportunity Project*, http:// goproject.gop.com/rnc_growth_opportunity_book_2013.pdf.

2. Charles Duhigg, "How Companies Learn Your Secrets," *New York Times Magazine,* February 26, 2012, http://www.nytimes. com/2012/02/19/magazine/shopping-habits.html?ref=general &src=me&pagewanted=all.

3. David M. Drucker, "GOP's New Turnout Machine Was in Top Gear," *Washington Examiner,* November 5, 2014, http://www.washington examiner.com/gops-turnout-machine-was-in-top-gear/article/2555760.

4. Telephone interview with Alex Lundry, September 19, 2014.

5. Ralph Vartabedian, "Cable TV Boxes Become 2nd Biggest Energy Users in Many Homes," *Los Angeles Times*, June 16, 2014, http://www.latimes.com/nation/la-na-power-hog–20140617-story .html#page=1.

6. Martha T. Moore, "Political TV Ads Are Beginning to Choose Their Viewers," *USA Today*, February 9, 2014, http://www.usatoday.com/story/ news/politics/2014/02/09/targeted-campaign-ads/5274937/.

7. DISH Network, "DIRECTV and DISH Revolutionize Political TV Advertising Landscape with Combined Addressable Advertising Platform Reaching 20+ Million Households," news release, January 26, 2014, http://about.dish.com/press-release/directv-and-dish-revolutionize-political-tv-advertising-landscape-combined-addressable.

8. Rentrak, "Win Big: How Rentrak's Advanced Targeting Helped Obama for America Shift the Media Buying Model from Madison

Avenue to Pennsylvania Avenue," http://www.rentrak.com/downloads/
Rentrak-OFA-CaseStudy.pdf.

Conclusion: Win the Future by Fighting the Past

1. Emily Badger, "We Have No Clue How Big the Peer-to-Peer Economy
    Is," *Washington Post*, May 21, 2014, http://www.washingtonpost.com/
    blogs/wonkblog/wp/2014/05/21/we-have-no-idea-how-big-the-peer-to-
    peer-economy-is/ (accessed December 14, 2015).
2. Jeff Barnard, "Maker of Budweiser Buys Oregon Craft Brewery,
    Sparking Outrage," *Boston Globe*, December 14, 2004, http://www
    .bostonglobe.com/business/2014/12/14/sale-oregon-craft-brewery-
    provokes-backlash/yI8h1DqUeeYWptVmjxdwTN/story.html.
3. Tripp Mickle, "Bud Crowded Out by Craft Beer Craze," November
    23, 2014, *Wall Street Journal*, http://www.wsj.com/articles/budweiser-
    ditches-the-clydesdales-for-jay-z–1416784086 (accessed December 15,
    2014).
4. Barbara Liston, "Craft Beer Distribution Battle Brews in the Flor-
    ida Legislature," Reuters, April 3, 2014, http://www.reuters.com/
    article/2014/04/04/florida-beer-idUSL1N0MT1DN20140404 (accessed
    December 15, 2014).
5. Madeline O'Leary and Chris Christoff, "Michigan Governor to Sign Bill
    to Ban Tesla Direct Sales," Bloomberg, October 22, 2014, http://www.
    bloomberg.com/news/2014–10–21/michigan-governor-to-sign-bill-to-
    ban-tesla-direct-sales.html (accessed December 15, 2014).
6. Karen Tumulty, "Obama Losing the Confidence of Key Parts of the Co-
    alition That Elected Him," *Washington Post*, September 11, 2014, http://
    www.washingtonpost.com/politics/obama-losing-the-confidence-of-key-
    parts-of-the-coalition-that-elected-him/2014/09/11/18a1c2da–391b–
    11e4-bdfb-de4104544a37_story.html (accessed December 13, 2014).

ABOUT THE AUTHOR

Kristen Soltis Anderson is a Republican pollster and is the cofounder of Echelon Insights, a public opinion and data analytics firm. She is a contributor at the *Daily Beast* and was named one of *Time* magazine's "30 Under 30" in 2013. She also served as a fellow at the Institute of Politics at Harvard University. She lives in Washington, DC.